Introduction to Lit

This book provides a complete guide to analyzing literary works, from an introduction of basic principles to the finer details.

Separated into three sections, the book covers:

- Principles—this looks at what literary analysis is, its three main components, and the various possible objects of analysis
- Main components—introduces nearly 30 aspects of text analysis, such as style, themes, social aspects, and context, and then goes on to introduce nearly 50 approaches, such as literary history, ecocriticism, narratology, and sociology
- The process of analysis—details the general structure of the analytical text, the structure of a pedagogical essay, the analysis of a theoretical element, possible "plans" for the analytical text, methods of argumentation, statements of opinion, hypotheses, the structure of paragraphs, and the use of citations.

This book is a synthesis of established scholarship with new, original insights, making it an ideal introduction to the study of literature as well as a valuable companion throughout further study.

Louis Hébert is a Professor at the Université du Québec à Rimouski (UQAR), Canada. He has published many books on semiotics and the methodology of literary analysis, in Quebec, France, and the UK, including *An Introduction to Applied Semiotics* (Routledge).

Introduction to Literary Analysis

A Complete Methodology

Louis Hébert

Translated from the French by Sam Ferguson

Routledge
Taylor & Francis Group

LONDON AND NEW YORK

Cover image: © Getty Images

First published 2022
by Routledge
4 Park Square, Milton Park, Abingdon, Oxon OX14 4RN

and by Routledge
605 Third Avenue, New York, NY 10158

Routledge is an imprint of the Taylor & Francis Group, an informa business

© 2022 Louis Hébert; Chapter 5, Louis Hébert and Sam Gormley

British Library Cataloguing-in-Publication Data
A catalogue record for this book is available from the British Library

Library of Congress Cataloging-in-Publication Data
A catalog record has been requested for this book

ISBN: 978-1-032-01727-3 (hbk)
ISBN: 978-1-032-01726-6 (pbk)
ISBN: 978-1-003-17979-5 (ebk)

DOI: 10.4324/9781003179795

Typeset in Bembo
by Newgen Publishing UK

Contents

5 Approaches to literary texts   77

Figures

Contributors

Author

Louis Hébert is a Professor at the Université du Québec à Rimouski (UQAR), Canada. He has published many books on literary analysis, methodology and semiotics, in Quebec, France, and the UK, including *An Introduction to Applied Semiotics* (Routledge).

Translator

Sam Ferguson is a translator specializing in translating academic texts in the humanities and social sciences from French to English. He completed a doctorate in French literature at the University of Oxford, spent several years working as an academic researcher and teacher, and has also published widely on French literature.

Co-author of Chapter 5

Sam Gormley is a Stipendiary Lecturer in French at Wadham College and Exeter College, University of Oxford. His teaching encompasses French literature, thought, and culture from the nineteenth century to the present day. Dr. Gormley's research focuses primarily on contemporary speculative fiction in French and English.

Introduction

This book offers the reader a resource that is, in my view, both useful and unique. Although there are many books that present literary theories or methods, there is a lack of works on methodology in literary analysis. The present work aims to fill this gap.

To my knowledge, there is no book to date that covers: (1) how to produce an analysis, from its basic principles to the formal aspects of a work of textual analysis (definitions, parts, and stages of the analysis, the structure, argumentation, presentation of opinion, use of citations, etc.); (2) most of the aspects that can be analyzed in a literary text (I identify about 30 of these: themes, actions, characters, rhythm, etc.); (3) most of the approaches that can be used to analyze these aspects (I identify about 50 approaches: literary history, themes, cultural studies, psychoanalysis, semiotics, etc.). The other books in this field address— often very successfully—only one of these three topics, either as a whole or in part.

Books offering an introductory overview of a subject can raise unrealistic expectations: readers hope to find in them both a complete coverage of the discipline and information on topics of specific interest to them. They expect not only to find a discussion of "their" topic, but that it will be treated in the way they expect it to be treated. Similarly, the professor or student using a handbook of this sort expects it to correspond almost perfectly to the content or writing tasks specific to the course in which it is being used. This is clearly impossible, and choices have to be made.

Part I introduces the principles of literary analysis: (1) a definition of analysis; (2) its various components (the corpus, the aspects to be analyzed, approaches, etc.); (3) the different phenomena that can become the objects of analysis (a creative work, theory, method, concept, the analysis of an analysis, etc.).

Part II addresses the three main components of analysis in greater detail: (1) aspects of the text (about 30, including style, themes, social aspects, context, etc.); (2) approaches (about 50: literary history, ecocriticism, narratology, sociology, etc.); (3) the corpus (types of corpus, their characteristics, stages of the treatment of corpora, the main problems encountered, etc.); (4) aspects that are specific to theatrical texts and performances (the definition of literary texts and genres, dialogue, stage directions, make-up, costume, music, etc.).

DOI: 10.4324/9781003179795-1

Part III addresses the process of analysis itself and the end product, the work of literary analysis, which I call the "analytical text": (1) the general structure of the analytical text (including its methodological, descriptive, and interpretive stages, with an example of an analytical text); (2) the structure of a pedagogical essay, that is, the sort of analytical text produced by school pupils and university students (types of essay, stages of writing); (3) analysis of a theoretical element (how to describe it, the skills that are required, etc.); (4) possible "plans" for the analytical text (dialectic, syllogistic, etc.); (5) methods of argumentation (the necessary qualities for an effective argument, presentation of about 60 types of arguments, etc.); (6) statements of opinion (types, necessary qualities, etc.); (7) hypotheses (definition, types, necessary qualities, etc.); (8) paragraphs (possible forms, logical structure, necessary qualities, etc.); and (9) the use of citations (parts of the citation, types, errors to avoid, etc.).

I wrote this book, not in a spirit of erudition, but of systematicity, primarily because I am by nature a systematist. The systematist is not satisfied to describe things as they are commonly described, but rather as they could be, or even should be described. The systematist takes apart the object of study, considers all the possible permutations of a phenomenon (and thus identifies "gaps" in the system), constructs typologies, finds logical errors, alternative paths, ambiguities, and previously unimagined options, and corrects, nuances, and completes the picture. The systematist looks for the relevance, richness, interest, systematicity, and precise details of the contents, and aims to express these in a precise and clear language.

As a result of this approach, although the book provides an overview of the subject, it also offers a great deal of new knowledge and know-how in literary analysis, which will be of use to university students and professors, as well as schoolteachers. The book focuses primarily on the analysis of literary works, but it is also relevant to the literary analysis of other objects of study (such as genres, theories, concepts, methods, themes, contexts, and literary events).

The first version of this book was published in French in 2014, as *L'analyse des textes littéraires: Une méthodologie complète* (Classiques Garnier). In 2020 I had the idea of publishing a version in English. I have completely rewritten the text for this new version, as my ways of looking at the field and my knowledge have developed since 2014, and I have also adapted the book with its new audience in mind. This rewritten text was translated into English by Dr. Sam Ferguson (with my active collaboration), and improved by his comments and suggestions. I received help from Dr. Sam Gormley for the sections on approaches to literary analysis that are more established in the English-speaking world, such as cultural studies. However, I have kept the "French" spirit of the book. While the fundamental principles of analysis are universal, the ways of seeing, presenting, and applying them may vary from one culture to another. In other words, I believe that the Anglophone reader will benefit from this encounter between two major intellectual cultures because it will produce a new way of looking at things. If cultural diversity is truly a virtue, this must also apply to literary studies, and cultural transfers must flow in both directions.

I would like to thank the many professors and researchers, in literature and semiotics, who have inspired me, and in particular my main intellectual mentors, whether I have met them or not: Joseph Courtés, Jacques Fontanille, Algirdas Julien Greimas, Jean-Marie Klinkenberg, François Rastier, and Claude Zilberberg. I am grateful to my students, for whom I had to learn, and from whom I learned. And thanks also go to Sam Ferguson and Sam Gormley for their enthusiastic and meticulous work.

To make comments or suggestions, the author can be contacted at: louis_hebert@uqar.ca.

Introduction to
Literary Analysis.

There are several
key components.

Part I
Principles

1 Definition of analysis

i.e: Really studying the center of your focus.

Broadly speaking, any phenomenon is either an entity (e.g., a human), a characteristic (e.g., this human is tall), a relation (e.g., he is the brother of such and such a person), or an operation (e.g., this human eats). An analysis is an operation that assigns one or more characteristics to an entity (the object) and this characteristic is related to the object (because the object possesses the characteristic).

To analyze any object (e.g., a text, a group of texts, a textual genre, an image) is thus to characterize it, that is, to stipulate that it possesses one or more specific properties (or characteristics). In logical terms, the object is then a *subject*, while the characteristic is a *predicate* that is assigned to the subject; the two together make up a proposition (in the logical sense of the term). A proposition is assigned a truth value, which will broadly be one of the following: true, false, or undecidable (when one cannot decide between true and false). The proposition with its assigned truth value is associated with a particular instance, an observing subject, who assumes responsibility for its content.

In the proposition "Water boils at 100 degrees Celsius," in the context of a scientific article: the subject is water; the predicate is the fact that it boils at 100 degrees Celsius; the truth value is true; and the instance that produces and assumes this proposition is the author of the article. The same principles apply to literary propositions such as "Macbeth is a monster," "Macbeth is not a monster," "Hamlet truly loves Ophelia," and "Hamlet does not truly love Ophelia."

Analysis is a cognitive operation, but the term "analysis" is also used to refer to a given text belonging to a textual genre that is closely focused on the operation of analysis, that is, the operation of characterization. A given analysis necessarily uses a method, which may be either more or less conscious, explicit, rigorous, relevant, and respected over the course of its application. A method is based on a theory, which may again be either more or less conscious, explicit, rigorous, relevant, and respected. Furthermore, a theory provides an image of the potential methods that can be derived from it, and a method provides an image of the potential applications that can be produced with it.

DOI: 10.4324/9781003179795-3

NOTE: OTHER PRESUPPOSITIONS

A method presupposes a theory. A theory presupposes an epistemology, a conception or theory of scientific knowledge, or at least of rational knowledge. An epistemology presupposes a gnosology, a conception or theory of knowledge in general. Finally, a gnosology presupposes a "consciousology," a conception or theory of consciousness (since any knowledge of something presupposes being conscious of this thing). In summary, the chain of presuppositions is as follows: application → method → theory → epistemology → gnosology → theory of consciousness.

The art of analysis consists not only in producing a precise and appropriate characterization, but also in convincing the reader that the characterization is in fact precise and adequate. To assess the value of an analysis, we can ask the questions: what do we know now that we did not know before the analysis, and better still, what do we know now that we could not have known without this particular analysis? In answering this question—especially in cases where the argument is powerful and clear—we should be aware of the hindsight effect, by which we come to believe that a point is so obvious that we did not need this particular analysis to arrive at that conclusion. Furthermore, even if another method (or a different analysis with the same method) could have led to the same result, the fact is that this analysis did so first.

2 Components of analysis

2.1 Introduction

I will mainly focus here on the analysis of literary texts, and more specifically on that of literary works (e.g., novels, poems), but my comments may be suitable, either with or without modification, for other forms of literary analysis (the analysis of literary forms, the lives of authors, a text devoted to theory, method, or an application of method, etc.). For a typology of possible objects for a literary analysis, see Chapter 3.

The analysis of semiotic products (e.g., written texts) is achieved through the combination and interaction of the following main components: (1) one or more corpora, (2) one or more approaches, (3) one or more aspects, (4) one or more configurations, and (5) one or more propositions.

1. A corpus, in the broad sense, is made up of one or more semiotic products (e.g., written texts), or parts of these products, chosen either based on the analyst's personal preference (a self-selected corpus) or based on "objective" criteria (a constructed corpus), which are the object of an analysis. In the narrower sense, it is made up of a complete semiotic product (not only extracts), or group of such products, selected for the desired analysis on the basis of objective, conscious, explicit, rigorous, relevant, and consistently respected criteria (see Chapter 6).

2. The approach is the general method—often already fully constituted (e.g., traditional thematic analysis, narratology)—with which the object of study is viewed. The method, in the broad sense, includes both the particular approach that is adopted and the particular use that is made of it for the analysis of a given object of study (including elements of general methodology in literary analysis). This particular use may modify the approach (by addition, omission, etc.), in its theoretical and/or methodological aspects. The approach—including both the general method associated with it and the other elements of method that are used—thus constitutes the "how" of analysis.

A given discipline may correspond to a general approach (e.g., linguistics, semiotics) and/or to specific approaches (e.g., for linguistics: the syntactic approach, the semantic approach; within semantics: the referential approach, the semic approach; and within semic semantics: Rastier's approach, Greimas's

DOI: 10.4324/9781003179795-4

approach, etc.). However, a given discipline does not necessarily have a corresponding approach at all (and not necessarily one that can be applied to literary objects of analysis, such as for nuclear engineering), and a given approach does not necessarily have a corresponding discipline (e.g., thematic analysis, deconstruction).

The concept of an "approach" differs from that of a "theory" in that a theory is not necessarily intended for direct application, and not every analysis is necessarily the conscious, explicit, and sustained implementation of a theory. However, as we have seen, every application presupposes a method (even if it is rudimentary, implicit, and not consciously recognized), and every method presupposes a theory (even if it is rudimentary, implicit, and not consciously recognized). For example, in literary studies, a traditional thematic analysis is not strictly speaking based on an explicit theory, and the implicit theory that it uses is itself rudimentary. In short, an approach is a mixture, in varying proportions, of theory and method. Generally, in a given application, one can distinguish between, on the one hand, the approach as a general model and, on the other hand, the adjustments that have been made to adapt it to the analysis of a particular object (e.g., for a given application, one might propose certain adjustments to the traditional thematic approach).

The abstract systematic description of an aspect of the text that has not yet been addressed directly or at any length by an institutionalized approach produces a proto-approach, that is, an approach that is not institutionalized but which may become so (compare narratology in its early days—when it was not yet institutionalized—and narratology today). Note that there are varying degrees of autonomy and institutionalization along the journey from being a proto-approach to being an approach. For example, as an approach, linguistics possesses a high degree of autonomy and institutionalization, with its own linguistic discipline, teaching programs, teaching posts, etc. In contrast, "rhythmology" does not enjoy the same autonomy and institutionalization. Those proto-approaches that do not attain full autonomy are then either subordinated, whether *de facto* or *de jure*, to an encompassing approach (e.g., literary rhythmic analysis is *de jure* part of poetics) and/or dispersed among several approaches (e.g., literary rhythmic analysis within the studies of versification, rhetoric, style, etc.). For a list and summary of possible approaches, see Chapter 5.

3. The aspect is the particular facet of the object of study that is being analyzed. To take a simple example, it is traditionally considered that a text can be divided without remainder (and in principle without overlap, but this is not actually the case) into two parts or two aspects: the content (the themes, in a broad sense) and the form (the way in which the content is presented). An aspect can be broken down into sub-aspects and sub-sub-aspects, etc. This is the case for aspects of content—which can be broken down into topoi (in the sense of conventional stereotypes of content, without any pejorative sense of being over-used, e.g., the topoi of impossible love, peaceful death) and general,

non-stereotyped (i.e., unlike topoi) themes (e.g., love, death, freedom)—and also for aspects of form—which can be broken down into tone, rhythm, etc. A given aspect may be treated by only one approach (e.g., the unconscious of the text can be treated only by the psychoanalytic approach) or by several approaches (e.g., wordplay may be treated by stylistics, rhetoric, linguistics, etc.). For a list and summary of possible aspects, see Chapter 4.

4. What I call a "configuration" is the particular element, belonging to the chosen aspect, that is to be targeted for analysis (e.g., "love" is a particular configuration belonging to the thematic aspect of a text). Aspects and configurations are therefore the "what" of the analysis. We must distinguish between configurations and sub-aspects. For example, if we consider that thematic analysis concerns either ordinary themes or topoi (stereotyped themes), then ordinary themes and topoi are sub-aspects of the thematic aspect, but not configurations. On the other hand, the particular topos of the scorned woman as it is deployed in *Hamlet* is a configuration.

5. What I call a "proposition" is the particular form that the configuration takes in the object of study according to the analyst, a proposition that the analysis must either validate or invalidate. The proposition is the particular "what" that the analysis sets out to prove. For example, "Hamlet is not truly in love with Ophelia" is a proposition pertaining to the configuration of love, which belongs to the aspect of themes. An analysis contains several propositions. The propositions may relate to a single configuration (e.g., the propositions "Hamlet is not truly in love with Ophelia" and "Hamlet would like to truly love Ophelia" relate to the same configuration). The proposition can be stated at the beginning of the analysis, or it can be temporarily delayed by presenting a question ("Is Hamlet truly in love with Ophelia?") or a matter to be verified ("whether Hamlet is truly in love with Ophelia or not"). In these cases where the proposition is delayed, however, the answer is really already known to the analyst. If one of these propositions is central to the analysis, it can be elevated to the status of a global hypothesis. A proposition is necessarily an answer to a research question or the outcome of the descriptive aims of the analysis. For example: "Does Hamlet love Ophelia?": yes; "How is the theme of love treated in *Hamlet*?": Hamlet loves Ophelia, Claudius loves Gertrude, etc.; "What is the thematic structure of *Hamlet*?": love is treated in such and such a way ..., death is treated in such and such a way ..., etc.

The proposition can therefore be described as "what is said about the 'what'" (in technical and logical terms, the "what" is the subject and "what is said about it" is the predicate). The proposition is supported by argumentation, which is made up of arguments of varying nature and quantity. Broadly speaking, the text encompasses the aspect, which encompasses the configuration, which encompasses the proposition.

We can distinguish at least 30 major aspects of the text and at least 50 major approaches. There are indefinite, if not infinite, numbers of possible corpora, configurations, and propositions.

[handwritten margin note: manifestation of narrowing of that aspects.]

2.2 Further information

Let us assume that any object of analysis, including the literary text, can be broken down into aspects (parts, components, facets, levels, dimensions, etc.) and that the various approaches used to analyze this object (analytical grids, models, devices, critical methods, etc.) largely differ from each other according to the aspect that they are aimed at. For example, the psychoanalytic approach, which focuses on the "psychoanalytic" aspect of the text (e.g., the unconscious, defense mechanisms), is very different from the stylistic approach, which analyses the "stylistic" aspect of the text (e.g., stylistic rhetorical figures, deviations and norms). However, two different approaches may focus on precisely or roughly the same aspect (such as traditional thematic analysis and semiotic thematic analysis). Some aspects are not applicable to all literary works and genres (e.g., versification does not apply, with very few exceptions, to the novel or to prose poetry).

It often happens that something that is a sub-aspect in relation to an aspect is also considered an aspect in its own right. For example, since a sign is made up of a signifier (e.g., the letters of a word) and a signified (the semantic content of that word), the signified is considered a sub-aspect in relation to the aspect that is the sign; at the same time, the signified can be seen as an aspect in itself (e.g., it is addressed as an object in its own right by thematic and semantic approaches). Sometimes, an aspect can encompass and exceed another aspect. For example, the analysis of contents encompasses and exceeds that of themes, since not all contents are themes, at least in the traditional sense of the word (e.g., grammatical contents such as singulars and plurals are not usually considered themes).

A given element of a text can be connected to several aspects. For example, the use of capital letters, which is a feature of the graphic and grammatical aspects of the text, can also be connected to semantic and rhetorical phenomena and aspects of the text, such as when the capital letter provides emphasis or serves to personify an entity (which also relates to the symbolic aspect).

A given approach may be valid for only one aspect. Such an approach may claim to be the only one that is able to address that particular aspect, or to be the one that is best suited to doing so. For example, narratology, in principle, aims to address only the narratological dimension of the text; stylistics, in principle, aims to address only the stylistic dimension of the text, for which, in principle, it is the most suitable approach. If the aspects overlap, at least in part, then several approaches may be capable of describing them. For example, we can broadly say that rhetoric is stylistics plus argumentation; it therefore follows that the rhetorical and stylistic approaches can be used to describe the same phenomena (bringing their own perspectives to bear).

Conversely, sometimes a single approach can be used to study several aspects of the text. However, in this case, these distinct aspects can generally be viewed as sub-aspects, encompassed by a single more global aspect. Thus, semiotics, the discipline that, broadly speaking, describes signs, applies both to signifieds (the contents of signs) and to signifiers (the forms that convey those contents), but these two parts constitute sub-aspects of the sign, which is the global object of semiotics. That being said, it is entirely possible to put together a composite approach, for example, by combining a narratological approach with a stylistic approach. As with all combinations, this would have to be legitimate (some approaches would be almost impossible to combine, as they are based on opposing principles, theories, or methods), interactive (it is not simply a matter of conducting a narratological analysis and a stylistic analysis at the same time, but rather of making these two analyses "converse" with one another), and relevant (it must make sense in terms of the aims of the analysis and of the text being analyzed). Finally, it is possible to use non-literary approaches to analyze a literary object (e.g., using criminology to study detective novels).

3 Objects of analysis

There are several possible types of objects for a literary analysis. In particular, we can distinguish between analyses that take the following phenomena as their object (whether in the singular or the plural, e.g., addressing either one or several literary works at the same time):

1. a literary (creative) work;
2. a corpus, when considered in itself and not for the texts it contains (e.g., a critique of the criteria used to construct a given corpus);
3. a method or approach (whether it is considered in itself or in its application to an object, e.g., a critique of traditional thematic analysis);
4. a theory (considered in itself, or in its integration in an approach, or in its application to an object, e.g., a critique of theories of reception or semiotics);
5. a theoretical concept (e.g., literature, genre, the topos in general, a given topos, the narrator, literarity, the sonnet, metaphor) or a methodological concept (e.g., induction, deduction, the parallel analysis of passages from a text);
6. a theoretical expression (e.g., the different definitions of the word "metaphor") or a methodological expression (e.g., the different definitions of the word "interpretation");
7. a theoretical text (e.g., Saussure's *Course in General Linguistics*), a methodological text (e.g., this book), or a text of applied analysis (e.g., analysis of Poe's analysis of his poem "The Raven");
8. another kind of literary phenomenon (e.g., the life of the author, the socio-historical context of a work, a literary event, etc.).

The analysis of a theoretical or methodological expression, even if it is only ever applied to a single object—for example, criticism on the work of the artist René Magritte uses the terms "bilboquet" and "grelot," referring respectively to a child's cup-and-ball game and a small bell, to name two strange recurrent forms—starts from a particular expression and examines the ways that it can be used, either by a single author or different authors, with a range of different conceptual meanings, which can sometimes be very diverse or even opposed to

DOI: 10.4324/9781003179795-5

one another. Conversely, the analysis of a theoretical or methodological concept examines the use of a particular concept, whether or not a single term has been used to denote that concept by different theorists, in different languages, at different periods (either by the same theorist over the course of their career, or by different theorists), etc. For example, one can analyze the concept of the sign, whether it is referred to in a given context as "sign," "signe" (in French), "signum" (in Latin), or "symbol" (in the broad sense, since this word can also denote a specific sort of sign).

In the analysis of one or more theoretical or methodological texts or texts of applied analysis, the analysis takes as its object one or more whole texts, whether these are articles or chapters of a publication, or entire books. This kind of analysis is not necessarily the same as the analysis of a theory, a method, or an applied analysis, since these may be elaborated over the course of several texts by a single author and/or by different authors (e.g., the development of psychoanalytic theory in Freud's works, and subsequently by other theorists), and a single text may develop several of these (e.g., Roland Barthes's development of different conceptions of photography in *Camera Lucida*).

E.A. Poe poem

The Raven vs. The Dove
- many have attempted to dissect The Raven. each believing that their analysis is the most accurate. conflicting views, but same analysis.

Part II

Components of analysis

4 Aspects of the literary text

4.1 Introduction

Rather than attempting to draw up an exhaustive list of the aspects of the text—an impossible feat, given the proliferation of aspects that follow from the various conceptions of the text proposed by different theorists in different periods—I have opted for a critical and systematist approach instead of an encyclopedic one. I shall present the aspects of the text as they are generally described, but also as they could be, or even should be described.

Certain aspects are encompassed within others. For example, the aspect of themes is encompassed within that of signifieds, while the ideological aspect is encompassed within the social aspect. Another example: analyses relating to feminism, gender, post-colonialism, etc. are notably focused on thematic, ideological, and representational aspects of the text, but these can of course be constituted as aspects in their own right.

Some aspects covered in this chapter (e.g., style) have direct counterparts in Chapter 5, which deals with approaches (e.g., stylistics). However, some of the specific approaches treated in that chapter correspond to a more general aspect in the current chapter. For example, whereas the chapter on approaches includes a section on mythanalysis, in the present chapter I have not provided a separate section on the "mythical" aspect of the text, although the latter is effectively treated as a part of several more general aspects, such as themes, topoi, beliefs, or ideology. In other words, one could envisage a larger number of aspects by considering each of the more specific aspects covered within the following sections. Moreover, each of the thousands of disciplines that exist can potentially be exploited in literary studies (e.g., criminology in studying a detective novel, mathematics in a "mathematical" novel), which then brings into view as many other possible aspects (e.g., a criminological or mathematical aspect).

It is likely that there are aspects that are not yet known to us, which may have been identified by little-known approaches or theories, or may come to be identified by future approaches or theories, just as the psychoanalytical aspect was identified only with the invention of psychoanalysis. Finally, aspects that do

DOI: 10.4324/9781003179795-7

not exist today may appear in the future, just as the internet and digital media aspects of some texts emerged only a few decades ago.

This list of aspects does not translate directly to a method of analysis, but should rather be viewed as a number of facets of the text that an analysis can address. It is not enough, for example, in order to produce a satisfactory analysis, to identify some phenomena in a text and to classify them according to the various types of aspects. If one addresses several aspects in the course of an analysis, one will usually choose aspects that are inherently complementary to one another (e.g., grammar and syntax, arrangement and rhythm), or for which one can establish the particular relations that exist between them in the analyzed work. One should therefore avoid "assorted" or "parallel" analyses, where one passes from one aspect to another without explicitly addressing the significance of the relations between them. For example, one should avoid undertaking an analysis that addresses both a poem's versification and its themes, without showing the relationships between these two aspects.

4.2 Beliefs, values, ideology, argumentation

An ideology is essentially made up of beliefs (true/false/undecidable, etc.), values (positive/negative/neutral/undecidable, etc.), and ethical precepts (things to be done/things not to be done/optional/undecidable, etc.). The analysis of these three kinds of modalities involves identifying the modalized objects and assigning them the appropriate modalities according to the different observers in question. For example, in most cultures, it is generally considered that killing one's fellow human beings is "negative," and that it is therefore among the "things not to be done." When two observers see things in the same way, there is modal consensus (e.g., a consensus of beliefs); when they differ, there is modal conflict (e.g., a conflict of values); when they change their minds, there is modal conversion (e.g., a conversion in ethical principles).

Approaches to the ideological reading of texts can differ in the following ways: they may be internal to the ideology in question (the analyst shares the ideology) or external to it (the analyst does not share the ideology); they may be objective or subjective; and they may be apologetic, neutral, or denigrating. For example, several readings of a text may agree that it conveys a communist ideology, but may differ as to whether they subscribe to this ideology, whether they describe it subjectively or objectively (and particularly without bad faith), and whether they approve of it or denigrate it. This denigration can amount to a work or even an author being "canceled" within the literary field, on the grounds that they are ideologically nonconforming, irrespective of their value or possible literary interest (e.g., historical) in other respects (e.g., the famous writer Céline has been discredited because of his expression of racist views). Consequently, to borrow the terms of the ancient philosophers, the Good and the True prevail over the Beautiful.

We must distinguish between, on the one hand, reference observing subjects and reference modalizations and, on the other hand, assumptive observing subjects and assumptive modalizations. Reference observing subjects and refer-ence modalizations are associated with the ultimate truth of the text (in general, the omniscient narrator of a text, for instance in a novel, is the reference observing subject). Assumptive observing subjects produce modalizations that may or may not correspond to the reference modalizations (e.g., the modalizations of a given character—such as the beliefs that they defend or embody—may be presented by the narrator as being false). The observing subjects are of different types: empirical (i.e., real) author (e.g., the real Shakespeare); constructed author (e.g., the image of the author derived from the text); narrator; characters; narratee (see section 4.22); constructed reader (the image that the text constructs of its expected/unexpected or desired/undesired reader); empirical (i.e., real) reader.

A value system is a hierarchical structure of values ("values" has here a more restrictive meaning than the one at the start of this section). It is a structure of thymic modalizations—attitudinal or axiological modalizations, which attribute the modalities "positive," "negative," etc., in varying intensities—which involve elements that are considered substantive or even transcendent (e.g., Coca Cola is generally not a value, in the narrow sense, but liberty and love generally are).

Argumentation is a process that aims to convince people of the veracity (i.e., truth) of a logical proposition, which is to say, the combination of a subject (the thing that we are talking about, e.g., Madame Bovary) and a predicate (what we are saying about the subject, e.g., that this character is bored). The proposition can be about a fact (e.g., it is raining: true), a belief (God exists: true), a value (liberty is positive: true), or an ethical claim (we must love each other: true). The term "argumentation" also refers to the whole set of arguments deployed to validate or invalidate a logical proposition (see Chapters 12 and 13 on argu-mentation and opinion).

4.3 Character, actant, actor, agonist

In the broadest sense, a character is an anthropomorphic entity involved (or that could be involved) as an agent (or subject) in the thematized (i.e., recounted by means of signifieds) and fictive action of a semiotic product (a text, image, etc.). For example, according to this definition, in a novel, an apple that falls by force of gravity onto someone's head is the agent of an action, that of falling on the head of the person, but it is not anthropomorphic. Conversely, characters include nonhuman but anthropomorphic entities such as: a magic sword endowed with consciousness, and therefore with will, in a fairytale; the com-puter HAL 9000 in *2001: A Space Odyssey*, which, for its own reasons, seizes control of the spaceship from its human occupants.

Semiotics prefers to use the concepts of actor and actant rather than the intuitive but problematic pre-theoretical concept of character. In the broadest sense, an actant is an entity that plays a role in a process (roughly speaking, an action) and/or an attribution (the assignment of a characteristic or property to something). An actor is an entity that fulfills at least two roles. For example, a man who washes himself is an actor since he is both the agent of the action (he does it) and the patient of this action (he "receives" it). Actors are therefore not limited to characters, even if the latter category is extended to include nonhuman anthropomorphic entities. Thus, the Dow Jones stock market index could be an actor in a financial text.

The system of interpretative semantics developed by the French semantician François Rastier distinguishes, non-exhaustively, between 16 roles, some processual and some attributive: (1) processual roles: accusative (an element affected by the action); dative (an element that receives a transmission); ergative (an element that does the action); final (a goal that is sought); instrumental (the means employed); resultative (an outcome); (2) attributive roles: assumptive (a point of view); attributive (a characteristic); benefactive (a beneficial element); classitive (a class of elements); comparative (a metaphorical comparison); spatial locative (a place); temporal locative (a time); malefactive (a harmful element); holitive (a whole broken down into parts); typitive (a type, or model, to which an individual instance, or token, relates or belongs). See Hébert, 2019 for an overview of Rastier's work.

From the point of view of a naive ontology (which defines kinds of beings, broadly speaking), an actor can correspond to: (1) an anthropomorphic being (e.g., a human, an ordinary or magical animal, a talking sword, etc.); (2) a concrete inanimate element, including objects (e.g., an ordinary sword), but not limited to them (e.g., the wind, the distance to be traveled); (3) a concept (courage, hope, freedom, etc.).

When we analyze an actor in the form of a human being (a character, in the conventional sense) we can distinguish between the following aspects: (1) physical (appearance, height, weight, etc.) and physiological (age, sanguine or nervous temperament,[1] etc.); (2) psychological (personality, desires and aversions, aspirations, emotions, feelings, attitudes, drives, etc.), intellectual (intelligence, knowledge, culture, etc.), and ideological (beliefs, values, morality, ethics, etc.); (3) relational and social (personal history, first and last names, social classes [political, economic, professional, etc.], marital status, family, spouse, friends, enemies, professional relations, etc.); (4) thoughts, words (and other semiotic products: drawings, etc.), and actions.

An agonist, in Rastier's theory, is an actor of a hierarchically higher level that encompasses at least two actors with identical or similar roles (Rastier, 2016: 77–78). For example, in *Hamlet*, Rosencrantz and Guildenstern generally form such an agonist. The actors included in an agonist may belong to the same ontological class (e.g., two humans, such as Rosencrantz and Guildenstern) or to different ontological classes (a human and an animal, a human and an object, an animal and an object, etc.). In the latter case, the actors are probably always connected by a metaphorical–symbolic comparison: for example, in *Of Mice and*

---

1 Note that temperament may be classified under either physiology or psychology, or both, depending on the theory in question.

Men, the small animals that Lennie loves and kills probably symbolize Lennie himself, in his fragility and in the self-destruction that he inevitably produces.

4.4 Collection

A literary collection is a document constituted by the grouping of several autonomous, often short literary texts, which together form a single work (e.g., a collection of formerly unpublished poems that has been structured by the author of the poems), or alternatively one that is composed of several works or parts of works. The individual parts may be literary creations (poems, short stories, novels, plays, essays, etc.) or texts of literary theory or criticism. The collection analyzed may be:

1. anthological (a selection of the best or most famous texts) and/or non-anthological (whether it contains a single book or several, such as in exhaustive compilations of an author's work, which are necessarily non-anthological);
2. posthumous (published after the author's death) or anthumous (published before the author's death);
3. ordered (a thematic and/or chronological order; the latter may be based on the date of the start of writing, the end of writing, the date of publication, etc.) or unordered;
4. undertaken by the author and/or an editor and/or a publisher;
5. composed of whole texts and/or excerpts (e.g., excerpts from novels in a school anthology);
6. composed of texts by a single author or multiple authors;
7. composed of texts belonging to one genre (e.g., poetry, erotic poetry) and/or belonging to several genres (e.g., nineteenth-century French literature).

One may find a "pattern" in the collection (either formal: chiasmus, inversion, etc., or narrative: from birth to death, etc.) that explains the sequence of texts, chapters, or sections (or simply their copresence). Let us consider some basic examples. In terms of the signified or content, a collection might be structured around: the four seasons (e.g., poems evoking spring, summer, etc. are grouped together, each forming a separate section), or the four elements (air, earth, fire, water). In Baudelaire's *Les Fleurs du mal*, the sequence of poems produces an overall narrative relating the narrator's pursuit of (generally ineffective) remedies to his *spleen* (the "Ideal," brotherhood, wine, revolt, death, etc.), each considered in turn. In terms of the signifier, a collection might be structured around an arrangement of texts based on the alphabetical order of their titles. Other criteria than signified or signifier can also be used, for instance the collection might be based on the chronological order of the writing of the texts.

The sequence of texts within the collection lends itself to an analysis from the perspective of segmentation, arrangement (see section 4.18), and rhythm (see section 4.17). We can distinguish in particular between semantic rhythms (of signifieds or contents) and expressive rhythms (of signifiers). For example, we might find semantic rhythms in the recurrence of themes from one unit to another (e.g., from one poem to another, from one short story to another, from one section to another). If we imagine a collection of four short stories containing the two major themes "A" (denoting, let us say, "love") and "B" (let us say, "death"), we might find recurring rhythmic combinations in the form A B B A (love, death, death, love), A A A B, etc.

The copresence of several texts within the same encompassing unit has the effect of modifying, inflecting, and determining their individual meaning and esthetic value, by virtue of the general principle that the global (here, the collection) determines the local. Consequently, a text in a collection does not have the same meaning as it does outside that collection. Each text in the collection is the context, with varying degrees of proximity, of the other texts in the collection (see section 4.7). For example, a given poem might be judged to be mediocre when viewed in isolation from the collection, but takes on a greater value within the collection thanks to its role as a pivot, a synthesis, a unit that highlights another element of the collection, etc. In terms of representativeness, some texts will be representative (or unrepresentative) of the collection to varying degrees compared with others, depending on the particular characteristics in question.

4.5 Connotation, denotation

The French linguist Catherine Kerbrat-Orecchioni suggests the following definitions and examples of the concepts of denotation and connotation in linguistics (these terms have other meanings in logic and philosophy):

> We can consider that the semantic content of any linguistic unit can be broken down into two types of components: *denotative features*, which are the only features that intervene directly in the referential mechanism [which makes it possible to connect the denotative features to the features of the objects being referred to], reflect the objective properties of the object denoted, and, in principle, are the only features involved in the truth value of the statement; *connotative features*, which certainly play a non-negligible role in the choice of the signifier, but whose relevance is determined by considerations other than that of strict adequacy to the referent. We will give two examples: (1) The content of "armchair" is opposed denotatively to the content of "chair" on the basis of the feature [of the seme] /with armrests/ vs. /without armrests/ [...] but the term also connotes the idea of comfort: even if all armchairs do not necessarily possess this property, the feature [comfortable] belongs to the "image associated" with the concept by the speaking masses, and overdetermines the semantic content of the item. (2) "Shoe" is opposed denotatively to "sock," but connotatively to "kicks" [i.e., a slang term for "shoes"]: these two terms have the same extension [i.e., they apply to exactly the same objects, the same referents];

it is therefore not the nature of the referent that determines the choice of signifier in this case, but the characteristics of the communication situation (a connotation of the "language level" type).

(Kerbrat-Orecchioni, 2002: 425)

I would add that a connoted term and its counterpart, which I would term the non-connoted counterpart (in fact, connotation is always symmetrical), may not share the same extension (inventory of referents): for example, "horse" (neutral) has a greater extension than "nag" (pejorative), whose extension is encompassed by that of "horse."

From an (exclusively) differential perspective, rather than a referential perspective, meaning is produced in the interaction between signifieds in language (as an abstract system) and in context (in a given text). From a referential perspective, if we consider that meaning (at least the important meaning) is produced in the matching of a concept to a referent (the entity aimed at by the concept) rather than consisting (exclusively) in the content of the concept, we have to see that this matching is only possible insofar as the features of the referent have been, beforehand or in the course of the current utterance, integrated into the concept in the form of replicas of them. The semantic meaning can be judged, in referential theories, to be secondary to the meaning produced in the matching of the concept with the referent. There are also asemantic referential theories: the theory of direct reference (without the mediation of a content) considers that direct matching applies either to all linguistic signs (or even to all signs), or to some of them (e.g., proper nouns and deictics), or to only one type of them (e.g., only proper nouns).

Referential theories with content (thus excluding theories of direct reference) must consider whether the concept replicates all the features of the referent, or only the set of features that are necessary for identifying the referent. The denotative content cannot reflect all the properties of a referent—especially given that these properties are probably infinite in number, even for non-physical referents—since language and a given text are machines whose effectiveness and efficiency are based on a principle of semiotic economy (a direct adaptation of the general principle of least effort). The problem is then that of stipulating which features are retained in language (more generally in a system) and in context (e.g., in a given text).[2] In the same way, any potential connotation must be validated as a connotation activated in and/or by the sign in the analyzed text (or even the sign outside the text).

Kerbrat-Orecchioni reminds us that, like any semiotic unit, a unit of connotation is broken down into signifier (Sa) (the form that conveys the sign) and

---

2 Kerbrat-Orecchioni, like others, considers that the signified is not the referent: it consists only of the distinctive features that are essential for distinguishing it from the other signs of the language and not of an exhaustive description of the designated objects, especially since any referent, even abstract ones, could have an infinite number of properties.

signified (Sé) (the content of the sign), even though "the term 'connotation' is often used only for connoted contents."

Connotation can be found in different places:

> Connotation can indeed be found in phonic, prosodic, or graphic material (a matter of "phonostylemes," regional "accent," the symbolism of the sounds, or phonic and typographic games …); it can make use of a morphological structure, a syntactic construction, a lexical unit, or even the discursive denoted content … As these various elements can be a source of connotations, we can see that their support can be, depending on the case, of a smaller, equal, or larger dimension than that of the word. On the other hand, connotators often function in networks: often the connoted content of a given text relies on a whole constellation of heterogeneous facts. But this does not mean that we should reduce all connotations to facts of "speech": although some of them are individual (specific to a subject, or to a textual idiolect), others are coded in language [e.g., the pejorative connotations of the suffix "-ard," in "coward," "dullard," drunkard," etc.].
>
> (Kerbrat-Orecchioni, 2002: 425)

As the author points out in relation to the denoted content, the connotative signifier can be a content, a signified. But we would add that the connotative signifier can also be a connotative content. For example, although for a misogynist speaker the word "woman" contains the connotative feature /negative/, for his interlocutor who is not a misogynist, the connotative seme (part of a signified also called "feature") /negative/ will cause the connotation /misogynist/ to appear, qualifying the text and the author (on seme, see section 4.19).

Rather than considering that the source unit of connotation is a connotative signifier and the target unit is a connotative signified, we can also consider the source unit to be an interpretant (i.e., a unit that has an effect on the content, which makes it possible to validate) and the target unit to be a seme and/or a signified.

Kerbrat-Orecchioni   proposes the following classification of connotative signifiers:

> —Connotations that enrich the representation of the referent through various associative mechanisms (every word connotes its own paronyms, synonyms, or homonyms [and co-occurrences]), or various types of play with the signifier (trope, pun, allusion, etc.).
>
> —"Stylistic" connotations, which indicate that the message proceeds from a particular sub-code (or "lect"): diachronic variants (with archaic or modernist connotations), dialectal variants (e.g., ["yous" as the plural form of "you," among some Scottish and Irish speakers of English]), "sociolectal" variants (terms specific to a sociocultural milieu), "idiolectal" variants (terms specific to an ideological structure [or to a specific speaker]), or "typolectal" variants (terms specific to a particular type of discourse, [just

as the use of "thou/thee/thy" in place of "you/your" is marked with a "poetic," as well as archaic connotation]).

—"Enunciative" connotations, which provide information about the speaker and the communication situation: some of the previous categories can also be found here (this is the problem of "levels of language," which are related to both style and enunciation), alongside "axiological" connotations (pejorative or meliorative), or affective connotations ("emotional" values, of which Bally attempted to draw up a list, and which Osgood's "semantic differentiator" aims to measure).

(Kerbrat-Orecchioni, 2002: 425–426)

Connotations relating to the enunciator (age, social status, culture, nationality, language, etc.) are governed by a general principle: every producer (and every production process) is reflected (positively, negatively, and/or by significant omission) in the product. Correlatively, any society is reflected in a product that is created within it, and which it determines (this is true of any other part of a product's context). Finally, any expected receiver (and therefore also any non-expected receiver) and/or any desired receiver (and therefore also any non-desired receiver) is reflected in the product (note that a receiver can be desired but not expected). One can also suppose that, if an empirical (given, concrete) receiver—whether or not it corresponds to the expected, constructed receiver—appreciates a product, it is because that receiver is reflected in that product in some way.

Connotations are sometimes valued in general (as in literary studies) and sometimes devalued in general (as in certain linguistic theories). Their "domain of relevance extends over all semiotic systems (connotations are indeed massively present in iconic, filmic, musical, gestural messages, etc.)" (Kerbrat-Orecchioni, 2002: 426).

4.6 Content, form

Traditionally, we consider that the content of a semiotic product is what is said (the themes or, more generally, the semiotic contents or signifieds) and the form is the way in which it is said. The content can be subdivided into a subject—what is being talked about—and a predicate—what is being said about it.

In the category of form we can place versification, genres, styles, rhetorical processes, tone, levels or registers of language, the lexical fields, rhetorical stylistic figures, sentence structure, the tenses and modes of verbs, punctuation, the structure of the text, narrative voice and perspective, etc. (Lafortune and Morin, 1996: x). It has also been said that style is the form of the text (Bénac and Réauté, 1993: 97).

In reality, this seemingly clear distinction continually runs into problems. In particular, the opposition between content and form does not coincide with the opposition between signified (content) and signifier (that which conveys the content). Although the content broadly corresponds to the signified and some elements of form relate exclusively to the signifier (e.g., several aspects

No	Content	Form	Example
1	expected degree	expected degree	The Earth is round
2	expected degree	unexpected degree	The Earth is rondiform
3	unexpected degree	expected degree	The planet Oxydia is round
4	unexpected degree	unexpected degree	The planet Oxydia is rondiform

Figure 4.1 A typology of combinations of content and form

of versification), other elements of form involve elements of the signified (e.g., tone, which may be comic, serious, etc.), or are even composed solely of the signified.

If we combine the content/form distinction and the deviation/norm distinction, we find the four situations indicated in Figure 4.1. The typology could be refined by distinguishing, within the category of content, between the subject and the predicate.

Content and form are traditionally considered to be independent from one another (this conception can be described as a "content/form theory"). This conception is closely related to essentialist theories (particularly Platonic idealism), according to which something is manifested by a form. It is also closely related to ornamentalist theory, which considers that a work of art consists of a (good) content ornamented with an attractive form (e.g., rhetorical embellishments).

Modern conceptions of this problem, which do not start from an essentialist position and which we can term "content–form theories," instead consider that a change in content necessarily involves a change in form and vice versa ("to die" does not have exactly the same meaning as "to pass away"; e.g., one cannot say "my plant has passed away"). In other words, just as Ferdinand de Saussure (a Swiss linguist whose *Course in General Linguistics* laid the foundation for much of the semiotic and structuralist thought of the twentieth century) postulates for the signifier and the signified, content and form are united by a relationship of reciprocal presupposition: if we change one, we change the other.

Works, movements, poetics, theories, genres, authors, etc., can be classified as either formalist or substantivist according to their focus on form or content respectively. Generally speaking, substantivism is valued over formalism. Victor Hugo expounded a substantivist view when he claimed that "poetry lies not in the form of ideas but in the ideas themselves" (Hugo, 1912: 5–6). On the other hand, some esthetic conceptions take the opposite view, such as that defended by the OuLiPo group. Ultimately, a valuable work of art is necessarily good in both content and in form.

The content/form opposition is homologous (i.e., it acts as an analogous pairing) to a series of traditional oppositions in our culture: soul/body, being/appearing, intelligible/perceptible, etc. We could add that it is homologous to the oppositions invariant/variable, general/particular, type (model)/token (concrete manifestation of the model), etc.

4.7 Context

The context of a unit is a "milieu" that "surrounds" it, made up of units (terms, relations between these terms, operations, etc.), whether or not they are of the same nature as it (e.g., words as the context for a word), and whether or not they have an impact on it by determining it to a greater or lesser extent. The impact of the context can apply to any or all aspects of a semiotic product (signifiers, signifieds, genre, style, etc.). We can extend the definition of "context" and distinguish the following types (by building on a typology from Rastier, 2001: 298): (1) the active context, that which has an impact on the analyzed unit; (2) the passive context, that upon which the analyzed unit has an impact; and then two inert contexts: (3) the non-active context, that which has no impact on the analyzed unit; and (4) the non-passive context, that upon which the analyzed unit has no impact.

We can distinguish between an internal context and an external context. The boundary between interiority and exteriority in this case is the boundary delimiting the semiotic product in question (e.g., a text). However, the closure of the semiotic product, which is always relative, is more difficult to grasp than it seems, not least because some semiotic products participate in a number of encompassing/encompassed relationships; for example, an oral text is a semiotic product, but the oral text together with its associated semiotic systems (e.g., gestures) also constitutes a semiotic product, which encompasses the first semiotic product. Oral and written texts can be associated with the following semiotic systems: facial expression, gesture, graphic presentation, typography, diction, music, images, illustrations, etc.

The internal context is either monosemiotic (e.g., ordinary text) or polysemiotic (e.g., illustrated text). The prefix "co-" can be used to designate an internal context, whether this context is of the same semiotic type or of a different semiotic type from the unit being analyzed. For example, in an ordinary text, the "co-text" of a unit refers to all the other textual signs. The co-text has as many zones of locality as there are levels of complexity. The main levels of a text are the morpheme (the smallest linguistic unit that can convey a meaning, e.g., "agri-"), the lexeme (roughly, a group of morphemes, e.g., "agriculture"), the period (roughly, a group of sentences), and the whole text.

We can distinguish between many forms of external contexts: biographical (whether viewed from a historical or psychological perspective; see section 4.16), sociological (see section 4.20), historical (both the "history" of ordinary people's lives and the "History" of famous people and events), sociocultural, artistic and esthetic, scientific, political, ideological, other works by the same author or by other authors, etc. The five main external contextual variables—which are all factors of relativity, meaning that phenomena can vary depending on them—are the producer, the receiver, time, space, and culture (which is a social and collective construction). Clearly, the time, space, and culture of the producer and the receiver may be the same or different (e.g., a foreign reader who is not contemporary with the novel that they are reading); it is therefore necessary to make a distinction between the context of production and the context of reception.

Just as the product always contains a reflection of the producer (whether deliberately or not), the process of production, the expected receiver (and therefore also any non-expected receiver), and the expected reception (and therefore also any non-expected reception), the context is also always reflected in the product (e.g., even a science-fiction utopia "speaks" of the contemporary era, even if it does so in a negative mode or by meaningful omission). These inevitable reflections of context may also be supplemented by explicit indications regarding the producer, the process of production, the context, etc.

Every product is affected by its context and, if only for this reason, reflects it; in principle, every product also affects to some degree, retroactively, the context in which it was produced, and which is thereby changed. An individual, minor text may have only a minor impact, or virtually no impact, on its context, but some texts have had a major impact and continue to do so (e.g., the Bible).

The approaches that are termed "contextual" (e.g., literary history for texts) on the basis that they methodologically—i.e., consciously, explicitly, and in a relevant way—exclude the immanence of the work, and approaches that are termed "immanent" (e.g., semiotics, rhetoric) on the basis that they methodologically exclude the context of the work are complementary rather than opposed to one another, since it is not possible to understand the work without a minimum of contextualization and internal description.

4.8 Deviation, norm

To be human is to be condemned to live according to norms and deviations, as well as other semiotic inevitabilities: being condemned to interpret and produce meaning, etc. Schematically, we can say that the natural sciences study laws and the sciences of culture study norms. The way in which we conceive and study norms, and correlatively, deviations, is therefore crucial and perpetually relevant for the sciences of culture.

Every semiotic product therefore relates to norms, either by conforming to them to varying degrees; by failing to fulfill them, or even "deviating" from them; by producing new norms that are opposed to or simply different from the norms in question; by not referring to the norms in question; or by being undecidable in relation to the norms in question.

All my observations can be applied, with some adjustments, to other arts. The concepts of norm and deviation can obviously be used to describe phenomena that are not necessarily literary or artistic: for example, comedy is always produced by a deviation (slipping on a banana peel is a deviation from "normal" conduct); physical and psychological ailments are conceived as deviations from the "norms" of health.

Literature has often been defined as a deviation from a norm, and this norm can vary from one theory to another (the scientific text, a theoretical "degree zero" of expression that would be the most direct way of expressing an idea, etc.). The literary text has been considered as containing more deviations than non-literary texts; and, within this category, poetry has been considered as containing more (and/or different) deviations compared with non-poetic literary texts. The literary texts produced by great writers have been viewed as violating norms, surpassing norms, and/or establishing their own norms. Rhetorical stylistic figures (e.g., metaphor) have also been defined as deviations compared to the ordinary, supposedly neutral way of saying things, as has style itself (see section 4.24). Other literary concepts are instead considered as norms: linguistic norms (grammatical, syntactic, and morphological rules, etc.), genres, narrative clichés (e.g., betrayal between lovers) or thematic clichés (e.g., the femme fatale), etc. Fortunately—for the sake of literature—this does not mean that these norms cannot be violated (e.g., Michel Tremblay's theater violated the norm of the Quebec theater of his time by introducing the popular language known as "joual").

The concepts of norm and deviation are associated with: (1) predictions, which may or may not be fulfilled (e.g., one expects a deviation, but it is the norm that is fulfilled); (2) wishes, which may or may not be fulfilled (e.g., one wishes for a deviation, but it is the norm that is fulfilled); (3) thymic attitude (euphoria, dysphoria, aphoria—i.e., indifference—etc.), which may or may not be produced (one may value the deviation or the norm, or be indifferent to it, etc.). Generally speaking, the products of mass culture (e.g., works that are unintentionally kitsch, such as sentimental novels or popular songs) value the norm, whereas products with a limited distribution (e.g., the "great art" of the "serious novel" or of "avant-garde music") value deviation.

The term "norm" implies, even if implicitly, the possibility of "deviation." The norm only possesses its value in relation to attested, probable, or simply possible deviations; clearly, the deviation only takes on its value in relation to the norm from which it deviates. The perspective is relative: that which is a norm relative to a deviation is also a deviation when seen in relation to that deviation. There are also deviations from the deviation, which are sometimes returns to the norm. The content of a norm or of a deviation is not inherently "normal" or "deviant," and the same phenomenon can be both norm and deviation, either at different times or simultaneously. For example, formal versification used to be the norm in poetry in Europe, but it is now a deviation relative to the current norm of poetry without formal versification (at least for "avant-garde" poetry). Yet even when formal versification was the norm in poetry, it was a deviation from standard, non-versified language.

A norm is always defined by a specific instance, an observing subject, whether collective or individual. For a given phenomenon, it can vary according to the usual factors of relativity: time, space, observing subject, culture, etc. This contrasts with the concept of a law, and notably a natural law (such as gravity), which is in principle immutable (or variable according to precise, fixed parameters) and not defined by an instance (unless we invoke God, Nature, etc.). I would argue that a norm is always defined within a system. For example, a language (or dialect) is one such system, but so are sociolects (which define discourses, genres, etc.) and idiolects (which define a writer's style, etc.). For example, Rimbaud and Verlaine's "Asshole Sonnet" is a deviation from the genre of the sonnet (and thus from the sociolect), which calls for a subject that is noble, or at least one that is not considered vulgar.

On the side of production, the norm indicates—prescriptively (in the broad sense, including all deontic modalities), and whether one is aware of it or not—the form that the semiotic product should take. On the side of reception, it can be used, from an evaluative point of view, to assess what has been produced. Finally, with regard to the immanence of the product, that is to say, with regard to a descriptive perspective focused on the product in itself, the norm corresponds to that which occurs with the greatest frequency; here we are concerned with a kind of statistical norm.

A norm can be seen as a unit that has a deontic modality assigned to it (i.e., relating to what the unit should "have," "be," or "do"). When the norm is viewed in logical terms, as a proposition, the unit becomes a subject (the thing that is being talked about) and the modality becomes a predicate (what is being said about the subject). We can distinguish between attributive deontic modalities (modalizing by a requirement to "have" or to "be"; e.g., a house must have a door) and action-oriented deontic modalities (modalizing by a requirement to "do"; e.g., a guitar must produce music). However, an action-oriented deontic modality can ultimately be analyzed as a type of attributive deontic modality.

Deontic modalities take four main forms (I have illustrated them here with the requirement to "have," but the same principles hold for requirements to "be" and to "do"): (1) prescription (must have); (2) prohibition or proscription (must not have); (3) permissiveness (there is no obligation not to have); and (4) optionality (there is no obligation to have, i.e., it is permitted to have or not to have). The first two modalities can be grouped under the label "obligation" and the last two under the label "option." A situation of freedom, in the narrow sense—which we could posit as case "0"—would concern that which is not assigned any of these modalities, and which is therefore undecided or indeterminate in this respect; a situation of freedom in a broader sense would also include the two optional cases (i.e., cases 0 + 3 + 4). Obviously, a given element can pass from one modality to another, such as from 1 to 4, from 0 to 1, etc. For example, the Enlightenment prescribed objectivity (modality 1); in reaction, Romanticism prescribed lyricism and subjectivity, so objectivity was then proscribed (modality 2). How, then, should we consider those elements that, without being obligatory, are nevertheless possible and frequent (e.g., a fairytale does not have to feature a dragon, but it is not uncommon)? I would say that modalities can be viewed as either categorical (without possible gradation) or as gradual. Where elements are not obligatory but are possible and occur frequently, this would then be considered a case of gradual prescription; this is effectively the same as a gradual optionality, since prohibition and optionality are, when gradual, inversely correlated (if one increases, the other decreases, etc.).

4.9 Generative seed

Generation is, together with genesis, one of the two possible perspectives from which we can consider production in general. Generation consists in the movement from a type (or model) to an actual product (a manifestation of the model, or token), or in the movement from a generative seed to its manifestation. Both of these cases are concerned with movement from a virtual unit to something that is "the same" but realized, manifested in reality. This movement can be described in terms of operations of transformation (addition, deletion, substitution, conservation, etc.) (see section 4.23).

Generic analysis (i.e., pertaining to genre) can be considered to be a generative approach insofar as it conceives of a given product (e.g., a given text) as the result of operations of transformation—even if the transformation is one of perfect conservation—starting from the type (e.g., the novel). Conversely, genetic criticism, which takes account of the operations of transformation between foretexts (e.g., drafts and proofs) and the final text, is obviously a genetic approach.

Other approaches are even more clearly attached to the generative perspective. Van Dijk considers that the content of a text can be summarized in a macroproposition that generates the whole content of that text; thus "I love you" might be the macroproposition of a particular sonnet by Louise Labé. These approaches, and indeed the concept of the "generative seed" as an aspect of the text, are open to a major criticism: this generative seed is very general in nature, and could easily apply to a large number of semiotic productions; the generative seed, at least when conceived at such a fundamental level, therefore has only a limited capacity for characterizing the text. According to Leo Spitzer, an Austrian literary critic specialized in stylistics, all the parts of the work (or at least the main parts) are isomorphic (have the same structure) in relation to each other, and the whole is isomorphic in relation to the parts; in this sense, each part is a micro-representation: that is, it constitutes a replication of the whole on a smaller scale (see the summary of Spitzer's argument in Guiraud, 1967: 73–77). The parts referred to here are the major aspects of the text (style, composition, plot, themes, etc.). The element that explains the structure is the spiritual etymon. For Spitzer, this etymon is a worldview. However, as we have seen, we can consider that there are generative seeds that are not worldviews. We can also consider that a work can possess several generative seeds. Keyword theory is another example of a generative theory, espoused by a number of structuralist linguists including Saussure and Jakobson. According to this theory, which is clearly open to criticism, a given text is generated by the various forms taken by the graphemes (roughly speaking, the letters) and/or phonemes of a given word or group of these units; in its more extreme version, this theory maintains that every text has a single corresponding keyword.

4.10 Genesis, variant, creation of the book

Genetic criticism is the study of drafts (and proofs, whether annotated or not), which are then conceived not as unwanted byproducts but as foretexts. It makes it possible to take account of the modalities, causes, and effects of the various operations of transformation (erasure, addition, insertion, conservation, etc.) that may take place between one foretext and another, or between a given foretext and the "final" text. It also makes it possible to take account of these same operations taking place between one version of a "final" text and another (e.g., the two different editions of *Les Fleurs du mal* that Baudelaire produced during his lifetime). More broadly, genetic criticism makes it possible to relativize the status of the work as a finished product, which is in fact only an arbitrarily chosen stopping point, or freeze-frame, along a path that could have continued, such that the "final" work would then have been only another "draft."

In principle, a foretext introduces variants in relation to another foretext of the same text, if another exists, and in relation to the final text. In addition to the modifications brought about by the author, there may also be those brought about, whether deliberately or not, by others involved in the editorial process (correction, or sometimes introduction, of errors, censorship, etc.). The various figures who play a role in the editorial process (publisher, series director, typesetter, etc.) also make choices, either with or without consulting the author, which have an effect on the text, even if these choices do not always strictly constitute modifications of the text: choices regarding the format of the book, the typeface used, the content of its covers, its printing, distribution, promotion, etc. When there are several different editions of a given text, we can compare textual variants and the variants relating to its medium of support. A given text may be supported in different formats, including a book (as a material object), an audiobook, a website, etc.

Genesis, translation, adaptation, internal rewritings (e.g., the differences between the three main sequences in "The Three Little Pigs"), etc., are comparable operations that can be included within the general categories, depending on the case, of either "transposition" (if there is a passage from one system to another: translation, adaptation, internal rewritings in different styles, etc.) or of "diaposition" (if there is no such passage, e.g., the internal rewritings of the three versions of "The Three Little Pigs") (see section 4.28 on transtextuality). These can make use of all the principal operations of transformation (see section 4.23 on structure, relation, operation). Genesis and generation constitute the two main perspectives from which we can consider production in general (see section 4.9).

4.11 Genre

Any semiotic product (written text, image, etc.) pertains (even if only negatively, e.g., by opposition, reaction) to one or more genres.[3] A textual genre can be defined from various angles, notably either as a program of norms (regulating the production and interpretation of texts of this genre), or as a type (a model) associated with this program, or as a class of texts that pertain to this type and/or program. The program constituted by the genre defines a type text (e.g., the model sonnet) to which actual texts (in this case, actual sonnets)

3 In fact, we can envisage three possible general perspectives, which we will illustrate with reference to literary texts: every literary text pertains to a genre (even if negatively); every literary text creates its own genre; and—an intermediate position—every literary text pertains to a genre, but every masterpiece creates its own genre.

correspond to a greater or lesser extent; the genre thus defines a class of actual texts (this corresponds to the logical and linguistic distinction between the "type" [the model text] and the "token" [the actual text]). The norms associated with a given genre are made up of prescriptions (elements that must be present), prohibitions (elements that must be absent), and other deontic modalities (permissiveness, optionality, etc.) that regulate the production and interpretation (reception) of texts (see section 4.8 on deviation and norm). The term "program" here denotes a coherent set of specific operations to be carried out. Genre, along with the corpus, the external context, etc., is one of the global units that determine local units (in this case, a given semiotic product).

Prescriptions and prohibitions may apply, depending on the case, to signifiers (e.g., a sonnet must contain rhymes of a certain type) or to signifieds (e.g., a sonnet should not, in principle, be vulgar, which gives rise to the parodic effect of Rimbaud and Verlaine's "Arsehole Sonnet"; a fairy tale may or may not contain an ogre). From another perspective, generic prescriptions and prohibitions may apply, depending on the case, to the content (what is being said) or to the form (how it is said).

A genre has "horizontal" relations with the genres with which it is interdefined within a generic field (e.g., drama and comedy are defined in relation to one another). It also has "vertical" relationships with the genres that encompass it (e.g., the detective novel is encompassed within the novel) or that it encompasses (e.g., the detective novel encompasses the various sub-genres of detective novel, such as the "locked room" mystery). Every text pertains to one or more genres of a given level, and several genres of different levels (higher and/or lower levels). We can use the term "super-genres" to refer to genres situated at a higher level than a given genre (as opposed to "sub-genres"). The most general genres of literature are probably the following: prose narrative (the short story, novel, fairytale, etc.), poetry, drama, and the essay; for a definition of these four genres, see Chapter 7.

Genres can be approached from any of the following three perspectives: (1) that of the producer and production (what genre does this production pertain to according to its producer?); (2) that of the product (what genre does this product pertain to according to the generic markers that it contains?); and (3) that of the receiver and its reception (what genre does this product pertain to according to the person who receives it, reads it, and interprets it?). In some cases, these perspectives will produce results that do not match. For example, a publisher might consider a work to be a novel (e.g., for marketing reasons), whereas its readers consider it to be a short story.

Artistic trends (e.g., Realism), movements (e.g., the Nouveau Roman), schools (e.g., Romanticism), periods (e.g., the medieval period), etc., are associated with certain genres, which may be more or less specific to those subdivisions. Like any other semiotic form, genres appear through the transformation of previous or contemporary forms, then transform and disappear in their turn, which may give rise to "new" forms, whether these are unprecedented or merely reinvented.

Some forms of literary analysis, and more generally some forms of semiotic analysis, consist in defining a genre, comparing genres (e.g., in order to define a generic field or to compare the different stages of evolution of a given genre), and classifying a text within one or more genres. More precisely, the main tasks of generic studies are: defining genres and the various levels of sub-genres and, possibly, super-genres (e.g., discourses, which, in Rastier's view, encompass genres); defining generic fields, in which related and competing genres are interdefined in relation to one another; observing the prefiguration, emergence, continuing existence, transformation (potentially begetting a derivative genre), disappearance, and resurgence of genres; and classifying semiotic products, such as texts, into genres. The classification of a text in a literary genre is a common form of analysis in pedagogical settings.

4.12 Language

In the broadest sense, language is the semiotic system from which oral and/or written texts are constituted. From an "environmental" perspective, language is the main semiotic environment of humans. From an instrumental perspective, language allows the expression of thought, or at the very least we can say that some thought, whether conscious or unconscious, is expressed in texts (oral or written). In this case, language is conceived as the means with which one expresses what one is talking about, that is to say, the means for expressing content; content necessarily manifests itself in a form, which is the way one talks about what one is talking about (see section 4.6). The study of language can include phenomena that linguistics has traditionally neglected (e.g., the phenomena analyzed in narratology) or those that it shares with other disciplines (e.g., the levels or registers of language are studied not only by linguistics but also by stylistics). Although not everything in a text is language (e.g., ideologies), everything in a text manifests itself through language.

In a narrow sense, language is a functional system, and the concrete texts (oral and/or written) that result from it and manifest it are facts of "speech." The canonical opposition language/speech (based on the opposition *langue/ parole* in Saussure's *Course in General Linguistics*) calls for some precisions. First, other systems interact with the language system in texts (see section 4.24 on style). Second, linguistics should not be limited to the study of language, but should also include the study of speech. Finally, linguistics should not be limited to the study of oral language and speech, or treat these as primordial, but must also take account of their written counterparts.

Traditionally, language is separated into domains that correspond to the various branches of linguistics: (1) phonetics (the study of linguistic sounds as physical stimuli), phonology (the study of minimal signifiers, i.e., phonemes, and other signifiers such as intonation); (2) morphology (the study of forms) and syntax (the positions of, functions of, and connections between elements); (3) semantics (the study of meanings [in context, in a given text] and/ or significations [out of context]); and (4) lexicology (the study of lexicons: of morphemes or word roots, of words, phrases, or fixed word groups, and of phraseologies or stereotyped sentences or phrases, such as proverbs). We can also add pragmatics to this list, which, according to one definition, is the study of speech (with which semantics, properly understood, is also concerned), while another definition describes it as the study of the relationship between linguistic signs and their users.

Insofar as the components of language are defined and governed by norms (even when they deviate from them), we can study, in a given text, the respect or non-respect of these norms (see section 4.8).

4.13 Mimetic mode

A mimetic mode (Rastier, 2001: 300) is the type of relationship that exists between the world created by the text (a constructed world) and the "real" world (the empirical world).

A number of different mimetic modes exist, which may be lexicalized (named) or not, associated with a single art or transartistic, either belonging to a single culture or transcultural, and either belonging to a single era or transhistorical. For example (with some overlaps): fantasy, the fantastical, the strange, empirical realism (e.g., in realism), transcendental realism (e.g., in Romanticism, Symbolism, Surrealism), magical realism, idealism, science fiction, absurdism, hyperrealism (in painting), naturalism (in French novels), symbolism, allegorism, impressionism (painting and music), expressionism, "fantacism" (humorous or dramatic), "poeticism" (in the novel or "poetic" painting), the mythical, the legendary, the historical, the biographical.

The analysis of the mimetic mode of a text consists in identifying the marks of the mimetic mode or modes involved. For example, for realism, these marks lie particularly in the presence of meticulous description (physical or psychological). As always, the elements that are identified are described in terms of the modalities (qualitative and/or quantitative) of their presence (or absence), and these are related to their causes and effects (e.g., on the meaning of the text). An analysis may also identify a new mimetic mode or draw up a typology of existing mimetic modes (or even of those that are conceivable but so far unattested).

The stipulation of the mimetic mode of a given production is relative, that is to say, subject to variation according to factors of relativity, including the global/local dimension (e.g., from one part of a text to another), time (e.g., from one era to another), and observer (e.g., from one culture to another or from one person to another). Let us consider some examples of the relativity of mimetic modes depending on the observers and time in question: Tibetan texts recounting the lives of the great masters are filled with supernatural events, yet they are considered by Tibetans to be both realistic and true. In short, these texts belong to the mimetic mode of realism for them—even though they relate events that are out of the ordinary—whereas for many other readers these texts belong to the mimetic mode of fantasy (more precisely, the mode of the "fantastique merveilleux" as defined by Todorov (1970), in which the presence of supernatural elements is accepted by the characters of the story). In the same way, the accounts of the extraordinary lives of Catholic saints, which in previous centuries were considered to be both realistic and true, are now mostly considered to belong to the mimetic mode of (Christian) fantasy.

4.14 Onomastics

Onomastics can be defined both as an approach and as the aspect that is analyzed by this approach. As an approach, textual onomastics is the study of the modalities (including possible natures, e.g., types of proper nouns), causes, and (both intended and unintended) effects (e.g., on the meaning of the text) of the presence (or absence) of proper nouns in a given text, or group of texts, or in one or more genres in the broad sense (e.g., in the novel, or even in literature in general). As an aspect, the onomastics of a text (in general or in a given text) is the set of proper nouns that belong to it and structure it, and the network of "meaning" (in the broad sense, including the "meaning" of signifiers) that they establish.

An actor is an entity—often, but not always, a character—that has a role in a text, whether literary or non-literary. A role refers to some form of participation in an action (e.g., the roles of the agent or patient of an action) or in a characterization (e.g., the roles of characterizer or characterized) (see section 4.3). The set of linguistic forms used to designate and potentially to characterize an actor constitutes that actor's "label" (Hamon, 1998: 107).

The main kinds of designators are therefore: (1) proper nouns (e.g., for Napoleon, the first "Emperor of the French": "Napoleon," "Bonaparte," "Napoleon Bonaparte"); (2) nicknames; pseudonyms; (3) pronouns (e.g., for Napoleon: "he," "him," etc.); (4) definite descriptions, which may be absolute (e.g., for Aristotle, "the most illustrious of Plato's disciples") or relative, e.g., "the man to whom you gave a tomato," or, for Napoleon: "the general," "the general portrayed with his hand in his coat"). There are also less traditional designators, such as (5) the use of adjectives and possessive pronouns (in "His hands were calloused," "His" referring to a character). The label of a given actor may not contain any proper nouns.

The natures of phenomena (their "being") and their functions (their "doing") can be considered from two main angles: mereological (pertaining to wholes and parts) and classificatory (pertaining to classes and classified elements). We can therefore draw up a list of the defining features of a phenomenon (which are the parts that make up the whole phenomenon). Like any linguistic unit, a proper noun can be characterized in terms of its linguistic aspects. We generally distinguish between the following aspects: morphology, semantics, syntax, and pragmatics. Accordingly, people have variously tried to define the proper noun: from a morphological perspective (it is capitalized, etc.); a syntactic perspective (it is often used without a determiner, etc.); a semantic perspective (according to the theory in question: it has no meaning, little meaning, some meaning, a lot of meaning, or a maximal degree of meaning); from a referential perspective (in principle it refers to a unique referent, except in cases of homonymy), etc.

These attempts at definition immediately lead us into difficulties. Not every capitalized element is a proper noun: exceptions include words at the beginning of a sentence, personified phenomena (e.g., "Death"), words printed entirely in capitals for emphasis, the names of social groups (the French, Christians), etc. Not all proper nouns lack determiners ("the Eiffel Tower"). Nouns such as "the moon," "the sun," although considered to be common nouns by some theories, have a unique referent like proper nouns. Nouns such as "the French," "the Quebecois," although designating many individuals, are also often considered to be proper nouns.

We can also construct a typology, that is to say, a classification of the various possible forms of a given phenomenon. Here is a short, non-exhaustive list of the types of proper nouns: anthroponyms are the surnames, patronymics, and/ or first names of people; to these we can add zoonyms (proper nouns commonly designating animals: "Fido," "Daisy," etc.) or even anthropomorphized singular objects (e.g., the names of swords, such as "Excalibur"). Toponyms are names of natural or artificial places ("Montréal," "Black Lake," "the Louvre," etc.). Chrononyms are names of historical periods ("the Middle Ages," "the Renaissance," etc.). Reonyms are names of objects or institutions (e.g., "the Eiffel Tower," when considered as an object), trademarks ("Viagra," "Coca Cola," etc.), company names ("Ford," "Walmart," etc.), and events ("Kristallnacht," "the Great War"). Inasmuch as titles of works are considered proper nouns, titrology is the branch of general and literary onomastics devoted to the study of these phenomena. In fact, any element of any ontological class can be assigned a proper noun. For example, the novelist Henri Bosco assigns proper nouns to individual trees (Bertrand, 2008: 75), not to mention the practice of lovers who assign proper nouns to a part of their partner's body. The anthroponym is generally treated as the prototype, or archetype, of the proper noun, in relation to which other types of proper noun are compared and defined, just as oranges and apples (rather than pomegranates and star fruit) are the prototypes of fruit.

Translations (in the sense of changes of linguistic categories) can occur: for example, a common noun can become a proper noun ("stone" and "Stone") and vice versa ("Picasso," the painter, and "a Picasso," to designate a painting by that painter). Internal translations (remaining in the morphological class of proper nouns) can occur. Thus, the anthroponym "Eiffel" (referring to the engineer Gustave Eiffel) becomes a toponym (and a reonym) in "the Eiffel Tower," and the first name "Roger" can become a surname (or vice versa).

In fact, natures and functions can be considered statically or dynamically, that is to say: either with regard to their possible transformations (emergence, continuing existence or transformation, disappearance, etc.); or in relation to historical time (from one period to another); or synchronically (in the same period); or in relation to the time of the story being told or the succession of the units of the semiotic product (e.g., the succession of words or chapters in a text).

Let us focus on anthroponyms and their primary, standard (e.g., non-metaphorical) use. Traditionally, a distinction has been made between denotative and connotative meanings, and approaches to referential semantics have considered the denotative content as being the only relevant meaning, or at least as the most important meaning.[4] There are five main theses concerning the denotative content (that which allows the objective identification of the referent) of the proper noun:

1. asemanticism (defended by logicians in general, e.g., Kripke, and several linguists, e.g., Molino): the proper noun is empty of denotative content;
2. hyposemanticism (Kleiber, Russel, etc.): the proper noun has a minimal denotative content (predicate of denomination, definite description);
3. mesosemanticism: the proper noun has the same denotative content as common nouns (I do not know of any supporter of this theory);
4. hypersemanticism (Bréal, Dauzat, etc.): the proper noun is overloaded with denotative content;
5. polysemanticism (Hébert): the proper noun, depending on its type, is asemantic, hyposemantic, or mesosemantic (although the opposition between denotative and connotative meaning is invalidated in this theory).

The same theses can be formulated with regard to the proper noun's connotative content (its more subjective content), although it is generally considered (e.g., by Roland Barthes) that proper nouns are hypersemantic in this respect.

In a literary text, a proper noun is often closely associated with one or more other words, which may or may not be present in the same text. The first type of association occurs through homonymy (where all letters and/or all sounds are the same in the two words). Two particular cases of homonymy arise: (1) from one proper noun to another (e.g., "Claudius," in *Hamlet* → "Claudius," as the name of a meteorite); (2) from a proper noun to a word of another morphological class (e.g., "White" → "white," an adjective indicating color). Homonymy can involve the phonic and/or graphic signifier. Here is an example in which there is identity of both the phonic and the graphic signifier (homonymy in the strict sense): "Stone" → "stone." The second type of association occurs through paronymy (partial homonymy): for example, "Leon" → "*leo*" ("lion" in Latin).

---

4 We must distinguish the logical meaning of the terms "denotation" and "connotation" from their linguistic meaning. Roughly speaking, in logic, denotation corresponds to reference and/or the referent, and connotation corresponds to linguistic denotation. We can use the expression "denotative content" to indicate that we are referring to the linguistic use of this term.

It is impossible to establish a link, on the basis of the similarity of signifiers, between words that do not share at least one common letter or sound: for example, "Peter" → "sad." However, other links may exist instead (e.g., in the proposition "Peter is sad").

The existence of a homonym or paronym for a given proper noun does not automatically mean that there is a significant connection between the two nouns. It is necessary to find elements of "proof" (called "interpretants") to establish the relevance of the association. In principle, any interpretation of such an association must be based on the potential meaning—whether the author was aware of it or not, and whether it is obvious or subtle—that was active at the time when the work was produced.

A proper noun can be analyzed with reference to the language to which it belongs ("White," in English → "white," also in English) or in another language ("Godot," as an apparently French name → "God," in English, in Beckett's *En attendant Godot*, a play that the author later adapted into the English version *Waiting for Godot*). The language to which the source or target word belongs may or may not correspond to the language of the context (e.g., an English proper noun in an entirely French text). Since there are several thousand languages (about 6,000), the use of a particular language in interpreting a proper noun must be justified.

"Polyglossia" is the term that I use for any copresence of two or more languages. We can also use the term "to polygloss," or "polyglossing," to refer to a process of rewriting that involves the passage from one language to another; "polyglossing" necessarily involves a situation of polyglossia.

In addition to the semantic contents that a proper noun may evoke through its association with other words, it can also evoke connotations in other ways: through linguistic associations (e.g., "Pierre" is a word in the French language); spatial ("Dupont" evokes a space that is more French than Quebecois, whereas the opposite is true for "Tremblay"); temporal ("Isidore" and "Wilbrod" sound like names from the nineteenth century in Quebec, whereas "Cunégonde" sounds medieval); evaluative ("Eutrope" is probably considered ugly by today's parents, whereas "Olivier" is a very popular name); sociological (in the Quebecois context, "Bob Tremblay" and "Hector de Saint-Denys Garneau" bring to mind the working classes and the aristocracy respectively, while "Hector" and "Oscar" bring to mind servants); etc. There are two possible scenarios: either the evocation has a semic impact (i.e., an impact on the semes, the components of the semantic content) as an interpretant (i.e., it activates an absent content, or neutralizes a present content, or decreases or increases the intensity of presence of a content that is already present), or it does not have such an impact. For example, in the expression "robbing Peter to pay Paul," the seme /English word/ could in theory appear in "Peter" and "Paul," but it probably does not for an English speaker. Obviously, the longer a text is, the more likely the evocations are to have a semantic impact. For a longer discussion of onomastics, see Hébert and Trudel, forthcoming.

4.15 Production, immanence, reception

The act of communication, which takes a semiotic product as its object, can usefully be considered as a structure. As such, it can be broken down into terms (Latin: *relata*, or *relatum* in the singular), the relations between those terms, and the operations or processes (or actions) that are applied to the terms, relations, or operations. The main elements of communication are three terms—the producer (e.g., the author), the product (e.g., the text), and the receiver (e.g., the reader)—and two processes (which also establish relations between the operator and the operands, and between the elements involved in the operation): production, which goes from the producer to the product, and reception, which goes from the receiver to the product. Note that the process of reception goes from the receiver toward the product, in that the receiver takes as their object the product created by the producer. The process of reception (reading, analysis, criticism, etc.), even if it is a simple act of reading (in the usual sense of the term), is always, or at least always involves, an act of interpretation.

However, there is also a process, which we will not consider here, that goes from the product to the receiver, in that the product is intended for and potentially transmitted to a receiver. We can call this process "transmission" and distinguish between two types of transmission: on the one hand, that of the document (e.g., a book) and the perisemiotic stimuli it conveys (e.g., ink marks forming letters), and on the other hand, that of the element for which the document is the support (e.g., the text conveyed by the book).

Just as the semiotic product is the result of the process of production, the reading (in the sense here of the product produced by interpretation) is the result of the process of reception; this reading can be converted into a text, which may be either oral (and then either fixed on some support, e.g., a recording on magnetic tape, or not) or written (and then necessarily fixed on some support). Other elements also play a role in the structure of communication, such as the external context (e.g., social, economic, political, cultural) and the semi-external context (including systems such as language, sociolect, and idiolect, and the forms that those systems define, such as genres, lexicons, and topoi).

The diagram in Figure 4.2 represents the simplified structure of literary communication I just described. The principles are valid for semiotic communication in general (and therefore, in theory, for any communication).

Semiotic analysis can focus on any of the five principal elements in this structure of communication: (1) the producer (e.g., through the author's biography); (2) the production (e.g., through the drafts of a novel); (3) the product itself (e.g., by analyzing the rhetorical figures in a poem); (4) the reception (e.g.,

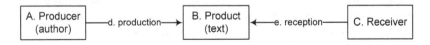

Figure 4.2 Simplified structure of literary communication

by comparing the interpretations that have been made of a given novel); and (5) the receiver (e.g., by studying the readership of a novel). To simplify matters we can reduce this to three broad perspectives: the producer and the production; the product in itself (in its immanence); and the receiver and the reception. For a typology of the 21 situations of analysis that this structure allows us to describe, see Hébert, 2014: 299–304.

As Molino (2018: 259) says: "The literary work consists neither in traces or meanings deposited forever, nor in the author's activity or intuitions, nor in the reader's interpretation, but it is rather the meeting of these three aspects of a single global reality." Consequently, if one wants to conduct an analysis from only one of these perspectives, it is necessary to carry out a methodological reduction, that is to say, one that is conscious, explicit, and relevant to the aims of the analysis.

We can distinguish between empirical elements (i.e., real or concrete, such as the real author) and their constructed (abstract) counterparts: the empirical producer (its being, intentions, messages, etc.) and the constructed producer; the empirical production and the constructed production; the empirical product and the constructed product; the empirical receiver and the constructed receiver (for texts, the model reader, and more generally the model receiver); the empirical reception and the constructed reception. A constructed element is the "image" of the empirical element that is provided by the element acting as a source of information (notably, of clues regarding the nature of the element in question). Each of the five empirical elements can be used as a source to produce a constructed version of any of the other empirical elements. For example, the empirical production can be used to constitute the constructed reception, the constructed product, the constructed author, etc. However, it should be noted that an empirical factor cannot be used as a starting point to construct its own constructed counterpart: for example, the empirical author cannot be used as a starting point to define the constructed author.

A number of different comparative relations can be established between an empirical element and its constructed counterpart: identity (or conformity), similarity, opposition (contrariness or contradiction), alterity. For example, the author constructed on the basis of the text can be very different from the real author. If we add further elements to the model of literary communication (e.g., code or system, world or referent, contact, context), we can also distinguish between the empirical and the constructed version of these elements. For example, Fouquier (1984: 138) adds the world to the model as an element, and distinguishes between the empirical world and the world that he refers to as "constructed." Following Jakobson (1960), we can add the elements of contact (between producer and receiver, or addresser and addressee) and code (more precisely, multiple codes, and even more precisely, systems), and distinguish between the empirical and constructed versions of these elements too.

Each of the three terms of semiotic communication has a principal operation associated with it: the presence or absence of an "intentionality" on the part of the producer; whether or not the intended elements are "marked" or integrated in the semiotic product; and whether or not the receiver perceives the marked elements. For example, an author may intend to inscribe a feminist element in their text; they may or may not succeed in marking this in the work, and they may or may not be aware of their success or failure to do so; and the marked feminist element may or may not be perceived by the receiver. Between each of these operations, there can be concordance or discordance: between the intention and the marking, between the marking and the perception, and also between all three of the operations.

The relations between intentionality and perception allow for the following four general situations, illustrated here with reference to the presence of a comic element in the text: (1) intention of comic element, perception of comic element (e.g., a successful joke); (2) intention of comic element, non-perception of comic element (e.g., a failed joke); (3) no intention of comic element, no perception of comic element; and (4) no intention of comic element, perception of comic element (e.g., a text that was intended to be dramatic, but is instead comical). Situations 2 and 4 correspond to failed communicative processes, but this failed writing and/or "erratic" reading (Saint-Gelais, 2007) can be creative and interesting. The same device (which, in technical terms, is a "Klein four-group") can be applied to other useful oppositions, such as deviation/norm, presence/absence of esthetic effect, (true) Art/kitsch, and dramatic/non- dramatic.

When the producer's intentionality aims at producing an effect in the receiver, we can add an operation that takes place at the same time as or after the operation of perception, that of experience. For example, one may well perceive the mark of a comic intention but not experience the supposedly comic element as being funny; in this case, perception and experience are not concordant. Consequently, we can distinguish between an intention that aims to leave marks in the signs of a text (signifiers and/or signifieds) and an intention that aims, through those marks, to bring about certain effects. We can distinguish between the following types of effects that might be intended: semiotic (e.g., a certain marked sign will lead to the production of a certain other sign or semiotic operation in the mind of the receiver), cognitive (intellectual), emotional, and physical.

Figure 4.3 summarizes the interplay between author, work, and receiver and adds some clarifications.

4.16 Psychology

The theory of anthropic levels (see Hébert, 2020: 62) broadly distinguishes between the following levels of human existence and experience, whether existing in reality or represented in semiotic products, including texts. First, the two fundamental levels: (1) immanent and (2) transcendent (whether one believes in them or not, one must be able to speak of spiritual transcendences), and potentially allowing for an intermediate zone, (3) the immanotranscendent. The immanent level is subdivided into three levels: (4) physical, (5) biological,

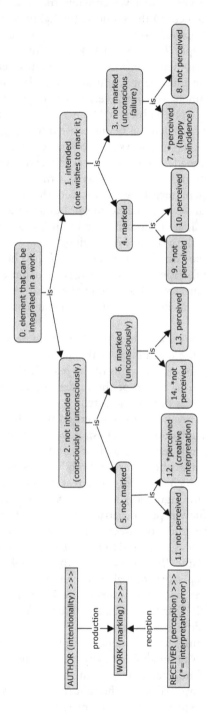

Figure 4.3 Intention, marking, and perception

and (6) cognitive. The cognitive level contains the following sub-levels: (7) physical sensation, (8) affect, (9) the semiotic (including speech), (10) the representational (mental "images," concepts), and (11) potentially other cognitive levels (not covered by types 7, 8, 9, and 10). Each of these ten subdivisions has a noumenal and a phenomenal version. The noumenal version refers to the object in itself (e.g., the immanent world as it is, aside from any question of perception); the phenomenal version refers to the object as it is perceived or interpreted by a subject, a given observer. Depending on the theory in question, the noumenon may be considered as being non-existent (e.g., according to solipsistic theories), or inaccessible, or partially or entirely accessible.

Psychology, in the broadest sense, is concerned with the cognitive level. It studies mental contents and processes, as well as the actions (gestures, words, etc.) that result from them, reveal them, and affect them in turn. In the case of a text, the psychological aspect relates to the author and the reader as well as to the actors in the text that are endowed with a mind, or a complex psyche (i.e., humans, animals, and anthropomorphized beings).

An analysis may focus on the psychological or psychoanalytical elements associated with a text: fantasies, drives, motivations, defense mechanisms, censorship, repression, dreams, complexes, psychoses, neuroses, phobias and other fears, affects, emotions, feelings, passions, temperaments, ego, superego, id, attitudes, ideals, etc.

These elements can be viewed from the three main perspectives of any production: the producer (the real author or the author constructed by the text); the product itself (e.g., the unconscious of the text, that of the characters); the receiver (the real, empirical reader, or the reader constructed by the text, the image that the text projects of its reader, etc.).

In a narrower sense, psychology is concerned with the sub-level of affects. Affects are (1) states, relations, processes, and cognitive contents, that are (2) produced by physical, semiotic, and/or cognitive or even transcendent stimuli, (3) experienced in the "affective body" of a sentient being (human, animal, etc.), and (4) which may be either real or thematized (integrated in the semiotic content, the signifieds) in a semiotic product whose content is either non-fictional (newspaper, magazine, etc.) or fictional (novel, drama, etc.). In this sense, the study of affect can be linked to the study of non-fictional characters (such as a real politician portrayed in a newspaper) or fictional characters (Madame Bovary, Hamlet). In principle, semiotic products simply reproduce the repertoire of real affects; in practice, there may be affects in semiotic products that have no equivalent in reality and, perhaps, vice versa. It is safe to say, however, that the frequency and intensity of affects are not exactly the same in these two different domains.

It is possible to identify several modalities of feelings (although I use the term "feelings" here, this point applies to any type of affect). We can distinguish between: feelings-as-stimuli (experienced in the physical body), feelings-felt (experienced in the "heart"), feelings-thought (experienced in the "head," e.g., "I love her"), feelings-expressed (in speech or with another semiotic tool, e.g.,

"I love you"), feelings-enacted (or activating, that which underlies an action), and feelings-proven (a voluntary or involuntary action that proves the presence of a given feeling, e.g., blushing as proof of love).

4.17 Rhythm

Three operations are necessary to produce a rhythm: segmentation (or articulation) into units, arrangement (a "placement" to be produced or recognized), and seriation (sequencing) of these units (see section 4.18).

These units can be of the following semiotic types: signifiers (or their parts, e.g., the phonological features of phonemes: /*vowel*/, /*consonant*/, /*open*/, /*closed*/, etc.); signifieds (or their parts, i.e., semes and cases, e.g., the semes /liquid/ and /comestible/ in the signified 'water,' or groupings of these parts: isotopies, semic molecules, etc.); or signs (i.e., the combination of a signifier and a signified, e.g., the word "water").

Succession may occur in time only, or in both time and space, as in the case of a succession of elements in a painting, for example, if the viewer's attention is led from left to right. Beyond a basic distinction between a spatial semiotics (image, sculpture, set design, etc.), a temporal semiotics (text, music, sound effects, etc.), and a spatiotemporal semiotics (dance, art installation, theater, cinema, etc.), we can distinguish between semiotic systems or languages: (1) with a fixed timing and sequence (e.g., a film shown in a cinema is not normally interrupted, slowed down, accelerated, reversed, etc.); (2) with free timing but fixed sequence (e.g., although one can go back or jump forward, in principle a text is read from one word to the next, but one can pause between two words); (3) with free timing and sequence (e.g., one looks at a painting for as long as desired, moving one's attention from one figure to another as desired, which is not to say that there are no conventions unconsciously influencing the way one looks at a painting).

Rhythm can be defined as a particular configuration—and its effect—constituted by at least two units of either identical or different "value," in at least two positions succeeding each other in time. In light of this definition, the minimal rhythmic configuration—that is, two units occupying two successive positions—will take one of the following four forms: (1) A, B; (2) B, A; (3) A, A; or (4) B, B (as "empty shells" without any value attached, "A, A" and "B, B" are identical, but the distinction between these cases becomes useful in the discussion of semiotic silence that follows).

In this minimal rhythmic configuration, the value of the units—one of the two values, or both of the values (in the latter case, the silences will be of different natures)—can be a "semiotic silence," in the sense of the absence of a "full" unit. If we take the four previous forms and give B the nature of a semiotic silence, we then arrive at the four forms: (1) A, Ø; (2) Ø, A; (3) A, A; or (4) Ø, Ø.

I do not define rhythm restrictively as the return of the same elements. This more expansive definition therefore allows rhythmic analysis to include—with respect to the repertoire of units—not only cases of fully repetitive rhythms (e.g., A, A or A, B, A, B), but also partially repetitive rhythms (e.g., A, B, A, C), and fully non-repetitive rhythms (e.g., A, B or A, B, C).

The repertoire of rhythmic patterns, even in very general terms, is extremely large. A rhythmic analysis will take account of the following main factors:

1. The number of successive positions in the rhythmic sequence. For example, a quatrain is a stanza composed of four verses, and an alexandrine verse is composed of 12 syllables. The structures produced by the succession of positions can be short, medium, long; dyadic, triadic, etc.; even or odd; etc.

2. The number of simultaneous positions in the rhythmic sequence. The number of simultaneous positions defines the planarity of the sequence. If there are no simultaneous positions, the rhythm is monoplanar; otherwise, it is pluriplanar (or polyplanar). For example, a verse and a stanza appear as monoplanar sequences when conceived, respectively, as a sequence of syllables or verses: a single syllable or a single verse occupies each successive position. However, if we view the signified as defining the relevant successive positions, and take the seme (a component of the signified) as the type of unit involved in the rhythm, we may find several "superimposed" semes in a given position, that is to say, in the same signified.

3. The number of units per successive position (including any overlapping units). For example, in a quatrain there is one verse per position; in an alexandrine verse, there is one syllable per position. Even if the rhythmic sequence is pluriplanar, the number of units in a given successive position may be lower than the number that is made possible by the rhythm's planarity. For example, there might be a biplanar sequence where one of the positions, unlike the others, is made up of a unit and a superimposed silence (this silence is then considered as a non-unit).

4. The total number of units that can occupy positions in the sequence. This is not the number of units per successive or simultaneous position, but the size of the repertoire of different units that can be chosen to occupy a given position. This number can, in principle, be either limited or unlimited. In order to represent a rhythmic pattern schematically, each unit of a different nature can be represented by a different letter. For example, A and B might represent the two rhymes of a quatrain in a sonnet.

5. The organization of the pattern. The main organizational patterns, with respect to the type of succession of units, are: (1) immediate succession (e.g., in the sequence A, B, there is an immediate succession from A to B); and (2) delayed succession (e.g., in the sequence A, X, B, where X = silence, there is delayed succession from A to B; however, there is immediate succession from A to X and from X to B). The main organizational patterns, this time with respect to the succession of the particular natures of the units, are: (1) grouping (e.g., A, A, B, B), (2) interlacing (e.g., A, B, A, B), and (3) embedding (e.g., A, B, B, A). In a tetradic (four-unit) rhythmic pattern with a double value (A and B), such as the rhyme scheme of a sonnet quatrain, these three main organizational patterns

correspond respectively to: couplet rhymes (A, A, B, B), cross rhymes (A, B, A, B), and envelope rhymes (A, B, B, A).

6. The type of units involved. In terms of the types of semiotic products in which they occur, rhythms are not limited to so-called "temporal" semiotic systems, such as music or literature. Rhythm is therefore not limited to poetry alone, and still less to versified poetry alone. For there to be rhythm, it is enough that at least two units (which may be the same unit repeated) are found in a sequence across at least two successive positions. We can therefore speak of rhythm in a pictorial work. Units can be of different natures, whether in a relation of simultaneity (e.g., a seme and a phonemic or graphemic feature occupy the same position) or in a relation of succession (an element of nature X will be followed by an element of nature Y). In the simplest cases, the units are all of the same kind, such as in the case of rhyme, where the units concerned are all phonemes.

7. The units that are actually involved. The units actually involved are the manifestations (or tokens) of the type of units in question (e.g., a particular seme or a particular phoneme that is used in the rhythmic sequence). To take the example of a quatrain in a sonnet, the rhymes might be in -*or* (A) and -*ing* (B).

8. The duration of the units. Rhythms can be: (1) isometric: all units have the same extent (either because of their inherent duration or through a process of "rounding" to standard values); (2) allometric: all the units have different extents; or (3) parametric: some units have the same extent as each other, and others do not. In terms of the length of the verses that constitute it, a stanza composed entirely of alexandrine verses (which therefore all contain 12 syllables) is isometric (and therefore monometric); a stanza containing alternating alexandrine verses and octosyllabic verses will be parametric (and therefore polymetric). It is possible to distinguish between rhythmic sequences with a major cadence and rhythmic sequences with a minor cadence. The former contain sequences of units of gradually increasing length (an upward slope), whereas the latter contain sequences of increasingly shorter units (a downward slope). There are, of course, other patterns, such as: rising units followed by falling units (a "roof-shaped" pattern), falling units followed by rising units (a "v-shaped" pattern), and a sequence of units of the same duration (a horizontal line pattern).

On the analysis of rhythm, see Hébert, 2019: 215–231.

4.18 Segmentation, arrangement

Segmentation is the process that projects or recognizes discontinuity within continuity (material, temporal, spatial, and/or mental). An example of this is the division of a text into sentences or words.

An arrangement is the particular configuration constituted by the segmentation that is applied to the semiotic product and the specific units that occupy each of the resulting segments; for example, the arrangement of a text of 100 words is made up of those 100 segments and the particular word that fills each of them (e.g., "The" for the first segment, "boy" for the second segment, etc.). We can distinguish between the arrangement of signifiers, referred to as "distribution," and the arrangement of signifieds, referred to as "tactics"[5] (following the terms used by Rastier, 2016). For example, when we analyze the sequence of actions in a story according to their order of appearance in the time of the story, we produce a segmentation based on the signifieds, relating to the thematized time of the events (represented in the signifieds) and not to real time, the time of our reality.

A given semiotic product can obviously be the object of many different segmentations, each of which should be based on different explicit and relevant criteria. For example, signifiers can be segmented on the basis of the following criteria, among others: sentence, word, or phoneme (or grapheme, in a written text). The different segmentations may correspond perfectly, a lot, moderately, a little, or not at all. In all cases, the relations between these different segmentations create a dynamic that produces effects in the semiotic product (e.g., effects of meaning), whether these effects are perceived consciously or not.

4.19 Sign, signifier, signified

The sign (e.g., the word "boat") is a unit composed of a signifier and a signified. The minimal linguistic sign is the morpheme (e.g., "agro–bio–logy" has three morphemes). The maximal sign is the text, or the set of texts by an individual author, or even the corpus in which the analyzed text is contained.

The signifier is the form of the sign that makes it possible to transmit its content, its meaning. There are four kinds of textual signifiers: (1) phonemic (phonemes, e.g., *b-o-t*) and related kinds (punctuation, intonation, etc.), and, more broadly, (2) sonic (timbre, pitch, power, etc.); (3) graphemic (graphemes or, broadly speaking, letters, e.g., *b-o-a-t*) and, more broadly, (4) visual (typeface, size, use of italic or bold type, arrangement on the page, iconic or abstract images formed by the words, etc.). Signifiers of types 2 and 4 are produced by means of perisemiotic physical stimuli (see section 7.4.1).

In the analysis of signifiers, we can look for significant repetitions of phonemes (alliteration, assonance, etc.) or graphemes, or groups of phonemes or graphemes, whether this is carried out within the framework of a rhythmic analysis or not (see section 4.17). We can also study their correlation (or not) with certain signifieds.

The signified is the meaning, or content, that is conveyed by a signifier. A signified can be broken down into semes or features, which are components of its meaning. The signified 'boat' can be broken down into the semes /means of transport/ + /on the water/, etc. A repeated seme forms an isotopy (e.g.,

---

5 This use of the word "tactics" is based on the etymology of the Greek *taktikhê*, meaning the "art of arranging, of disposing."

the seme /liquid/ occurs twice in the expression "to drink water"). A repeated group of semes forms a semic molecule (e.g., /feeling/ + /positive/ in the expression "love and friendship"). Semic molecules include characters (or, more broadly, actors; see section 4.3), topoi (or stereotypes of content; see section 4.27), etc. Various typologies of semes exist: figurative / thematic / axiological (Greimas and Courtés; see Courtés, 1991: 163ff), inherent / afferent (Rastier, 2009), denotative / connotative (see section 4.5).

The types of semes that we can expect to find are: (1) semes associated with oppositional classes with a high degree of generality (e.g., /abstract/ vs. /concrete/, /animate/ vs. /inanimate/, /human/ vs. /animal/ vs. /plant/ vs. /mineral/, /positive/ vs. /negative/, etc.); (2) semes associated with classes corresponding to fields of human activity (/food/, /architecture/, /seafaring/, /linguistics/, etc.); (3) semes associated with other classes than those already mentioned (/seasons/, /citrus fruits/, /utensils/, etc.); and (4) semes that do not form classes but define characteristics (e.g., /round/, /sweet/, /famous/, /yellow/, etc.). A signified always contains several semes. It can contain all four kinds of semes, for example "grapefruit," which contains the semes: /concrete/, /plant/, /food/, /citrus fruit/, and /yellow/.

When we list the lexical signs (morphemes, words, expressions, phraseologies) that contain a given seme in a given text, we identify the lexical field of this seme; for example: "black," "winter," "the Great Journey," "death" might constitute the lexical field of the seme /death/ in a poem. I would add that the semes that, in a given text, accompany a given seme in the lexical units where that seme is found constitute the semantic field of that seme. For example, if, in a given text, the seme /death/ is generally or always accompanied by the semes /darkness/ and /negative/, these semes constitute its semantic field (and vice versa).

Semes or signifieds can be identical from one sign to another. They can also be opposed (e.g., the signifieds 'night' vs. 'day,' the semes /dark/ vs. /light/). Homologation is a relation between (at least) two pairs of opposite elements (e.g., opposite semes) such that, given the oppositions A/B and C/D, A is (always or mostly) to B as C is (always or mostly) to D. For example, in our culture, white is to black as life is to death, etc.

Most of the concepts discussed here with respect to signifieds can also be applied to signifiers: semes then become phemes (e.g., the status of a grapheme or phoneme as either a consonant or a vowel corresponds to a phemic feature), isotopies become isophemes, semic molecules become phemic molecules, etc.

Correlations can be found between, on the one hand, semes, isotopies, and semic molecules and, on the other hand, phemes, isophemes, and phemic molecules. See Hébert, 2019: 143–169.

4.20 Society

A given semiotic product, such as a text, is necessarily a social product and contains marks of this social dimension. We can therefore study the sociality of the text, that is to say, how one or more societies or social elements are represented and/ or have an impact on the text and, conversely, the social impact that is produced (or not) by this particular text. The concept of society is interdefined with, among others, the concepts of the individual, the social group, culture, ethnicity, the nation state, the people, civilization, and country. Without entering into the detail of these concepts, let us simply note that a sociology must necessarily be complemented by an individuology, which considers not only how a given individual is socially determined (and determines, or not, the society in question), but also how that individual dissociates him- or herself—whether deliberately or not, consciously or not, and in reality or merely in appearance—from these determinisms (e.g., those of the social classes to which they belong).

Five major social phenomena can be analyzed: (1) social classes (of age, gender, socioeconomic groups, etc.), (2) institutions (state, church, education, army, financial institutions, the literary establishment, etc.), (3) ideologies (systems composed of beliefs, values, and ethical precepts), (4) sociolects (the pre-established discourses of ideologies, including their associated vocabulary and typical stylistic rhetorical figures), and (5) social discourses (everything that is said, written, filmed, etc., within a society, including about the society itself and about other societies; according to Angenot, 1989: 13).

The analysis of sociality can obviously address any of the three main dimensions of literary analysis: production (author, intention, writing, etc.), the work itself, and its reception (reader, reading, criticism, analysis, etc.). An analysis of sociality with a perspective focused on the work itself will be devoted in particular to identifying and characterizing the "society of the text," in its instances (individual actors, collective actors, and institutional actors; institutions; ideologies; etc.), relationships, qualities, and processes.

The theory that real society is "reflected" in the text presents a number of traps for the unwary. In particular, one must take into account the following three kinds of reflection, and not only the first, most obvious one: direct reflection (Abraham Lincoln as Abraham Lincoln), reflection by the opposite (Abraham Lincoln as an outright racist), and reflection by significant omission (a text about politics during the American Civil War that does not mention Lincoln). Furthermore, one must take into account not only the reflection of one element in another single element, but also reflections formed either by fusion (two or more phenomena from real society are reflected in one phenomenon in the text) or by separation (one phenomenon from real society is reflected in two or more phenomena in the text). Finally, one must also take account of transpositions (e.g., from the serious to the parodic). If one wishes to "measure" the degree of fidelity with which real society is reflected in the text, one should avoid valuing a larger reflection and devaluing a smaller one. A personal worldview on the part of a writer can explain the absence of a "faithful" reflection in the text, and this worldview may, to a greater or lesser extent, give rise to a coherent distortion of reality (in accordance with the way that reality is generally conceived by a given society or social group, in light of the fact that reality in itself, or "the real," is probably ultimately inaccessible).

One should also keep in mind the principle that the society of the text has an autonomy in relation to real society, even if the text is in a realist mode. In particular, the characteristics of real social elements are not necessarily relevant to the corresponding elements in literary texts, even those that are the most realist. For example, members of the bourgeoisie in a novel probably eat more caviar than the real bourgeoisie do. In other words, care must be taken when applying the theory, methods, and data of sociology to the sociology of literature.

Real society is one of the contexts of the text (see section 4.7), and in fact constitutes the "reservoir" from which all socially determined contexts (esthetic, economic, etc.) are derived; this notably excludes the "raw" physical context (although even the most elementary physical perceptions are also shaped culturally and therefore also socially) and those of the determinisms (for definition, see p. 61) derived from the author that are not socially defined.

Social classes in the broad sense include: social classes in the narrow sense (working class/middle class, proletariat/bourgeoisie, aristocracy/commoners, etc.), socio-professional classes (intellectuals, workers, professionals, etc.), age classes (young/old, teens/pre-teens, etc.), geosocial classes (rural/urban, provincial/metropolitan, etc.), economic classes (rich/poor, etc.), generational classes (baby boomers/Generation X, etc.), gender classes (male, female, non-binary, transgender, etc.). Some social classes are deeply connected to the identity of individuals: woman/man, non-traditional gender/traditional gender, racialized/non-racialized, discriminated/discriminating, etc. These oppositions are generally homologous with the opposition dominant/dominated. Some classes are thus, to varying degrees, identity-based, culturally oriented, and more or less permanent (e.g., age classes are temporary).

A social class is associated with a corresponding ideology (or several complementary, or even contradictory, ideologies). Any social class is seen through the distorting prism of the speaker's own social class (this is a situation of irreducible subjectivism, wherein absolute objectivity is impossible). Therefore, in principle, a member of the bourgeoisie will tend to idealize the bourgeoisie in its real and textual manifestations (but often a member of a class is unaware that they are a member of that class, and will therefore not recognize themselves in representations of this class, e.g., many rich people do not consider that they are rich!). In short, we can consider, through a particular application of the Sapir–Whorf hypothesis (that two observers cannot share the same perceptions if they do not share the same linguistic background), that social class determines the way we see the world.

Social classes can be structured by dyadic oppositions (e.g., bourgeoisie/proletariat, aristocracy/commoner), triadic oppositions (e.g., working class/middle class/upper class), or other forms of opposition. Depending on the requirements of the analysis, it may be sufficient to use a general typology (e.g., middle class/working class), or a more specific typology may be needed (e.g., upper middle class, lower middle class, etc.). The dominant/dominated opposition is a very useful general opposition, which can be applied in the following situations, among others: in the family and the couple (husband/wife, parent/child, etc.); in social classes in the narrow sense (e.g., bourgeoisie/proletariat); in social roles (e.g., masters/servants); in social status (e.g., man/woman, parent/child, white/black, majority/minority); in cultures (North/South, West/East).

One or more social classes can be associated with the following literary phenomena: author and reader; production and reception; narrator and narratee; character; ideology, institution, sociolect, and social discourse; situation, plot, and event; theme and topos; other formal elements (genres, stylistic rhetorical figures, etc.); and other literary phenomena (movements, events, etc.).

What sort of objects do social classes apply to in "real life" and, indirectly, in semiotic products? In principle, social class has a bearing on all possible social and even individual facets of life: material products (e.g., champagne for the rich); symbolic products (semiotic products, concepts, etc.; e.g., novels as bourgeois products); cultural practices and tastes (e.g., the avant-garde for intellectuals); gestures, posture ("heixis"; e.g., the upright, aloof bearing of aristocrats); clothing; language (accent, vocabulary, etc.); emotions (e.g., the lyricism attributed to artists); sensory perceptions (e.g., the disgust that certain city dwellers experience when exposed to the odors of the countryside).

For some social classes (in the broad sense), we can distinguish between class of origin/class of belonging; class of belonging/class of destination; class of habitus/class of position (Bourdieu, 1981: 75).

The class of origin is the class to which a given element belonged or still belongs, especially in a person's youth. The classes of origin and belonging can be the same or different, or even opposite. Examples of cases where the class of origin is different from the class of belonging, in French, include the "parvenu" (e.g., the nouveau riche) and the "contre-parvenu" (e.g., someone who has fallen in status and/or wealth from the nobility, a member of the bourgeoisie who decides to live like a member of the proletariat).

The class of destination (or aspiration) is the class to which an individual or collective social actor aspires. The (desired) class of destination should be distinguished from the class of arrival, which may or may not correspond to the desired class. When a social actor aspires to belong to another class, in principle they aim for a class that is higher than their current class of belonging in one respect or another. For example, Saint Francis of Assisi, who enjoyed high economic and social status from his class of origin (from his family background), opted to live as a poor man among the poor because "theirs is the kingdom of heaven."

The class of habitus is related to one's way of life, and an individual is often unconscious of this kind of class affiliation. Conversely, the class of position is related to a consciously held ideological position, whether it is expressed (in speech or otherwise) or not. These two classes can be in opposition to each other with regard to a given phenomenon. For example, members of the French "caviar left" (or "champagne socialists") are pro-proletarian in terms of position but bourgeois in terms of habitus. It should be noted that one can belong to a class of habitus that is different from one's actual class of belonging: thus, a person who was born as a peasant and remains a peasant may nonetheless have certain aristocratic behaviors, and another person who was born as an aristocrat and remains so may have some peasant behaviors. Habitus can be broken down into different facets of thought, speech (and more generally of semiotic production), and action.

Between two classes linked to the same element, three types of "trajectories" (Bourdieu, 2016) are possible: social progression (increase), social maintenance or conservation, and social regression (decrease). We can add three further social trajectories to these, by negation of the three initial trajectories respectively: non-progression, non-maintenance or non-conservation, and non-regression. For example, we can speak of social non-progression in a case where social progression was expected, but social conservation or regression occurred instead. These six social trajectories can be associated in various ways with thymic evaluations (euphoric/neutral/dysphoric, or positive/neutral/negative) and thus form various frameworks for "social stories." Thymic evaluations are more complex than they appear. For example, a character may regret (dysphoria) their rapid social progress if, for example, they wanted to remain a peasant but became the president of their country out of duty.

We can distinguish between three types of relations between social actors (societies, individuals, institutions, and collectivities, including classes): irenic (e.g., a relationship of collaboration), neutral (e.g., a relationship of indifference or non-aggression), and polemical (a relationship of conflict, whether open or not).

4.21 Space

Time, space, nature, and culture (including semiotic systems, such as language) are the main environments, or contexts, in which humans are immersed. As such, they are all—with the exception of nature, of which certain aspects, such as the laws of nature, are always and everywhere the same—factors of relativity. The context determines the product and is reflected in it (either directly, or negatively, or by significant omission).

Time and space, at least from the naive or everyday perspective, have a real, objective existence (but some theories consider that they do not, such as Buddhism, which considers that time and space are ultimately mere concepts). Time and space can also be thematizations, since they are integrated in the semantic contents of semiotic products, and indeed of every semiotic product, with a small number of exceptions (e.g., time can be thematized even in painting). While time is not material in itself—although it is measurable and associated with material phenomena—real spaces have physical dimensions. Time and space are also representations (in the broad sense of mental images, rather than the narrow sense of visual images); these representations represent either physical phenomena, semiotic phenomena (i.e., thematizations), or other representations. Space is therefore a physical, semiotic, and cognitive construction.

Space is, in a first sense, the substrate in which three-dimensional phenomena are deployed, and the effect of this deployment. It is a more or less open field in which physical and biological phenomena take place, as well as—indirectly—the mental phenomena that are correlated with them. Just as time is associated with both a position and a duration (defined by the difference between two temporal positions), space corresponds both to a position (defined in two or three dimensions) and to an extent (area or volume). But, unlike time, it also corresponds to a form. Contrary to objective time (which flows from the present to the past), space does not inherently possess an orientation and a flow; it can, however, be traversed by fields of force that are strictly spatial, according to certain theories and also—since any theory in principle can be realized in the semiotic products of fiction—according to certain fictional texts. Space is also, in a second sense, the particular organization of any natural place, or one that is constructed as such; we can refer to this meaning of space more specifically using the term "spatial organization." By this conception, space corresponds to a phenomenal field and the phenomena that occupy or characterize it. Spaces can be, and usually are, encompassing and encompassed. Here is an example of a chain of concentric spaces: room < house < neighborhood < city < region < country < continent < earth, etc., up to the level of the entire universe (which is a self-inclusive space). To simplify matters, we can distinguish between space (the container) and place (the spatial organization contained within space). What we identify as a given space and/or place is in reality a form that is isolated on a more or less ad hoc basis (e.g., we arbitrarily opt to interrupt the continuous contiguity between "two" spaces, which were in fact one and the same space, such as the room and the house, the house and its grounds, the individual property and the neighborhood, etc.). The same principle applies to time.

In the same way that events (including even an unchanging state of affairs) take place in time, physical or biological elements occupy space, and therefore events—whether physical, biological, or cognitive, and whether natural or cultural—also take place in space, either affecting it or not.

Space can be natural or artificial (constructed by humans or animals). Natural space cannot be perceived by humans without the mediation of a cultural grid: when we look at a piece of virgin forest, we cannot help but superimpose our conceptions regarding nature. In other words, a space that is natural with regard to its production is never entirely or purely natural with regard to its reception. It is therefore useful to distinguish between (using terms drawn from phenomenology) the pheno-space (the space such as it appears to us) and the noumeno-space (the space such as it is in itself). The question then arises as to whether one ever has access to noumeno-space or only to one or more of its pheno-spatial versions.

Just as a temporal position is related to a given state of a given culture (e.g., a play written in the nineteenth century reflects the culture of its time to some extent, even if negatively or by significant omission), space is also related to a given culture (e.g., a play written in France reflects French culture to some extent).

Just as we can distinguish between five main sorts of time that interact in a textual (or filmic, musical etc.) product (see section 4.26), we can distinguish between five main sorts of spaces related to those same products: (1) space of production (associated with the author and the writing process: places where the author writes, places that "inhabit" or have previously inhabited them); (2) space thematized within the product: (2.1) space shown or represented, (2.2) space that is evoked or implied (e.g., a character in prison—a represented space—dreams of the beach—an evoked space);[6] and (3) space of reception (associated with the receiver and reception: places occupied by the receiver at the moment of reception, places that inhabit them or have previously inhabited them). We can undoubtedly also speak of a non-thematized evoked space (e.g., a character who wears a mask may evoke the space of ancient Greece for those familiar with the masked theater of this period), but this inferred space may also be thematized (and not only a mental image for the receiver).

In the case of a play, the space of production is threefold: the space of writing, the space of the preparation of the staging (in the director's mind and concretely in rehearsals), and the space where the play is performed.

Moreover, if we take into account the constructed author (e.g., the image that the text gives of the author), the constructed production (e.g., the image that the text gives of its production), the constructed reception (e.g., the image that the text gives of its reception), and the constructed receiver (e.g., the image that the text gives of its receiver), we will obtain as many new kinds of spaces again.

One can view the page (or double-page spread) of a written text, or the surface of a painting, etc., as spaces, which are subject to various spatial structurings and arrangements. In this respect, the words of a written text are not only linked in time but also arranged in space, even in an ordinary text that does not make a complex use of spatiality (as a calligram does).

In analyzing spaces, we can take account of: (1) the number of spaces (dyadic space, triadic space, etc.); (2) the extent of spaces; (3) their form (cubic, unbounded, etc.); (4) their "furnishings" (people and objects that exist in them, processes that take place in them, etc.); (5) the distances (quantitative and qualitative) between spaces; (6) their relationships: irenic (peaceful, collaborative, etc.), neutral, polemical; (7) literal spaces (often realistic, e.g., a bourgeois living room, but not always, e.g., a Martian space station) and metaphorical spaces (e.g., a bourgeois living room as a symbol of Hell in Sartre's play *No Exit*); (8) movements (of characters, objects, etc.) from one space to another and within a space; (9) their openness (e.g., public streets), relative closure (e.g., houses), or virtually complete closure (e.g., a labyrinth, prison); (10) their accessibility or inaccessibility (e.g., the unattainability of utopian spaces); (11) their private or public nature; (12) their positive, neutral, or negative character; (13) a

---

6 A space that is evoked by a character through memory, fantasy, etc., is a represented space from the perspective of the character involved in the memory, fantasy, etc.

measure of the mobility of characters, objects, etc. (the number of movements, distance covered, etc.); (14) the configuration of the movements in the space (straight lines, curves, etc.); (15) the iconic (realistically represented), stylized (e.g., caricatured), or symbolic nature of the spaces; (16) their real (e.g., the real Eiffel Tower), realistic (e.g., the Eiffel Tower in a realist novel), or fictitious (e.g., Eldorado, Olympus) nature; (17) their natural and/or cultural (human-produced) character; and (18) their immanent or transcendent (Heaven, Hell, etc.) nature, etc.

4.22 Story, narrative, narration, action

The words "story," "narrative," and "narration" are highly polysemous, so it is important to understand the particular way in which I use these terms here and elsewhere in this book. The story, in the narratological sense, is the structure of states and processes (roughly speaking, actions)—ordered by chronological successions and simultaneities—that is thematized within a given semiotic product (text, image, film, etc.), in the sense that it is integrated into that product's contents (the signifieds). The story may be fictional (e.g., in a novel) or real (e.g., in a television news report, a newspaper), to varying degrees. By this definition, the story therefore excludes events that happen in "real life" but that are not recounted in some way. For example, if someone slips on a banana peel, this only becomes a story when it is physically reenacted, for example, on stage or among friends, or narrated in words.

The narrative is the shaping of the story through the process of narration; for non-textual products, or products that are not exclusively textual, we can speak of "monstration" rather than "narration" ("mimesis" and "diegesis" respectively, in Aristotle and Plato's terms). The narrative is therefore produced by the process of narration (or monstration). For example, in the narrative, the events of the story can be presented in chronological order (narrative 1 of a given story) or in reverse chronological order (narrative 2 of the same story).

In short, the story is what is being talked about, and the narrative is how it is talked about.

The narrator (or monstrator) is the thematized instance (embedded in the contents of the text) that produces the narrative, and the narratee is the thematized instance to which the narrative is addressed. Narrator and narratee are the textual counterparts of the empirical and extratextual instances that are the real author and the real reader; they also correspond to the constructed author and the constructed reader, that is, the image that the text presents of its author and its reader respectively.

An action is a process, whether thematized or not, produced by an anthropomorphic being (e.g., a human, an intelligent alien being). A process may be produced by an anthropomorphic being (e.g., in the case of a murder) or not (e.g., in the case of a falling tree killing a passerby).

An action consists in the change, or more precisely the transformation, from a first state (S1) to a second state that is opposed to the first (S2 = ¬ S1; in logical notation, "¬" indicates negation). If we include the transformation itself as the second stage in the sequence, we arrive at a triadic conception of action. A state is a triplet consisting of a subject, an object, and a junction (either a conjunction: "with the object," or a disjunction: "without the object"). For an action to exist, it must be the case that the subject of the two states is the same, and that the object is the same, but that the junction is different. For example, S1 consists of the prince without the saved princess (disjunction), and in S2 this becomes the prince with the saved princess (conjunction).

In a semiotic product, such as a text, transformations involve actors (including characters) who produce, whether deliberately or not, actions and/or receive their effects. Actions can be subdivided into three main categories: actions in the narrow sense (i.e., "doing"), words (i.e., "speaking," and producing other semiotic products that can be treated in the same way, such as images, etc.), and thoughts (i.e., "thinking," whether the thoughts are formulated verbally or not). These categories can be combined to produce nine possible permutations. For example, we can distinguish between an action-enacted (kissing someone), an action-said ("I'm going to kiss you"), an action-thought ("I could kiss him"), etc.

An artistic work generally interweaves several types of arc, or mathematical curve, that are interconnected to varying degrees, including: an actional arc (which measures the intensity of the actions), an emotional arc (which measures the intensity of the affects), a dramatic arc (which measures the intensity of the plot), and an esthetic arc (which measures the esthetic intensity). These arcs can be considered from three perspectives: that of the author's intention, the analysis of the internal marks within the work, and the effect on the receiver.

The different types of arc may or may not coincide. For example, the final explosion that destroys the villain's military-industrial complex in a James Bond film is certainly the culmination of the actional arc, the emotional arc (at least for the characters), and the dramatic arc, but this does not mean that the maximum esthetic intensity is achieved at the same time (although this is undoubtedly the effect sought by the producer and director).

4.23 Structure, relation, operation

Facts do not exist, only phenomena (the "facts" as they appear to us). More precisely, and in philosophical terms: the noumenon (the object in itself, e.g., a carrot) does not exist, or is unreachable, so we are condemned to have access only to the phenomenon (the object as it appears to a given subject, e.g., a carrot, which is perceived as delicious by a rabbit, and inedible by a wolf). Any phenomenon (and any noumenon) can usefully be interpreted as a structure, and a structure can be interpreted as a system (in one of the two senses of this word, namely, that of a whole whose parts are interdependent). A structure is an entity made up of terms, relations, and operations. A relation is a link that is established or recognized either between a unit and itself (a reflexive relation) or between a unit and one or more other units (a transitive relation).

Structuralism considers that relations are primordial and define terms (unlike ontological perspectives, which consider that terms are primordial and that relations are produced afterwards); one could also go further than this, and maintain that operations are primordial and produce both relations and terms.

The operations that make it possible to transform one term into another are known as operations of transformation; the other major sort of operation is an operation of characterization (the fact of recognizing one or more characteristics or properties in a given phenomenon). Operations of transformation either (1) produce objects, in the broad sense, including mental objects (either by creation *ex nihilo*, by deriving an actual instance from a type, by deriving a type from many actual instances, or by construction from pre-existing materials); (2) destroy objects (either by annihilation, i.e., without leaving any residue, or by complete deconstruction); or (3) transform objects. For our purposes, the main phenomena involved in the operations of transformation are signs, signifiers (notably of a phonemic or graphemic type), and signifieds or contents.

The main operations of transformation acting on substances are:

1. addition (+): a → a b
2. deletion (-): a b → a
3. substitution (- and +): a b → a c
4. displacement (- and +): a b → b a
5. separation (- and +): ab → a b
6. fusion (- and +): a b → ab

The main operations of transformation acting on intensities are:

1. increase: e.g., poor → very poor
2. decrease: e.g., very poor → poor

We also need to add a non-operation (of characterization or transformation) to this list, which is the "operation" of conservation. It can concern substances or intensities. It is either marked (unexpected, such as when a professor does not enter the classroom at the start of a class, a situation of non-addition) or unmarked (expected, such as when an elephant does not enter a classroom, another case of non-addition).

There are many families of relationships. Let us consider some of them in more detail.

1. The main comparative relations are those of: ipseity (A is identical to itself), identity (one A is identical to another A), opposition (contrariness: day and night, contradiction: day and non-day), alterity (glory and a hippopotamus), similarity (an egg and another egg), non-metaphorical analogical similarity (an egg and a bald man's head), metaphorical analogical similarity (a woman and a flower), analogical similarity by non-metaphorical homologation (day is to night as the sun is to the moon), and analogical similarity by metaphorical homologation (spring is to winter as youth is to old age).

2. The main temporal relations are those of simultaneity, succession (either immediate or delayed), and simultaneity-succession (two phenomena overlap partially).

3. The correlative relations fall into two categories. First, the categorical correlations (with no gradation or degrees) are simple presupposition (the presence of a wolf presupposes the presence of a mammal, but a present mammal is not necessarily a wolf), reciprocal presupposition (one side of a sheet of paper presupposes the presence of its reverse side, and vice versa), and mutual exclusion (a door is either open or closed, it cannot be both at the same time). Second, the gradual correlations (with gradation or degrees) are positive (or direct) correlation (the more there is of one thing, the more there is of another thing; e.g., where there is more poverty, one will find more health problems) and inverse correlation (the more there is of one thing, the less there is of another thing; e.g., where there is more education, one will find less poverty).

4. The relations of causality involve cause, causation, and effect, and the relations of determination involve a determinant, determination, and a determined (element). Water, soil, heat, light, and a seed cause a tree; a constant wind from the north determines the tree in its inclination toward the south. Presupposition, mutual exclusion, positive correlation, and inverse correlation are not necessarily accompanied by causation or determination. In short, correlation is not necessarily causation (but all causation is also correlation). For example, there is a correlation between the level of ice cream sales and the number of deaths by drowning, but it cannot be said that ice cream causes drowning. There is actually a third underlying factor, that of the weather: when it is hot, people both consume more ice cream and swim more.

5. The main types of relations of globality/locality are mereological relations (involving wholes and parts), set relations (involving classes and elements classified in classes), and type relations (involving types or models and tokens or manifestations of a model: e.g., the type "tree" in my mind and the manifestation of an actual tree that I find in a forest).

See Hébert, 2019: chapters 1 and 2.

4.24 Style

Style, like all important concepts, has been given many definitions. Style has been seen as the form of the text (how it is written or spoken) as opposed to its content (what it says) (see section 4.6). We can define style more specifically, as far as texts are concerned (although the concept goes beyond the textual), as the set of choices made by an enunciator between all the possible means of expression that are presented by language and other textual systems, insofar as these choices manifest a deviation from the zero degree of enunciation, which is to say, the most logical and simple formulation. For example, the expression "He left for a very long journey" is a deviation from the degree zero, "He died."

It should be noted that, by this definition, there is style only if there is a deviation; however, one might also consider the realization of the norm, especially if it is not expected, as a style. One can therefore define style, not in relation to a degree zero, but rather in relation to the expected degree (which may be the degree zero or a deviation from it). In both cases, style produces (and is produced by) a deviation from a norm (see section 4.8). Norms are defined within and relative to systems. My own typology includes the following systems: anthropolect (norms common to human beings as a whole), cultorolect (norms common to a given culture), sociolect in the broad sense (norms common to a given social group), sociolect in the narrow sense (Rastier) (norms common to a particular social practice, and which notably define genres: literary, philosophical, medical, etc.), dialect (in the sense that Rastier gives to this word as a system of language, a system which is obviously social), idiolect (norms common to a given textual producer), textolect (norms common to a given text), and alect (the non-systemic part of a text). See Rastier, 2016: 48–49.

Style can also be defined, restrictively, in relation only to idiolect (Rastier, 2001: 302) (e.g., the style of Baudelaire, or that of Yeats). But whereas this conception of style is particularizing, other conceptions are more generalizing. For example, we can speak of styles associated with particular genres, such as the romantic style, or those associated with general ways of writing: simple, florid, restrained, sublime, artistic, esthetic, impressionistic, noble, figurative, etc. (Bénac and Réauté, 1993: 225). We are then largely concerned with tone and mimetic modes (see section 4.13). Let us add to the list the following styles or tones, which are broadly opposed to the sublime: derisory, vulgar, disgusting, grotesque, flawed, clumsy, kitsch, ordinary, banal, sordid, chilling, scatological, etc. Tone is traditionally defined as the way of writing adopted by an enunciator, which conveys their mood, feelings, and attitudes toward the subject matter. I would add that tone relates not only to one's point of view regarding what one is talking about, but also to one's choice of what to talk about. For example, a light tone will necessarily favor the selection of light subjects (such as drinking sparkling low-alcohol rosé wine by the pool on a summer evening), although it can also be used to deal lightly with "heavy" or "serious" subjects (such as the meaning of life and death). In this sense, tone is similar to worldview, but a given worldview may be associated with several different tones, which a given writer may variously choose between from one work to the next (see section 4.30).

However we define style, we must remember that it concerns both signifieds (the contents) and signifiers (phonemes, graphemes, etc.).

A norm is realized in a text by an operation of conservation of the norm that is found in the system in question (e.g., the language system), whereas deviations in a text are produced by operations of transformation of the norm (conservation can be seen as a non-operation of transformation). The possible types of transformation include addition, deletion, substitution, displacement, fusion, separation, etc. (see section 4.23 on structure, relation, operation).

More specifically, deviations are created by writing processes (but these also produce non-deviations, if they are expected, for instance by the reader, or according to the rules of the genre). These writing processes include stylistic figures. A stylistic figure—or, with different shades of meaning, a rhetorical figure, a linguistic figure, or a writing process—is (1) an interpretive path (a sequence of interpretive operations and results), (2) which is stereotyped and (3) named (e.g., it is a metaphor), or at least could be named, (4) involving the signifier (e.g., phonemes or graphemes) and/or the signified (the contents, the meanings). This interpretive path is used (5) in the production of a text (e.g., the writer wishes to produce a metaphor) or (6) in the reception of a text (the reader must perceive that there is a metaphor and understand it, or alternatively the reader might not see or understand the metaphor, or might even see a metaphor where there is none).

The figure consists of a perceived degree and a conceived degree (Klinkenberg, 1996: 83). The perceived degree is, as the name indicates, what is perceived at first analysis (although any "perception" is already an interpretation). From the perceived degree, we then pass to the conceived degree. The conceived degree corresponds to the norm and the perceived degree to the deviation. For example, in the case of the metaphor "I shook hands with a flower," where "flower" stands in for "woman": the perceived degree is "flower" and the conceived degree is "woman." Let us now consider an example that concerns signifiers. In the expression "What the fork!" the perceived degree is "fork" and the conceived degree is the f-word. We pass from one degree to another by means of one or more operations of transformation (including that of conservation, which keeps things the same as they are at the beginning). For example, we pass from "fork" to the f-word by substituting letters or phonemes.

Between the perceived degree and the conceived degree there necessarily remains an invariant element, which is preserved or is simply identical (e.g., the common letters shared by "fork" and the f-word, and the idea of beauty shared by "flower" and "woman"). There are obviously also variant elements (variables) between the two terms in these sequences, in the sense of elements that differ, or are even incompatible (e.g., "flower" contains the seme /plant/ whereas "woman" contains the seme /human/).

The main stylistic figures can be grouped into the following families (which I have adapted and expanded from Pilote, 1997: 319–324):

1. figures of analogy: comparison (metaphorical), metaphor (*in praesentia, in absentia*), allegory, personification;
2. figures of opposition: antithesis, antiphrasis (ironic or euphemistic), oxymoron, opposition, paradox (real or apparent), contradiction;
3. figures of substitution: metonymy, synecdoche, periphrasis, circumlocution, synonymy, euphemism (also a figure of attenuation of an element perceived as negative)/counter-euphemism (also a figure of amplification of an element perceived as negative);
4. figures of emphasis: repetition, redundancy, pleonasm, anaphora/epiphora (the last two figures are also figures of construction);
5. figures of amplification: hyperbole, accumulation, ascending gradation (the last two figures are also figures of construction);

6. figures of attenuation: euphemism, litotes, ellipsis (in some cases, also a figure of construction), reverse or descending gradation (also a figure of construction);
7. figures involving sonorities or spellings: onomatopoeia, assonance, alliteration, rhyme, imitative harmony (also a figure of analogy), homonymy (homophony, homography), paronymy, anagram (anaphone), palindrome, paronomasia, pun, prosthesis, epenthesis, paragoge, apheresis, syncopation, apocope, substitution, metathesis, separation, fusion (also a figure of construction);
8. Figures of construction: chiasmus (with or without opposition), alternation, embedding, crossing (e.g., in cross rhymes), inversion (also a figure of permutation), ellipsis (of words, phrases or narrative, etc.; also a figure of omission or deletion), insertion (also a figure of addition), anacoluthon, parataxis, major/minor/other cadence (rising, falling, falling then rising, rising then falling, neutral, linear, or with multiple peaks and falls), zeugma (also a figure of omission).

4.25 Theme, thematic, thematic structure

Traditionally, a theme is defined as the main topic of a text. For example, revenge is the theme of *Hamlet*; ambition and love are the themes of Stendhal's *The Red and the Black*. Moreover, the theme usually, if not always, reflects large existential concepts (life, death, glory, love, redemption, freedom, femininity, etc.). In the broadest sense, a theme is a semantic element, generally repeated, found in a given corpus, even if this corpus is limited to a single text (or more broadly, a single semiotic product: image, film, etc.).

In this sense, a theme is not necessarily a conceptual, general, existential, and highly valued or devalued element (love, hope, death, glory, freedom, truth, etc.); it can just as well be another conceptual element (entropy, grammatical plural, tenses, love of cats, etc.), a general concrete element (animate beings, in the broad sense of living beings), a particular concrete element (cats), a large concrete element (e.g., the Eiffel Tower), or a trivial one (e.g., chewing gum). Themes can also include states (the fact of remaining the same rather than changing), processes (actions, such as that of picking a flower), instances (e.g., a particular flower), qualities (e.g., the blue of the flower), and relations (e.g., the flower is in a pot), etc. In this broad sense, thematic analysis notably includes action analysis and the analysis of characters (more precisely that of actants, actors, and agonists; see section 4.3), ideologies, and rhetorical stylistic figures that involve content (see section 4.6).

Considered as an unanalyzed whole, a theme corresponds to a seme (a component of content, of the signified) whose repetition constitutes an isotopy: for example, the seme /death/ repeated in the phrase, "His death, his last journey, saddens us all." Considered as an analyzed whole, a theme corresponds to a group of recurrent semes (semes that are repeated together), and therefore constitutes a semic molecule: for example, the rather unusual theme of /yellow/ + /viscous/ +

/harmful/ is found embodied in various dishes in *L'assommoir* by Zola (see section 4.19 on sign, signifier, signified, and Rastier, 2016: 56–57).

A thematic structure is a grouping of at least two themes that are united by at least one relation that is made explicit by the analyst:[7] for example, if, in a particular work, love (theme 1) causes (relation) death (theme 2), these three elements form such a structure.

In the traditional sense of the word, a thematic is a grouping of at least two themes whose relationships are not necessarily made explicit by the analyst. In short, it can, in principle, be a simple inventory of copresent themes. A thematic structure, by definition, makes explicit the relations between the themes that constitute it. Let us postulate that, in principle, any theme can be analyzed and transformed into a thematic structure and vice versa. For example, we can understand love as a theme in itself or as a triadic thematic structure comprising two terms and a relation (which would ideally be reciprocal): "X loves Y."

A theme may be stereotyped, in the sense that it may be defined relative to a given systemic level. It then takes on the value of a topos, in the broad sense of a conventional stereotype of content (e.g., thwarted or impossible love, betrayal, etc.) (see section 4.27 on topos).

The symbol is a thematic structure of metaphorical analogical comparison, which combines a symbolizer (e.g., weighing scales) and a symbolized (e.g., the concept of justice). Different levels of symbols can be distinguished (see section 5.44 on stylistics).

Meaning is produced only through difference.[8] One of the forms of difference—along with similarity (e.g., between a day and another day) and alterity (e.g., between a day and a hippopotamus)—is opposition (e.g., between day and night or between day and non-day). Opposition can be represented by a slash placed between the two opposite terms (e.g., day/night). Oppositions are usually dyadic, that is, they consist of two terms, but there are oppositions with more than two terms: the future, the present, and the past form a triadic opposition; the four seasons form a tetradic opposition; and the spaces of agriculturist narratives often form the tetradic opposition forest/countryside/village/town. For the sake of simplicity, I shall comment here only on dyadic oppositions, but these statements can be adapted to apply to non-dyadic oppositions.

The fundamental question to address when undertaking an analysis is: Where to begin? One way to begin the analysis is to look for identities and oppositions

---

7 When analyzing several themes, it can be useful to provide the reader with the analyzed text, if it is sufficiently short, and to use specific colors to highlight the words associated with certain themes (indeed, a single word may relate to several different, even contradictory themes).

8 We could say that meaning is produced through identity and difference, especially since the theme is often defined as the repetition of the same semantic element and isotopy as the repetition of the same seme (a component of a signified). However, to say that an element is repeated presupposes that the various repetitions of this same element are identified and distinguished (e.g., by the different positions that they occupy in the sequence of words). They are therefore different from each other in this respect at least. Ultimately, every instance is a hapax, unique, unrepeated and unrepeatable.

either on the level of the signifier (the vehicle of the content, such as phonemes) or that of the signified (the content). Since we are talking here about thematic analysis, we will limit ourselves to identities and oppositions between signifieds. For example, one could certainly look for the theme of light in the work of the Quebec author Anne Hébert, but we will arrive at a deeper analysis if we look for both light and darkness. We can achieve greater precision by constructing a semiotic square (see Hébert, 2019: chapter 3) on the basis of a given opposition; we will then go from two analytical classes (e.g., light, darkness) to ten analytical classes (e.g., light, darkness, non-light, non-darkness, light and darkness at the same time, neither light nor darkness, and the other double combinations of the first four elements mentioned).

We can note whether both terms of an opposition are present in the semiotic product being analyzed (e.g., a painting that uses both black and white), thus forming a "semiotic contrast," or whether only one of the terms is present (e.g., a painting that uses white without any black), forming what we will simply call a "non-contrast." We can also note whether the opposition is synthetic or analytical. An opposition is synthetic if it occurs between elements considered as a whole, for example between white and black. It is analytical if it occurs directly between the parts of the whole only, and therefore indirectly between the wholes that possess these parts. For example, a hammer and a hippopotamus are not opposed synthetically but analytically, if we consider, for example, that the former is small and the latter is large. A synthetic opposition can always be transformed into an analytical opposition; for example, what creates the opposition between white and black is the opposition between their properties, respectively, of luminosity and darkness. Between any pair of elements, we can always find an analytical opposition, even between two "identical" objects (e.g., one is found on the left and the other is found on the right).

Once we have identified oppositions in a given text, we can try to link them to form a more complex structure. One of the possible relationships between two or more oppositions is that of homologation. Homologation occurs when one of the two terms (A) of the first opposition (A/B) corresponds to one of the two terms (C) of the second opposition (C/D), while the other term (B) of the first opposition corresponds to the other term (D) of the second opposition. We then say that A is to B as C is to D, or, in a symbolic format, A : B : : C : D. For example, if light (A) is to darkness (B) as positive (C) is to negative (D), we find a relationship of homologation between these two oppositions: since light (A) corresponds to positive (C) and darkness (B) corresponds to negative (D). When the homologation produced constitutes an inversion with respect to the expected homologation, we can speak of counter-homologation. For example, Sade produces such a counter-homologation by associating, against the norms of society in general, vice with positive and virtue with negative. For more detail on homologation, see Hébert, 2019: chapter 1.

It is not necessarily possible to group all the oppositions identified in a given text into a single relationship of homologation. It may then be possible to form two or more homologations; for example, the opposition A/B may be homologous to C/D and opposition E/F homologous to opposition G/H, without A/B also being homologous to E/F, etc. Obviously, an opposition may not be homologated to any other opposition that is identified by the analysis, or that is simply present in the text (while not being mentioned in the analysis). Furthermore, oppositions may be linked by relations other than homologation. For example, an opposition may relate to only one term of another opposition. For example, it might be that both light (A) and darkness (B) are related to the single term positive (C), rather than light being positive and darkness being negative.

4.26 Time

Time is the substrate in which simultaneities and successions occur. It can also be seen as the effect produced by the succession of units, whether accompanied or not by simultaneities. It is also a frame of reference—which may be relative (before, after, etc.) or absolute (1912, 1913, etc.), precise (e.g., at 4 p.m.) or imprecise (e.g., between the first and thirty-first of the month, a few months ago), direct or indirect (inferred from clues)—associated with one or several units. Duration, or temporal extent, is the difference between an initial and a final temporal position. Time can be seen as being amorphous (without variations in its nature and without, in itself, exerting an impact on things) or, on the contrary, as being endowed with qualitative variations and as determining the elements that accompany its "flow."

Let us first distinguish between three main kinds of time: (1) thematized time, related to the chronological sequence of states and processes (actions) of the story recounted in a semiotic product (even in a short expression such as "he will marry," which tells a mini-story); (2) the time of arrangement (see section 4.18), produced by the succession—whether this succession is imposed strongly (e.g., in a film), moderately (e.g., in a book), or weakly or unconstrainedly (e.g., in a painting)—of the "real" semiotic units (signs, signifiers, or signifieds) of the semiotic product. These two kinds of time may or may not coincide (e.g., they will not coincide if the second event from the story is presented in the first sentence of the text, and the first event of the story is presented in the second sentence of the text). Thematized time, whether fictional (e.g., in a novel) or reflecting real time (e.g., in a daily newspaper), is a simulacrum of (3) real time. Real time can be subdivided into (3.1) objective time ("clock time") and (3.2) subjective time (e.g., even if they have the same duration in objective time, pleasant moments pass more quickly than unpleasant ones). We can also distinguish between (1.1) thematized time that is represented or shown, and (1.2) thematized time that is merely implied or evoked; for example, a work of fiction might depict characters from the twenty-first century (represented thematized time) who evoke, by talking about the subject, the time of Antiquity (evoked thematized time). We can probably also speak of a non-thematized evoked time (e.g., a character wearing a mask might evoke the time of Antiquity, even if this historical period is not talked about, for those who are familiar with the masked theater of that time), but perhaps we should consider this inferred time as also being thematized, and not merely a mental image.

If we relate time to the three instances of semiotic communication and its two processes, we can distinguish between five kinds of time: (1) the time of the producer (of the author); (2) the time of the production of the work (the duration of reflection, of the total period of writing, of the time spent in actual writing); (3) the time of the product itself (e.g., the thematized time or the time of the arrangement); (4) the time of the reception of the work; and (5) the time of the receiver (see also section 4.20 on space). With regard to the time of the producer and that of the receiver, we must distinguish between the time of their own existence and the possible other times that inhabit them. For example, a contemporary author might be fascinated by the medieval period, and this fascination might affect the content and form of a work whose action is in principle contemporary. Clearly, then, time is not only an undifferentiated frame of reference or duration, but can also be correlated to a culture; the same principle is also true for space.

In addition to the five kinds of time identified above, if we take into account the constructed author (e.g., the image that the text provides of the author), the constructed production (e.g., the image that the text provides of its production), the constructed product (e.g., the image that the production provides of the text), the constructed reception (e.g., the image that the text provides of its reception), and the constructed receiver (e.g., the image that the text provides of its receiver), we will find as many new kinds of time.

Since rhythm can be defined as the linking, in at least two successive temporal (and/or spatial) positions, of at least two elements (even the same repeated element), the study of rhythm presupposes the study of time (see section 4.17, or for more detail, Hébert, 2019: chapter 15).

When analyzing the relationship between the context of production and the work itself, it is necessary to take into account the possible interval between the date of publication and the date of conception. For example, a work may have been conceived, at least in broad outline, long before its publication date, and it may have been written over the course of a long period of time. In this case, the work will reflect the time of its conception and composition more than its date of publication, and if the period of conception and composition is long, the work will necessarily reflect that period as a whole, rather than any particular moment within that period. In the case of theater, another date must be added to the equation, namely the date of the first performance of the play, which sometimes occurs several years before the publication date of the theatrical text.

Moreover, a text might have been written in one era—with its story either taking place in that same era or in another (past or future)—but might reflect—whether the author is aware of it or not—another era entirely, for example, in terms of the beliefs, values, or ideology that are at stake (e.g., an ideology or esthetics that is nostalgic for the past may manifest itself in a contemporary text and story).

This raises the question: how should we identify the time of the action of the story told, the time of the conception of the work, and the time of the work's ideological or esthetic framework?

The process of identification makes use of the determinations that are present in the text. A determination is a phenomenon that affects the way of being of another phenomenon, and is inscribed within that other phenomenon by the very fact of its action upon it. For example, a constant south wind may determine the growth of a tree, so that it tilts northward. In a text, determinations can be representations. An example of a historical determination of this sort would be the representation of a real historical figure in a novel. But determinations may also take other forms. An example of a non-representational historical determination would be the presence of forceful stylistic figures, as an indication that the text may be related to the Romantic period. Determinations can be used as clues for inferring the different temporalities at stake. Temporal clues in the work can be drawn from signifiers and/or signifieds. For example, the presence of an archaic or defunct spelling of a word (a signifier) might reveal the date of conception or publication (or republication) of the text that uses it.

Temporal clues can be explicit (e.g., if a historical event is referred to directly or implicit (e.g., if a historical event or scientific discovery is hinted at indirectly). They may be absolute (e.g., an event happened on such and such a date) or relative (e.g., it happened before such and such a date or event), precise (e.g., February 24, 1920, at 8 p.m.) or imprecise (e.g., a day in the 1920s).

It is possible to identify seven main dyadic temporal relations. Simultaneity (or concomitance) is the relation between terms associated with the same initial and final temporal position, and thus with the same temporal extent (duration). It is possible to distinguish between (1) strict simultaneity (the situation referred to in our definition) and the following types of (2) partial simultaneity: (2.1) inclusive simultaneity (the duration of the first term is entirely encompassed by that of the second, but exceeded by it), (2.1.1) inclusive simultaneity with coincidence of initial positions, (2.1.2) inclusive simultaneity with coincidence of final positions, (2.1.3) inclusive simultaneity without coincidence of initial or final positions, and (2.2) simultaneity-succession (partial simultaneity and succession). (3) Succession is the relationship between terms where the final temporal position of one term is prior to the initial position of the other. (3.1) Immediate succession concerns cases where the initial position of the second term is situated immediately after the final position of the first term; otherwise, there is (3.2) delayed succession. It is possible to distinguish between (3) strict succession and (2.2) simultaneity-succession, a form of partial simultaneity and succession. Figure 4.4 represents these temporal relations.

These temporal relations all have their spatial equivalents, and therefore, by generalization, constitute relations of extent, whether this extent is spatial or temporal; but other spatial relations also exist.

Following Lessing in his *Laocoon* (1836 [1767]), we can distinguish between the arts of time (literature, music, etc.) and the arts of space (painting, sculpture, etc.); of course, there are mixed arts that involve both time and space (theater,

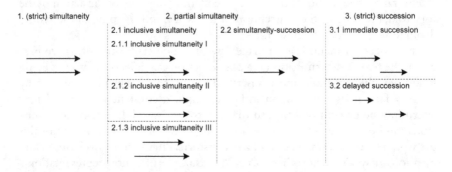

Figure 4.4 Dyadic temporal relations

cinema, etc.). Beyond a basic distinction between a spatial semiotics (image, sculpture, set design, etc.), a temporal semiotics (text, music, sound effects, etc.), and spatiotemporal semiotics (dance, installation art, theater, cinema, etc.), let us distinguish between these semiotic systems or languages: (1) those with a fixed timing and sequence (e.g., a film shown in a cinema is not normally interrupted, slowed down, accelerated, reversed, etc.); (2) those with free timing but fixed sequence (e.g., although one can go back or jump forward, in principle a text is read from one word to the next, but one can pause between two words); (3) those with free timing and sequence (e.g., one looks at a painting for as long as desired, moving one's attention from one figure to another as desired, which is not to say that there are no conventions unconsciously influencing the way one looks at a painting).

4.27 Topos

The simplest definition of a topos ("topoi" in the plural), in the sense that interests us here, is that of a stereotype of content. The word "stereotype" is used here in a neutral sense, and has no pejorative (or meliorative) meaning. The stereotype of content (what is said), that is to say, of the signified, is therefore interdefined with the stereotype of the signifier (that which conveys the meaning) and the stereotype of form (the way it is said). Obviously, a signifier can be seen as an element of form. For example, making a connection between romantic love and eternity is a stereotype of content, whereas expressing it in French with a rhyme between "amour" (love) and "toujours" (always, forever) adds a stereotype of form (see section 4.6).

A work is essentially made up of topoi of different systemic levels and different degrees of generality/particularity (I will return to this), and the non-stereotyped part of the thematic contents of a work is small, even in an apparently avant-garde work. There are thousands, perhaps tens of thousands, of topoi (more precisely, of sociotopoi). It is the topoi in a work that make it readable, or at least more economical, by making use of the implicit. This is not to mention the pleasure that there is, from the perspective of analytical detachment, in tracking down the topoi in a text, or alternatively, from the perspective of naive or deliberately unreflective fascination, in rediscovering a familiar topos and enjoying it again (just as a child likes to be told the same story over and over again).

Let us look more closely at the relations between topoi and lexicons of lexies (words or expressions) and phraseologies (stereotyped sections of sentences, such as proverbs). Topoi are sometimes lexicalized by words, expressions, or phraseologies, which may be used and recognized to varying extents: the righter of wrongs (a character who comes to the rescue of the oppressed), thwarted love, impossible love, the improbable hero, improbable love, redemption, set a thief to catch a thief, like father like son, etc. However, the vast majority of topoi are probably not lexicalized (or even consciously recognized): for example, there is no established term for the opposition love/ambition, a person who becomes distracted because they are in love, etc.

We can distinguish between thematic topoi (e.g., the flower at the edge of the abyss, the villain dressed in black) and narrative topoi (e.g., the beautiful woman who loves an ugly man). However, many thematic topoi can be converted into narrative topoi and vice versa: for example, the thematic topos of the femme fatale (e.g., Eve in the Bible) can become the narrative topos of the woman who causes a fatal event.

In my typology of systems, we can distinguish between the anthropotopos (common, in principle, to all humanity, e.g., the wise old man), the culturotopos (common to a given culture, e.g., the importance of food in French culture), the sociotopos (common to a given social group, especially in relation to a given genre, e.g., the capitalist villain in Marxist novels), the idiotopos (limited to an individual, for example, the topos of literature as emptiness in the work of Stéphane Mallarmé), the textotopos (limited to, and repeated within, a single text), and the atopos (either a thematic content that is part of the system of language, such as love, or an item of thematic content that has the potential to be a topos but is actually a hapax, not repeated anywhere, not even in the same text, e.g., let us say—hereby creating one such hapax—the potential topos of an ant that eats Hawaiian sushi). As I see it, the system of language does not in itself contain topoi; thus, the content of "love" is not a topos, but the situation, or the plot of love as deployed in a novel is one, and overly possessive love is one too.

A topos is a content and, as such, it can be analyzed in terms of semes (individual components of content). A topical grouping of semes can be seen either as a simple collection of semes or as a structure, which is then made up of a unit made of terms (semes) and of relations between these terms (cases). For example, the topos of the femme fatale, containing the semes /woman/ + /fatal/, can be viewed as the following structure: /woman/ → (ATT) → /fatal/ (ATT: attributive, characteristic). For a list of cases, see section 4.3.

A topos is a type (a model) that corresponds to a greater or lesser number of occurrences (manifestations of the model, or tokens). One, several, or all the elements that together constitute the type can be either generalized or particularized. For example, the topos /poet/ + /despised/ + /by the people/, which is found in the work of Victor Hugo and Charles Baudelaire, can be generalized to the topos /superior being/ + /despised/ + /by inferior beings/ (a topos we could call "persecution of a superior benefactor"). This then makes it possible to extend this same topos to Jesus, Socrates, the man in Plato's cave, etc.

4.28 Transtextuality: intertextuality, autotextuality, etc.

Gérard Genette (1982: 8), a narratologist whose work has provided a large number of terms and concepts widely used in literary criticism, distinguishes between five forms of transtextuality, that is, a significant textual relation that takes as its starting point a literary text (oral and/or written): (1) paratextuality (the relation of a text with its preface, title, etc.), (2) intertextuality (quotation, plagiarism, allusion, etc.), (3) metatextuality (the relation of commentary of one text by another), (4) hypertextuality (when a text is attached to an earlier text that it does not comment on but rather transforms [parody, travesty, transposition, etc.] or imitates [pastiche, forgery, etc.]; the former text is then the hypertext and the latter is the hypotext), and (5) architextuality (the relation between a text and the classes to which it belongs, such as its genre). The elements that are referred to as paratexts may, depending on the status that we decide to give them, participate in intertextual relations (in the broad sense that I give to the term) if we consider them as external to the text, or in intratextual relations if we consider them as internal to the text, or in strictly paratextual relations.

I prefer to define intertextuality in a broader sense than Genette does, and to include in this category the types of relations that he terms intertextuality, metatextuality, and hyper-/hypotextuality; of course, Genette's distinctions are still relevant.

Intertextuality and architextuality can be considered either as global relations (established between wholes) or as local relations (established first between parts and then, indirectly, between wholes). In the latter case, the starting term is considered as a part of the text and the second term as a part of another text (intertextuality) or as a part of a textual type (architextuality). There are also local–global intertextual relations: for example, a part of a text may refer (globally) to another text or a genre as a whole (e.g., in a particular sentence in a novel, a character states, "I have read *Hamlet*," thereby referring to the whole of that play).

A given text (A) may have a direct intertextual relation to a second text (B), or it may have an indirect intertextual relation to B by means of a direct intertextual relation to text C, which itself has a direct intertextual relation to text B. Two texts may seem to have a direct intertextual relationship between them, but in reality they both, possibly in ignorance of one another, have a relation to a third text, which the analyst is unaware of, or alternatively they may draw from the same reservoir of available forms that are either anonymous (not attached to one author in particular) and/or anoperatic (not attached to one work in particular), whether they are prevalent or not at a given time.

A particular case of this is when one of the two linked texts is the very one that has participated, through its canonical role, in constituting the reservoir of available forms. For example, a modern treatise on feminism that is unaware of Simone de Beauvoir's work might nevertheless take up ideas from *The Second Sex*, since these ideas are widely disseminated and have come to be seen as self-evident. Obviously, the resemblances between texts can also be the result of pure chance, which gives rise to so many apparently meaningful coincidences.

We can extend the concept of hypertextuality to encompass adaptation (e.g., a novel adapted as a novel for children, or as a film, or vice versa), translation, and even internal rewritings (e.g., the three main sequences in the story of "The Three Little Pigs"). These transformations from one text to another may be labeled as either transposition (if there is a passage from one system to another, as in the case of translation or internal rewritings from one style to another) or diaposition (if two texts or parts remain within the same system, as in the example of "The Three Little Pigs"). I am using the word "transposition" here in a more general sense than Genette does. A transposition makes an element *x* of a system *a* become an element *x'* of a system *b*. Transposition therefore concerns the transformative passage of the "same" element from one system to another.

Autotextuality is the general name for any (reflexive) relation established between a semiotic product and itself (at the level of the whole and/or at the level of the part). It can take several forms: from the text as a whole to itself as a whole, from the whole to one of its parts, from a part to the whole, and, finally, from a part to that same part. In contrast, a relation between one part of a whole and another part of that same whole is a case of intratextuality (e.g., if we compare two characters who are found in same text). Using another criterion, we can distinguish between three kinds of autotextuality. Autorepresentation (a product represents an image of itself) and autoreflexivity (a product "reflects" on itself) are necessarily relations of autotextuality: that which is self-representing or self-reflexive necessarily refers to itself. Moreover, self-reflexivity presupposes a relation of self-representation: in order to "reflect on itself," the product must necessarily present itself in one way or another as the object of its own discourse. However, not all autorepresentation gives rise to autoreflexivity; for example, if a camera films the monitor to which it is connected, we see the monitor in the monitor in the monitor, etc., but it is difficult to see any sort of autoreflexivity in this. Finally, autoreference will be understood here as a relation of autotextuality that appears without autorepresentation or autoreflexivity; for example, in the famous political slogan "I like Ike" (for the election of the American president Dwight D. Eisenhower, nicknamed Ike), the sound effect draws attention to itself, without there being either autoreflexivity or true autorepresentation. Autorepresentation and autoreflexivity are also instances of the phenomenon known as *mise en abyme*.

4.29 Versification

Versification may vary from one language to another and, for the same language, from one time period to another.

Versification is a set of textual aspects, codified to varying degrees, which are specific to texts that are (1) versified (in the sense of being divided into verses, either by line breaks on the written page, or by means of the verbal delivery of the speaker), and/or (2) follow a rhyme scheme, and/or (3) follow a scheme of syllabic measurement and arrangement, which generally corresponds either to a quantity-based system (e.g., in this system, an iamb, in a verse of iambic pentameter, is a metric foot containing one short syllable followed by one long syllable) or to a stress-based system (e.g., an iamb contains one unstressed syllable followed by one stressed syllable). In some cases, versification is concerned with textual aspects that are shared with other textual forms (e.g., alliteration, assonance, and rhythm are also found in prose texts, and even in visual poetry). All combinations of the three main aspects of versification are possible: a text can be versified or not, follow a rhyme scheme or not, and follow a scheme of syllabic measurement and arrangement or not. Some combinations are common (e.g., in verses, with syllabic measurement and arrangement, with rhyme; or in modern poetry, in verses, but no syllabic measurement and arrangement, and no rhyme) and some are uncommon (e.g., not in verses, but with syllabic measurement and arrangement, and with rhyme).

The main aspects encompassed in versification are: meter (pentameter, hexameter, etc.) and metric foot (iambic, trochaic, anapestic, dactylic, spondaic, etc.); the grouping of verses into stanzas (e.g., a quatrain, a stanza consisting of four verses); the arrangement of verses in relation to rhyme; richness (the number of identical sounds shared by rhyming elements); caesura and other forms of division; accents, scansion, and rhythm (see section 4.17); fixed forms (such as the sonnet) and uncodified forms.

Most of these aspects pertain to signifiers (the arrangement of verses, the richness of rhyme, etc.), but some belong either to signifieds or to signs as a whole (the combination of a signifier and a signified): e.g., the prohibition against rhyming words of the same root, such as "happiness" and "unhappiness." In addition, signifieds can be associated with elements that belong to the signifier. These meanings may derive from the signifieds of the words correlated with these signifiers (e.g., words ending in -*ard*, such as "coward," "dullard," or "drunkard," often have negative connotations, and a poem could use words with the same sounds, for instance *v* and *f*, each time it speaks of love). These meanings may also derive from other sources (e.g., the effect of softness produced by vowels, the effect of energy or violence produced by consonants, the semantic effects produced by the stability and symmetry of successive verses of equal length, etc.).

A text is either divided into verses or not. A text that is not (strictly) poetic can still be divided into verses (e.g., the plays of Jean Racine, or the novel in verse written by the Quebecois author Réjean Ducharme, *La fille de Christophe*

Colomb); a poetic text can also be written without being divided into verses (as is the case of prose poetry, which is common in modern poetry).

4.30 Worldview

A worldview is the particular conception or representation of the world of a given producer, class, or type of producers (e.g., a literary school, a social class, a nation, a culture, the whole of humanity). Let us give a simple example of worldview: the art historian Wilhelm Worringer (1907) sees in the geometrical and schematic pictorial representations produced by the ancient Egyptians the symptom, among this people, of an anguished relationship to the world.

Theoretically and methodologically, a distinction must be made between the real, empirical worldview of a producer (the one "in the head" of a producer), and the constructed worldview that an analyst derives from the factors of communication (producer, production, product, reception, receptor), and especially from the producer's products (and these two worldviews can be very different indeed). The constructed worldview is developed by using the product as a source of clues, but also, potentially, by using it as a source of thematized information (e.g., if a text speaks directly about the author's worldview). The constructed worldview of a producer is conveyed, in a way that may be more or less direct, explicit, and deliberate, in one, several, or all of the producer's products (e.g., several literary texts by the same author). The use of the product as a source of clues about the worldview of the producer is based on the (fairly safe) premise that the product always tells us something about the producer (and the process of production), and that it can therefore tell us in particular about that producer's worldview.

On the other hand, a particular "view" can also relate to something other, and more limited, than an overall conception of the world. Let us give some literary examples: we can analyze, for a given literary phenomenon (a text, corpus, genre, topos, etc.), what appears to be the author's view, image, representation, or conception of themselves, literature, a culture, a class or social group, a language, a genre, love, etc.

Often, and perhaps always, the vision can be rendered in the form of one or more logical propositions: for example, "The world is rotten," "Humans are inconstant." Potentially, it may be possible to link together the logical propositions pertaining to a given worldview (or other "view"), thereby constituting structures of varying degrees of complexity (to the point that they may constitute a fully developed ideology). For example, the proposition that the world is rotten (P1) implies (relation) that parts or all parts of this world (P2), for example humans, are rotten. A logical proposition consists of a subject (what we are talking about, e.g., the world) and a predicate (what we are saying about it, e.g., that it is rotten).

The worldview can be that of the producer themselves (e.g., an author), but it can also be a thematized worldview, such as that of a "character" depicted in the product (either a real one, such as a politician represented in a newspaper, or a fictitious one, such as a character in a novel). In this case, the thematized worldview may be consistent with that of the producer (in the examples just mentioned, the journalist and the novelist respectively), or different, or even opposite. There is also a worldview embedded in the language itself, before its use in a given text, since language already contains an interpretation of the world.

The analysis of a worldview—and, to a lesser extent, the analysis of some other kind of "view"—generally belongs to the domain of generative studies. Indeed, it is often postulated that a worldview generates the product, either partially or entirely. For example, Spitzer considers (and this is probably excessive) that an author's worldview informs not only the themes but all aspects of the work (e.g., its style) (see section 4.9).

5 Approaches to literary texts

5.1 Introduction

Now that I have discussed the main aspects of the literary text, I shall draw up an alphabetical list of the possible approaches to the literary text, once again without claiming to be exhaustive, and trying as far as possible to avoid repetition with the previous chapter. I shall provide a short, necessarily simplistic summary of each approach, as well as mentioning the names of some of the critics and theorists associated with them. As approach and aspect are linked (e.g., one cannot talk about stylistics without talking about style), this chapter will overlap in places with Chapter 4 on aspects of the literary text. For each approach I shall present what the approach is, in my view, but also suggest what it could be, or even what it should be.

I apologize to the reader who does not find, in the list below, the approach that they would wish to find (or if they find it subsumed under another approach), and also to the reader who finds an approach that they would rather not see. For example, some people might object to the presentation of such a specific approach as onomastics, but this happens to be an approach that I have studied in detail in my previous works.

Some overlaps exist between approaches. For example, we can consider that poetics encompasses narratology, that rhetoric and stylistics share much in common, that linguistics is the semiotics of languages and is therefore included in the latter, etc.

A given analysis may adopt either a single approach or a combination of approaches. In principle, any combination of the 50 or so approaches is possible (e.g., literary history and semiotics). Furthermore, any discipline (there are thousands of them), at least in principle, can be used to analyze literary texts, with the use of its own methods and/or by focusing, within the literary text, on the part that corresponds to the usual object of this discipline: anthropology, chemistry, mathematics, geography, criminology, etc. For example, criminology can be of some use in the study of crime novels. If literary studies are combined with another discipline (such as criminology) to analyze the same object (such as a novel), there is multidisciplinarity; if the theories and methods

DOI: 10.4324/9781003179795-8

of one discipline are transferred to another, there is interdisciplinarity (e.g., if linguistic concepts and methods are imported into literary studies). In addition, new approaches will inevitably come to be either invented or developed on the basis of existing theories, methods, or applications.

Eleven of the sections in this chapter were written by Sam Gormley, either alone or with my collaboration, in which case this is indicated at the end of the section in question. The inset "notes" in these sections were all written by myself.

Before beginning the alphabetical list of approaches, I shall provide some typologies of approaches to semiotic products. My comments will focus on literature, but they can also be generalized, either with or without adaptation, to any artistic semiotic product, or even to all semiotic products.

5.1.1 Internal and external approaches

All approaches are, to varying degrees, either (1) internal (or immanent, in the sense that they treat the text in itself), such as narratology, rhetoric, stylistics, linguistics, semiotics; or (2) external, such as literary history, literary biography, the study of literary context, etc. Sometimes a single approach can be either internal or external depending on the circumstances (e.g., psychoanalysis of the author is external to the text, whereas the psychoanalysis of characters is internal to the text).

External approaches, insofar as they methodologically (that is to say, consciously, explicitly, and in a relevant way) exclude the immanence of the work, and internal approaches, insofar as they methodologically exclude the "context" of the work, are more complementary than they are opposed to each other. It is not possible to understand the work properly without a minimum of contextualization, and an external approach that is not informed by the text itself would be completely abstract, or irrelevant, or would risk being incompatible with the text. Struggles for precedence or pre-eminence between internal and external approaches are fruitless. An internal approach is not in itself a simple auxiliary to an external approach that would provide the definitive meaning of the work, and vice versa. An external approach is not a necessary and unending prerequisite before the analyst can legitimately undertake an internal approach. Each type of approach, subject to its scientific validity, is in principle complete in itself. Internal approaches integrate the external elements from their own point of view, whereas external approaches integrate internal elements from their point of view.

5.1.2 Approaches that are interior and exterior to literary studies

The approach may be either interior to literary studies—that is, developed within the domain of literary studies for application in that domain (e.g., narratology, sociocriticism)—or exterior to literary studies (e.g., when geographical, criminological, or sociological methods are applied without significant adaptation to a literary corpus). A given approach can have an external version (e.g., psychoanalysis, sociology, general semiotics) and an internal or internalized version (e.g., psychocriticism, sociocriticism, or literary semiotics respectively). More specifically, we can posit a scale consisting of four positions between two given disciplines, such as history, history of literature, literary history, literary studies. The two intermediate forms internalize the approach of the other discipline within their own respective disciplines: history of literature internalizes literature in history, and literary history internalizes history in literary studies. Literary semiotics internalizes literature in semiotics, whereas semiotic literary studies (such as this book) internalizes semiotics in literary studies.

5.1.3 The typology of Cerisuelo and Compagnon

The critics Marc Cerisuelo and Antoine Compagnon (n.d.: n.p.) distinguish four main families of approaches or forms of criticism: (1) contextual or explanatory models (e.g., philology, literary history, sociology, psychoanalysis); (2) deep or interpretive models (e.g., Gaston Bachelard's and Jean-Pierre Richard's thematic analysis, psychoanalytic analysis of texts); (3) textual or analytic models (e.g., rhetoric, poetics, semiotics, narratology); and (4) gnostic or indeterminate models (e.g., esthetics of reception, deconstruction, intertextuality). From the perspective of the gnostic models, the meaning of semiotic products is not given but rather constructed, and it can be paradoxical (the work says one thing but means the opposite) or completely relative (any meaning attributed to the work is equally valid, or alternatively any interpretation is misinterpretation).

5.1.4 A typology based on Jakobson

Drawing on Jakobson's model of language functions (see Hébert, 2019: chapter 16), families of approaches can be distinguished according to the factor (aspect) of communication involved: (1) producer and production (e.g., biographical criticism, genetic criticism), (2) receiver and reception (e.g., theories of reception or reading), (3) the message (e.g., narratology, stylistics, poetics, semiotics), (4) context (e.g., literary history, history of ideas, history of mentalities), (5) code or system (e.g., linguistics for the language system, genre for genre systems, stylistics for the idiolectal system specific to a given author), and (6) physical contact (through a particular channel, support, or document) or psychological contact between producer and receiver (e.g., phonetics, information theory and its concept of noise, media analysis).[1]

---

1 We can further distinguish between approaches that focus primarily on signifiers (e.g., versification, sound analysis, phonology), or signifieds (meaning, in the broadest sense), or forms of both (e.g., a lexicological approach). Approaches that ultimately aim at "meaning" will focus either on primary meaning (e.g., the plot of "The Three Little Pigs") or on secondary meanings (e.g., the psychoanalytic meaning, such as instances of the pleasure principle and the reality principle, present in "The Three Little Pigs"). I am drawing here on Courtés's (1991: 61–63) distinction between types of meanings.

5.2 Cognitive poetics

Cognitive poetics is a school of literary criticism that applies the principles of cognitive science to the interpretation of literary texts. Related to the fields of reader-response criticism (which argues that the experience of the reader is a vital starting point for literary criticism) and stylistics, cognitive poetics is part of a wider "cognitive turn" in literary criticism that highlights and analyses the intertwined nature of reading and biological–neurological processes through the application of empirical cognitive models. Commonly analyzed aspects of texts include metaphor, world-building, and figure–ground perception. Peter Stockwell notes that:

> the foundations of cognitive poetics obviously lie most directly in cognitive linguistics and cognitive psychology, together forming a large part of the field of cognitive science. The basic insight behind these disciplines is in realizing that forms of expression and forms of conscious perception are bound, more closely than was previously realized, in our biological circumstances.
>
> (Stockwell, 2019: 6)

As Stockwell argues: "reading literature is a natural process, a natural object of exploration," and since literature itself "necessarily involves an activating consciousness," it can be analyzed from a scientific perspective. Cognitive poetics can thus be defined as a "science of reading" (Stockwell, 2019: 2). As indicated in the section on theories of reading, there are different kinds of readings and readers, all of which offer potential fields of study for cognitive poetics. Cognitive poetics starts from the assumption that reading is not a disembodied process but one that involves complex cognitive responses. The argument can subsequently be made that "a theory of literary reading inspired by embodied cognitive science is uniquely able to capture these reader-response dynamics and account for them in terms of specific psychological processes" (Caracciolo, 2018: 12). Cognitive poetics is therefore concerned with asking the question: what happens when we read literature?

George Lakoff and Mark Johnson's *Metaphors We Live By* (1980) is widely held as a precursor to cognitive poetics. The book rethinks the idea of metaphor as a rhetorical device used in poetry, instead arguing that metaphors are cognitive mechanisms which reveal the "conceptual metaphors" that structure our habitual understanding of the world (e.g., *life* is a *journey*, an *argument* is a *war*). Expanding this view, cognitive poetics claims to be able to offer "a unified explanation of both individual interpretations as well as interpretations that are shared by a group, community or culture" (Stockwell, 2019: 5).

NOTE: DO THE SCIENCES OF CULTURE NEED TO DRAW ON THE NATURAL SCIENCES?

We would argue that, while there are clear advantages to the use of a scientific approach to account for the role of the body and the mind in literary studies, one must avoid succumbing to a potentially hegemonic enthusiasm. Ultimately, all human activities involve the body and the mind, but this is not a sufficient reason to claim that any valid approach in the sciences of culture must necessarily be based on the biological and cognitive sciences (or, more generally, on the natural sciences), or must necessarily draw on them. If this were the case, since everything ultimately depends on the physical world, the mother science would have to be physics, or, for example, quantum physics more specifically. However, a discipline can legitimately and productively place itself on "higher levels" without necessarily having to pass through the "lower levels," even if it benefits from the critically integrated knowledge of these lower levels. If this were not the case, then logically it would first be necessary to completely elucidate the problems situated on the lower levels—which physics, for example, is far from having done, and will probably never do—before being able to move on to the higher levels.

Authors: Reuven Tsur, Peter Stockwell, Joanna Gavins, Mark Turner, George Lakoff, Mark Johnson, etc.

Sam Gormley and Louis Hébert

5.3 Comparative literature

Comparative literature is the discipline and study that compares texts and textual forms (genres, themes, topoi, etc.)—but also different types of semiotic products (e.g., film and text, or even film and film) and their associated forms—that in principle arise from different cultures (and possibly from different languages), in order to bring out their identities, similarities, oppositions, and alterities, and to establish the causes, modalities of presence, and effects of these different comparative relations.

Not all literary comparisons necessarily belong to the approach of comparative literature. It is also necessary, in principle, for the comparison to consider two semiotic products (or forms) from two different cultures. However, the concept of different cultures is a relative one. For example, one can more confidently speak of two separate cultures in the case of the global West and the East, or France and the United Kingdom, than in the case of the northern and southern states of the US. However, we can speak of the internal diversity of a given culture in a number of different ways. For example, in the first case mentioned above, we can consider the internal diversity of Western culture, which includes different cultures such as those of France and the United Kingdom. Internal diversity also applies to the different forms taken by the "same" culture at different points in time. For example, metaphor in Elizabethan England can be compared to metaphor in British works of our own time. Finally, internal diversity can be found within the same culture and historical period. For example, metaphor may appear in a certain way in Western literary texts and in another way in Western cognitive science.

Comparative literature is by definition intertextual (in the broad sense, not relating only to written texts) and intercultural. It is often interlinguistic, intersemiotic, interartial, and intermedial (see sections 5.16, 5.17. 5.21 and 5.48). It is also, in principle, multidisciplinary or interdisciplinary, and therefore intertheoretical: "comparative literature rebuilds a space for dialogue and questioning that had been largely dislocated by the processes of specialization and disciplinarization at work since the nineteenth century" (University of Montréal Department of Comparative Literature, n.d.). One could go as far as to say that Germanists and Italianists do not "speak" to one another, nor nineteenth-century specialists and twentieth-century specialists, nor literary scholars and painting specialists, and that these neighboring fields have a need for disciplinary meeting spaces, such as that provided by comparative literature (although some other disciplines, such as semiotics, can also provide such a meeting space).

Moreover, interculturality can arise in relation to any of the main poles of literary communication: author, text, reader (e.g., between the author's culture and that of the reader, or between two cultures present in the head of a bicultural author). In particular, interculturality can occur within the text itself. For example, the action of an American novel may take place in Italy. More precisely, in a given text, the presence of another culture can be produced by thematic representations of the other culture (as in our American novel set in Italy) and/or by other kinds of marks providing clues regarding the other culture (e.g., an American novel is set in the US, but we feel the influence of Italian culture from the use of a characteristically Italian stylistic figure). All the same combinations that we mentioned here in the case of interculturality also apply to intertextuality, interlinguality, intersemioticity, interartiality, intermediality, multidisciplinarity or interdisciplinarity, and intertheoricity.

Like any analysis of a semiotic product, an analysis using a comparative literature approach must choose between an emic approach (which uses categories of analysis internal to the product and its associated culture) and/or an etic approach (which uses categories of analysis external to the product and its associated culture). Let us take the example of love in *Hamlet*. In an emic approach, we would use the categories of love as they existed at the time in English society, and consider whether they are adopted or not, or transformed, or refuted in the play. In an etic approach, we could, for example, analyze the same play using the categories of love developed within a psychological theory of our own time. In this respect, the analysis of two objects from different cultures can be done in several ways, which can also be combined. One can use a distinct emic (internal) approach for each object; or one can use the categories of analysis of the first object to analyze the second object, and possibly vice versa; or one can use the same etic (external) approach for both objects; and finally, one can use a different etic approach for each object.

Authors: René Étiemble, Pierre Brunel, Yves Chevrel, Robert Escarpit, Northrop Fry, etc.

5.4 Cultural materialism (New Historicism)

Cerisuelo and Compagnon present cultural materialism as follows:

> The theory of history has changed, and the effect of this has also been felt
> in the reading of texts, including literary ones. Contrary to the positivist
> dream, the past is accessible to us only in the form of texts [and other semi-
> otic products: images, etc.], which are themselves inseparable from those
> that constitute our present. History is not singular, it is composed of a
> multiplicity of contradictory stories or narratives, and it does not have the
> unique meaning that totalizing philosophies have seen in it since Hegel.
> History is a narrative, which describes the present as well as the past [or
> even an imagined or desired future], and it is analyzed itself as text, or lit-
> erature, by the theorists of history. [...] Like the hermeneutics of reception
> and deconstruction, the new history abolishes the barrier between text
> and context, which had been a central principle of all literary criticism,
> on the grounds that contexts are themselves only narrative constructions,
> or texts. *There are only texts.* The American school of New Historicism
> (Stephen Greenblatt, Louis Adrian Montrose, Arthur F. Kinney), which is
> inspired by Foucault and emphasizes the power relations of which all his-
> tory, as discursive formation, is the product, is interested in those who are
> excluded by discourse and power. American cultural materialism, which
> is also influenced by Althusser's definition of ideology and the cultural
> studies of the British critic Raymond Williams, now rarely deals with lit-
> erature, which is suspected of elitism owing to its canonical character, but
> instead prefers to address all forms of culture, and particularly popular
> culture.
>
> (Cerisuelo and Compagnon, n.d.: n.p.)

In short, for this approach, the content of the past, present, and future can be
considered only through texts (and other semiotic and non-semiotic products)
and the study of those texts ultimately produces more texts (even if they are
oral ones), especially in the form of narratives. In this respect, all textual aspects
can in principle be addressed and all textual approaches used. In other words,
the (historical) context of literary texts is also textual. Consequently, intertextuality too is generalized. Moreover, as the principle of relativism dictates, there
is not one history but many histories, with different points of view. And there
is not only History with a capital "H" (that of important characters and major
events) but there is also history with a lower-case "h" (e.g., the everyday lives of
ordinary people). In particular, we can distinguish between heterohistory (e.g.,
the history of African Americans produced by Euro-Americans) and autohistory
(e.g., the history of African Americans produced by themselves). I believe that
both such histories are valid and complementary. Acknowledging the principle
of relativism ("everything is relative") does not necessarily mean that one will
fall into the trap of absolute relativism, whereby any interpretation is worth as

much as any other. We should instead adopt a critical relativism, which carefully and rigorously assesses the value of each interpretation (the view that the Earth is flat is a relative belief that can, or even must, be discarded). The important thing is not who is speaking, but who is telling the truth (in the knowledge, however, that the truth is difficult to discern). Otherwise, even if one's intentions are appropriate and good, one can fall into the trap of *ad hominem* judgment. However, we must arrive at the truth in cultural sciences through the critical confrontation of points of view, especially if they are different, and the endogenous point of view (e.g., that of autohistory) is an important perspective to be to be taken into account.

See Cultural studies (section 5.5); Deconstruction (section 5.6), and Reception (theories of) (section 5.36).

Authors: Stephen Greenblatt, Adrian Montrose, Arthur F. Kinney, etc.

5.5 Cultural studies

As defined by Grossberg et al., cultural studies is:

> an interdisciplinary, transdisciplinary, and sometimes counter-disciplinary field that operates in the tension between its tendencies to embrace both a broad anthropological and a more narrowly humanistic conception of culture. [...] It is typically interpretive and evaluative in its methodologies, but unlike traditional humanism it rejects the exclusive equation of culture with high culture and argues that all forms of cultural production need to be studied in relation to other cultural practices and to social and historical structures.
>
> (Grossberg et al., 1992: 4)

Within Anglophone academia, cultural studies is primarily associated with the Marxist theorist and sociologist Stuart Hall, who, together with Richard Hoggart, founded the Centre for Contemporary Cultural Studies at the University of Birmingham in 1964. "British cultural studies" arose at a specific historical and political moment that saw rising multiculturalism in UK society, the increasing influence of US consumer culture and mass communications, and the rise of the New Left. It sought to analyze the constantly shifting dynamics of ideology, ethnicity, class, capital, and national identity as they manifested in cultural objects, practices, and texts. Cultural studies starts from the recognition that culture is not stable but rather a highly contingent and mobile set of fluctuating practices (and as such it is a strongly contextualist school of thought). It views culture as a site of struggle and contestation rather than of fixed values. Perhaps as a logical result of this starting point, the field of cultural studies itself "has no distinct methodology, no unique statistical, ethnomethodological, or textual analysis to call its own" (Grossberg et al., 1992: 2), but rather represents a politically engaged (typically leftist) commitment to "the study of the entire range of a society's arts, beliefs, institutions, and communicative practices" (Grossberg et al., 1992: 4). Hall himself contributed influential work to a wide range of fields, including the study of diasporic identity, communication and television media, semiotics, and institutional power.

Cultural studies deploys a number of theoretical terms and frameworks— often adopted from the social sciences—that have since become fundamental in textual scholarship, including the concepts of hegemony, agency, and identity. A cultural studies approach thus entails dissecting popular and dominant discourses in order to reveal the workings of ideological processes on everyday life. While its potential objects of study are limitless, cultural studies analyses are particularly useful for the study of film, media, and popular art.

Cultural studies can be considered as an intellectual branch of a larger current that seeks to "democratize culture," and more generally society. This current itself is encompassed by the current of individualism, centered on the value of the individual, which is itself multiplied by the mass of individuals. This democratization has the potential to yield benefits in terms of material (financial) and symbolic capital, since the works of popular culture by definition are of interest to a greater number of people, and are often well adapted to production in series, and even to industrialization (as opposed, for example, to installation art or land art).

Authors: Stuart Hall, Raymond Williams, Angela McRobbie, Pierre Bourdieu, Anthony Giddens, etc.

Sam Gormley and Louis Hébert

5.6 Deconstruction

Sorin Alexandrescu summarizes as follows the operations that are constitutive of deconstruction:

> discovering the opposition that dominates a given text and the privileged term in this opposition [an opposition consists of two opposite terms]; revealing the metaphysical and ideological presuppositions of the opposition; showing how it is undone and contradicted in the very text that is supposed to be founded by it; reversing the opposition, such that the previously non-privileged term is now brought into relief; displacing the opposition and thereby reconfiguring the problematic field in question. It must be emphasized, then, that deconstruction consists neither in the simple reversal of a hierarchy nor in the wholesale rejection of an opposition; on the contrary, the opposition is maintained, while reversing its internal hierarchy and shifting its locus of articulation.
>
> (in Greimas and Courtés, 1986: 62)

For example: (1) In Jacques Derrida's *On Grammatology* (1967), a foundational work of poststructuralist theory, the author exposes the following opposition, which he finds to be common in linguistic and philosophical discourse (here,

"+" indicates the valued term and "–" indicates the devalued term): speech (+)/writing (–); (2) he reverses the opposition to produce the new opposition: speech (–)/writing (+); (3) he then shows—in opposition to ideological and metaphysical presuppositions underlying the initial opposition—that everything is ultimately writing and that nothing, not even writing, can be said to be original (and thereby truly valued). He thereby dissolves, in a sense, the opposition.

In logical terms, deconstruction consists in establishing a homologation between two oppositions (in the example given above, speech/writing and +/–), then producing a counter-homologation, which reverses the relationship between those terms (speech/writing and –/+). Let us recall that homologation is a relation between at least two oppositions (A/B, C/D, etc.) where we can say that A is to B as C is to D, etc.; for example, in this case, speech is to writing as positive is to negative. If we consider this approach in terms of truth status: whereas Aristotle used the dilemma (a proposition is either true or false, with no other possible position) and rejected the tetralemma (a proposition is either true, or false, or true and false, or neither true nor false), and Buddhist philosophers adopted the tetralemma, which they called *catuṣkoṭi*, only to refute it (ultimate reality lies beyond the tetralemma, and none of the four possibilities or the combination of them are relevant for describing it), deconstruction, we could say, dissolves the dilemma into a "monolemma": if everything is writing, the speech/writing opposition collapses.

Still speaking from the perspective of truth status, we can say that the apparent relation of homologation (speech/writing and +/–) is not the real relation between these terms, and the real homologation is actually the inverse of that. Finally, we can say that what appears to be a dyad (speech/writing) is in fact a monad (everything is writing).

Deconstruction is based on the principle that the work contradicts itself: it says or postulates one thing while demonstrating the opposite. On the contrary, hermeneutics postulates that the work—even if it is apparently or superficially contradictory or even indeterminate, as is the case for many modern works—is coherent, which makes it possible to explain the obscure passages or elements by using passages or elements whose meaning is clearer, or at least to propose a new synthesis that incorporates both the obscure and clear elements.

Deconstruction, as practiced by authors such as Jacques Derrida, Paul De Man, J. Hillis Miller, or Geoffrey Hartman, uses the following concepts in particular: grammatology, *différance*, archi-writing, trace, spacing, supplement, hymen, phonologism, logocentrism.

Authors: Jacques Derrida, Paul De Man, Joseph Hillis Miller, Geoffrey Hartman, etc.

5.7 Dialogism

This is how Robert Barsky presents the theory of dialogism proposed by the influential Russian critic and theorist Mikhail Bakhtin:

The act of reading is thus comparable to a conversation. Bakhtin is only moderately interested in the opinion of either of the speakers; the most important aspect of dialogue is its power to give rise to unexpected statements, and to ideas and opinions that do not belong to either speaker, but are essentially the result of their interaction. [...] When applied to the novel, this theory assumes that a complex dialogue develops in the text, first between the author and their characters (especially the hero), but also, through the intermediary of the characters, between the author and the reader. In this sense, the reader also becomes a character, placed in a particular situation, and whose point of view sheds light on a singular interaction (that of the text), in an equally singular way, that is to say, according to the context of reading the work. If the reader rereads this same text, their "situation" will necessarily have changed, if only because the text is already familiar to them.

(Barsky, 1997: 55)

Since literary texts present several voices in dialogue, they can be said to be polyphonic to varying degrees (Bakhtin finds that this is more true of the novel than of poetry, considering the latter to be monological, which seems contestable). This dialogue is not produced only by the (spoken or written) dialogues between characters, but could also be established, for example, between the opposite actions carried out by two characters.

I would add that several dialogues must be taken into account: between author and reader, between characters, between narrator and narratee (the instance to which the narrator addresses himself or herself), and sometimes between narrator and character. The category of "characters" here includes the authors of statements reported by the characters themselves (e.g., the author of a newspaper article that is quoted by a character) and, even when they are not characters in the conventional sense, the narrator and the narratee. We can add to this the distinction between the empirical instance and the constructed instance. For example, the empirical, real author corresponds to the constructed author (e.g., the image that the text provides of the author), whether or not this image accurately resembles the empirical author. Finally, we must take into account the distinction between the "underlying" and "overlying" enunciator. For example, if, in the nineteenth century, an author makes a misogynistic statement, they are thereby acting as the overlying enunciator in relation to the underlying enunciator, which is the whole society of the nineteenth century in general (or the average citizen); they are, in this sense, the spokesperson—acting either more or less consciously, and more or less deliberately—of that underlying enunciator.

To the extent that literary texts confront several discourses, they are said to be interdiscursive. The word "discourse" is highly polysemic, and in this case it refers to all the expressions produced by a given enunciator. Each character bearing an ideology (or several) "becomes an *ideologue*, in the Bakhtinian sense of the term, and each of their words becomes an *ideologeme*" (Barsky, 1997: 63).

An ideologeme is a component part of a given ideology. As mentioned above, this ideology attached to a character can actually be related to an underlying enunciator.

The method for producing a dialogic analysis may include the following steps:

1. Identify the speakers or enunciators.
2. Identify the ideologies and connect these to the speakers who support them, including underlying enunciators.
3. Break the ideologies down into ideological aspects (beliefs, values, and ethics), and connect these to either explicit or implicit ideological propositions, which are made up of a subject (what one is talking about) and a predicate (what one says about it).
4. Compare (with reference to relations of identity, similarity, opposition, alterity, etc.) the propositional content of the different ideologies.
5. Identify instances of ideological and/or propositional consensus, conflict, and conversion.
6. Potentially, identify an archi-ideology, which the author is not necessarily conscious of, and which arises from the interaction between the different ideologies, as their sum total or as a new synthesis.

Authors: Mikhail Bakhtin, Julia Kristeva, Tzvetan Todorov, André Belleau, etc.

5.8 Digital media (new media) studies

Digital media studies—also referred to as new media studies—is an interdisciplinary field of humanities scholarship that examines the impact and roles of new technologies on traditional forms of analysis; the evolving habits and practices of readers and publics in response to new technologies; and the new forms and genres emerging as a result of the introduction of digital media. Digital media studies broadly overlaps with the fields of art and design, communications, and information studies; in this respect, it draws heavily on the pioneering work of Marshall McLuhan, whose slogan "the medium is the message" (1964) renewed scholarly interest in emergent modes of mass communication. As Lisa Gye puts it:

> academics studying digital media come from a broad palette of more established disciplines—critical theory, media studies, literary studies, art, political economy, information technology, philosophy and so on. What binds us is our interest in the ways in which digital media are reshaping our media landscape.
>
> (Gye, 2007: n.p.)

Digital media studies has much in common with the social sciences in its emphasis on broader patterns of engagement, consumption, and criticism with respect to new digital media, including social media, virtual environments, and user-generated content. Digital media and new media studies adopt a

wide-perspective attitude, conscious as it is of the major impact of global con-
nectivity (over the internet) on previously more localized patterns of cultural
consumption. More recently, theorists have challenged the distinction between
"old" and "new" media, citing the ways in which relatively early technological
developments (e.g., the camera, the telephone) have retained a foundational
importance in our contemporary media landscape.

In principle, intermediality differs from digital media studies in that the former
is concerned, on the one hand, with all media, whether old, new, or emerging,
and on the other hand, with their interaction (see section 5.16). However, digital
media studies may also address the media ecosystem, even if only the part of it
concerned with new media, and in this respect its approach is also intermedial.

Authors: Marshall McLuhan, Lev Manovich, Janet Murray, Jean Baudrillard,
Graeme Turner, etc.

Sam Gormley and Louis Hébert

5.9 Ecocriticism

Ecocriticism (or environmental criticism) is the study of "the relationship
between literature and the physical environment" (Glotfelty and Fromm,
1996: xviii). Note that the physical environment can be cultural (e.g., a resi-
dential building), but the primary focus here is the natural environment.
Ecocriticism is interdisciplinary, has no unified methodological or explicit theoretical basis, and can take extremely diverse forms, but practitioners are generally united by a "spirit of commitment to environmentalist praxis" (Buell,
1995: 430). For example, ecocritical analysis might entail close reading of a
literary text to reveal wider cultural attitudes toward the environment; to show
how an author envisages non-destructive interactions between humanity and
the natural world; or to demonstrate how popular genres (dystopia, post-apoca-
lypse, etc.) serve as vehicles for environmental messages. In theory, it is possible
to pursue an ecocritical analysis of any given artistic text from any period—
whether literary, filmic, or visual—by examining what it does or does not say
about the natural environment.

First-wave ecocriticism chiefly sought to reassert the importance of North
American nature writing from the nineteenth and twentieth centuries, including
Henry David Thoreau's *Walden* (1854), Aldo Leopold's *A Sand County Almanac*
(1949), and Edward Abbey's *Desert Solitaire* (1968). Themes of wilderness, soli-
tude, and closeness to nature predominated in ecocritical writing of the 1990s,
which made use of a broad critical distinction between "nature" and "culture"
as the basis for textual analysis. In anthropology, the term "culture" is used to
refer to everything that is not natural and that is produced by humans (and
by certain animals), but although humans are cultural beings, they also belong
to nature through their bodies—although these too can be culturalized (e.g.,
tattoos, surgery, etc.)—and the natural physical or mental products of those
bodies. Moreover, it should be noted that there is also animal culture, especially

concerning the non-innate knowledge that is transmitted from individual to individual (e.g., knowledge of feeding grounds for a pod of whales). Broadly speaking, we can distinguish between pure nature (e.g., algae), culturalized nature (e.g., algae integrated in a sculpture), naturalized culture (e.g., a metal boat wreck covered with algae), and pure culture (e.g., a metal boat).

Contemporary ecocriticism is a constellation of diverse critical methodologies, and overlaps significantly with animal studies, nonhuman studies, indigenous studies, ecofeminism, new materialism (a recent development within feminist theory that broadly focuses on concepts of animacy and agency in the nonhuman world), and Anthropocene theory. In its second and third waves, ecocriticism expanded to include the study of literatures not in English and literatures of the Global South through the lenses of environmental justice, (post)colonialism, and global warming. Owing to its broadly activist roots and sociopolitical thrust, ecocriticism has sometimes been situated in opposition to so-called "French theory" and its skeptical interrogations of language and representation. However, in its modern form, ecocriticism is attuned to the ways in which politics and culture have always shaped discourses around nature and the environment (e.g., the concept of "wilderness"). As Timothy Clark (2014: 75) notes: "one crucial but dubious function of the concept of nature has been to lend seemingly unchallengeable foundations to very contestable claims." Ecocritics thus leverage referential instability to reveal how seemingly self-evident terms about nature obscure cultural and political bias.

NOTE: THE CRITIQUE OF "NATURE"

One can, like Timothy Morton, undertake to radically deconstruct the idea of nature. We can assume that—with the possible exception of a transcendent entity—we never have access to noumena (things in themselves), but only to phenomena (things as they appear to us). Consequently, we never have access to a noumenonature, a nature in itself (as it really is, in the absence of a filtered interpretation). The famous question remains unanswerable: what is the sound of a tree falling in the forest if no one is there to hear it? In particular, nature is always already perceived through cultural filters, which become established in the human from an early stage, both in phylogenetic terms (regarding the history of humans as a species) and in ontogenetic terms (regarding the development of an individual human, from as early as the fetal stage). For example, can we look at a forest without our cultural filters, which "add" (there are also subtractions) to the "raw" forest considerations such as the function of a forest in an ecosystem, its possible uses by humans, its economic and ecological value, the fact that we like or dislike forest, etc.? In other words, we do not have direct access to the "nature" of the forest; at best, we have access to a laborious, complex, intellectual reconstruction of that "nature," which would be less deforming than another, apparently more immediate (but actually more "mediated") perception of the forest. Just as the concept of nature then becomes blurred, so too does the concept with which it is interdefined, that of culture. Indeed, culture itself is subject to the same relativization as nature. How could we have direct access to a noumenoculture? In particular, if cognition emerges from physical matter and processes (if not from the brain alone), and thus from the natural world, how could we perceive anything other than a naturalized culture? But then, our vision of nature is also always pre-naturalized, even though we can never reach a noumenonature. Obviously, the above hypothesis regarding the emergence of the mind can be contested, but that of the determination of the mind by the physical (and vice versa) is beyond dispute.

Authors: Lawrence Buell, Ursula Heise, Timothy Clark, Joni Adamson, Stacy Alaimo, Timothy Morton, etc.

Sam Gormley and Louis Hébert

5.10 Feminism, feminist criticism, gender studies

Feminism is a political, cultural, and philosophical movement which advocates for the equality of women and men, and which seeks to liberate women from the confines of patriarchal structures. Gerbier (2006: 320) defines feminism as "the doctrine that presides over the defense of the rights and dignity of women," and considers that "the general thrust of feminism lies in the inconsistency between the affirmation of the theoretical equality between the sexes [but even this theoretical equality is not supported by all individuals, groups, institutions, and societies] and the observation of the actual inequality between the sexes."

Since its emergence as a social movement with the campaigns for women's suffrage at the turn of the twentieth century, feminism has evolved through a number of distinct phases. Simone de Beauvoir's seminal study *The Second Sex* (1949) was a watershed moment for second-wave feminism and became a crucial touchstone for its assertion that "one is not born, but rather becomes, a woman." This anti-essentialist stance (i.e., the recognition that biology cannot dictate a woman's destiny) provided momentum for feminists of the so-called "sexual revolution" between the 1960s–1980s, who argued for the emancipation of women from the domestic or professional (e.g., nursing) roles commonly assigned to them. Fundamental to this emancipatory aspiration was the invention of the contraceptive pill and the gradual legalization of abortion in the 1960s and '70s. Third-wave feminism appeared in the US in the 1990s and introduced a wide range of new intersectional perspectives on previously side-lined communities, including transgender women, women of color, and women with disabilities. Since the 2010s, fourth-wave feminism has been largely associated with questions of women's empowerment, often articulated through the medium of digital media (e.g., the influence of the #MeToo movement).

The distinction between "gender" and "sex" (which Beauvoir was already hinting at in 1949) is a vital one in contemporary debates within feminism and related disciplines (see section 5.33 on queer studies and queer theory). Gender, in the broadest sense, refers to the socially and culturally constructed aspects of femininity and masculinity. As theorized by thinkers such as Judith Butler, gender refers to a set of social meanings performed by individuals across time and transmitted across generations, thereby legitimizing a seemingly natural gender binary. Indeed, the fields of philosophy, sociology, and anthropology have long recognized a distinction between sex and gender in human cultures. Sex refers more narrowly to the biological differences (chromosomal, genital, physiological) between men and women.[2] Gender studies, which grew out of feminist and queer literary studies, takes the constructedness of gender identity as its starting point for critical analysis. Like many contemporary critical disciplines, gender studies encompasses an extremely wide range of concepts and texts; it might be described as a critical attitude that entails close attention to the shifting construction and uses of gender and gendered expression in literature, film, and related cultural texts.

One can look in literary texts and forms (and all semiotic products and forms), with regard to all textual aspects, for the marks of the affirmation of a theoretical equality and especially the marks of a real inequality. One can also look for how feminist doctrine has been represented, whether positively or negatively, directly or indirectly, consciously or unconsciously, in a given text or corpus. One can analyze texts by men or women that speak of women, and also—since the two sexes and traditional genders are interdefined—of men. Finally, taking into account the three main dimensions of the analysis of literary communication, we can identify, in general or for a particular work or corpus, the possible differences between *écriture féminine* and an *écriture masculine*; between work created by a man and work created by a woman; and between the reception (reading, criticism, analysis, etc.) carried out by men and women.

Modern feminist scholarship is situated within this nexus of debates around equality, representation, and gender. Feminist literary criticism can take many forms: critical analyses of the representation of women in texts written by men; the recentering of overlooked texts written by women; and the close analysis and critique of the uses of gendered language. Feminist approaches to texts are also concerned with differences in ways of reading and of doing criticism; as Ellen Rooney (2006: 4) asserts: "feminist literary theory maintains that women's reading is of consequence, intellectually, politically, poetically; women's readings signify." Feminist scholarship in the 1960s and '70s was significant for its focus on women's social condition and lived experience as the basis of a radical form of embodied criticism. The influential French theorist Hélène Cixous developed the concept of *écriture féminine* in the late 1970s to describe a challenging, boldly gendered (feminine) style of writing liberated from the de facto language of patriarchy. In recent years, contemporary feminist critics have focused widely

---

2 It should be noted that science does not bear out a hard-and-fast biological distinction between the two sexes, but rather identifies two broad tendencies within the human population with considerable scope for variation.

on questions of genre, form, and canon, alongside analyses of the representation of women in literature.

Authors: Mary Wollstonecraft, Simone de Beauvoir, Betty Friedan, Audre Lorde, Angela Davis, bell hooks, Judith Butler, Hélène Cixous, Julia Kristeva, Luce Irigaray, etc.

Sam Gormley and Louis Hébert

5.11 Genetic criticism or textual genetics

Genetic criticism is the discipline that analyzes the comparative relations (identity, similarity, opposition, alterity, etc.) and operations of transformation (addition, deletion, substitution, permutation, increase, decrease, fusion, separation, conservation, etc.) between a foretext (a "draft") and another (earlier or later) foretext, and/or between a foretext or group of foretexts and the final text, from the point of view of their causes, modalities, and the effects of their presence (or absence) (see section 4.23 on structure, relation, and operation).

This study of the internal diachrony (succession in historical time) of the different states of a given work is one of the forms that can be taken by the study of intertextuality (see section 5.17).

Authors: Jean Bellemin-Noël, Pierre-Marc de Biasi, etc.

5.12 Geocriticism

In the broadest sense, geocriticism is the study of the causes, modalities, and effects of the presence (or absence) of spaces in semiotic products, including literary texts.

The practice of geocriticism therefore depends on the definition of space and its typologies. These spaces can be: (1) those of production (the spaces that the producer inhabits or those, whether real or fictitious, that "inhabit" the producer), (2) those of the product (thematized spaces, integrated into the content of the work, whether these spaces are entirely fictitious or correspond to some degree to real spaces), and (3) those of reception (the spaces that the receiver inhabits or those, whether real or fictitious, that inhabit the receiver). The study of the first type of spaces is the domain of geopoetics; the study of the second type of spaces is the domain of geocriticism in the narrow sense; the study of the third type of spaces is the domain of what I propose to call geoesthetics, and which remains to be established as an actual field of study (on geoesthetics, see Poirier-Roy, 2020). Existing geopoetics seems to consider only the concrete spaces in which writing takes place. A complete geopoetics could include analyses that focus either on concrete spaces or on the spaces that inhabit the producer, or analyses that take into account the interaction between the two kinds of spaces. The same principle applies to geoesthetics.

Geocriticism in the narrow sense can take two main forms: either one studies the thematic representations of a given space in several semiotic products (e.g., representations of the Eiffel Tower or the bourgeois living room in several novels); or one studies all the spaces that are thematized in a given semiotic product (e.g., in a given novel). The same principle applies to geoesthetics: either one studies the influence of a space on the reception of one or more given semiotic products or in general; or one studies the influence of different spaces on the reception of a given work. This is a general principle: an approach can take a particular element as its starting point (e.g., the Eiffel Tower) and then consider the whole that includes it (e.g., the works that represent or refer to the Eiffel Tower), or it can take as its starting point a whole (e.g., a particular novel) then consider the elements of this type that it contains (e.g., all the thematized spaces in a given novel).

Geocriticism concerns the representation (more precisely, the thematization) of spaces in the text (more broadly, in a given semiotic product: image, text, etc.). When it considers the determining effect that space has on the text—whether this determination results in a representation of space or some other impact, such as the choice or structure of genres, signifiers, signifieds, etc.—it becomes a matter of geopoetics. It still remains to define the status of the determinations arising from space represented in a text when this space is not also the concrete space where the writing took place and/or one of the spaces that inhabit the author. Obviously, when a text takes a given space as its principal space, especially if this space is one of the principal themes, we can assume that this space inhabits the author. There are degrees in the strength with which such spaces inhabit an author. We can distinguish between two stages of geopoetic analysis: the first stage relates to the time when the forces of geodetermination are exerted on the process of writing; the second stage relates to the time when these forces have actually impacted (by marking) on the text. At the moment of writing, the author may allow themselves to be directed by these forces, or may amplify them, or, on the contrary, the author may attenuate them, counteract them, change them, or attempt to do so. While the second phase can be analyzed by the author as well as by another analyst, the first phase is probably more easily accessible to the author, whether they analyze it at the time the force is exerted or afterwards. The same two stages apply to geoesthetics, that is, the study of the determinations of space on the interpretation of the semiotic product. Since the concept of space is a broad one, one must take care in choosing the extent of this concept that is used for a given analysis. For example, if I write in a room where I have some Beethoven playing, is the specific influence produced by this music relevant to a geopoetic analysis? How far should we, and can we go in listing the contents that fill the space? An expansive definition would lead us to a broader concept of contextopoetics and contextoesthetics respectively. The context includes not only the spatial dimension, but also the temporal, the social (cultural, etc.), the individual (biographical, emotional, etc.), etc. (see section 4.7 on context).

Since time and space are interdefined, this inevitably leads to the concept of a chronocriticism. Literary history and narratology constitute parts of such a chronocriticism (see sections 5.20 on literary history and 5.24 on narratology).

Time, space, nature, and culture are the main environments, or contexts, in which humans are immersed. As such, they are—with the exception of nature, of which certain aspects, such as laws of nature, are always and everywhere the same—factors of relativity (but there are other factors of relativity), meaning that phenomena can vary depending on these factors.

Authors: Bertrand Westphal, Robert Tally, Christiane Lahaie, etc.

5.13 Hermeneutics

Hermeneutics is:

> [the] theory of the interpretation of texts. Historically derived from the task of establishing ancient texts, *philological hermeneutics* establishes the meaning of texts, inasmuch as it depends on the historical situation in which they were produced. As for *philosophical hermeneutics*, which is independent of linguistics, it seeks to determine the transcendental conditions of all interpretation.
>
> (Rastier, 2001: 299)

Most, if not all, approaches use, whether consciously or not, and explicitly or not, concepts drawn from material or philological hermeneutics: the principle of the internal coherence between aspects and between passages of the text, and that of the external coherence between those aspects and the contextual facts causing and determining the work; the distinction between literal/figurative meanings; etc. In a certain way, even deconstruction (see section 5.6) participates in hermeneutics by taking almost the opposite approach.

We can distinguish between a general material hermeneutics, as a theory of the interpretation of semiotic products, and several specialized material hermeneutics (of the text, of the image, etc.). As a discipline, hermeneutics belongs to the subdivision of the sciences of culture (as opposed to the natural sciences) that can be called the "sciences of meaning," whether we are speaking of a general hermeneutics or the specialized hermeneutics of a single type of semiotic product (e.g., linguistic semantics, the hermeneutics of painting). The part of semiotics that is primarily interested in meaning belongs to the sciences of meaning, whereas the part of semiotics that is primarily interested in signifiers (e.g., the phonemes of a text, the lines of a drawing) belongs to the "sciences of form," which also includes linguistic morphology, which specializes in textual forms. In the sciences of meaning, signifiers are taken into account only as a means to grasp meaning and not for themselves. Semiotics is probably the only discipline that is interested in both the signifiers and the signifieds of all semiotic products; there are other "semiotic sciences," but they are specialized, such as literary studies, art studies, etc.

Authors: Friedrich Schleiermacher, Wilhelm Dilthey, Martin Heidegger, Hans–Georg Gadamer, Peter Szondi, Paul Ricœur, Leo Spitzer, Jean Starobinsky, etc.

5.14 History of ideas

According to "an interpretive tradition already widespread in Antiquity and the Middle Ages [...], literature was, from its beginnings, a practice of fiction that both conceals and reveals profound ideas" (Hallyn, 1987: 241). Fernand Hallyn distinguishes between two major traditional currents in the history of ideas. The first current (Paul Hazard, Lucien Febvre, René Pintard, Jean Ehrard, Robert Mauzi, Roland Mortier, Arthur O. Lovejoy, etc.) is devoted to writing the history of individual ideas. These ideas can be conceived as being either precise or diffuse. In the second current, the ideas form "an anonymous intertext to which writers are indebted and which they transform, but whose precise or unique origin or source cannot be defined" (Hallyn, 1987: 242). As with any approach, one can either take as one's starting point the particular element, here an isolated idea, and search for it in a set of texts (let us call this a top-down approach), or one can start from a set of one or more texts and identify all the isolated ideas that it contains (let us call this a bottom-up approach).

According to Hallyn, in the history of ideas one should avoid the trap of focusing exclusively on the signified (the contents), and should also study signifiers (the forms that support the signified). I would add that one should avoid the trap of focusing exclusively on the signified (the content, what is said), and should also study the form (how it is said). The two terms of an opposition—here signifier/signified, and form/content—can, methodologic-ally, be studied separately, but in fact they are inseparable. Traditionally, the recognition of this interdependence between the two terms emphasizes the influence of the "material" on the "intellectual": the influence of the body over the mind, the signifier over the signified, the literal meaning over the figurative meaning, the form over the content, the medium over the message, the support (e.g., a book, a website) over the "supported" (e.g., the content of a book, of a website), etc. In the most extreme cases, the concrete term entirely displaces the abstract term, such that the influence is total and unidirectional: "The message is the medium" (Marshall McLuhan). Obviously, the influence can, or even must, be seen as reciprocal.

The second current consists in a synthetic approach, which is that of *Geistesgeschichte* promoted by the Schlegel brothers, Wilhelm Dilthey, etc. (this word comes from *Geschichte*—"history"—and *Geist*—"spirit," in the same sense as in *Zeitgeist*). "In this current, all the cultural productions of an era—be they literary, artistic, political, scientific, or other—are linked to a general attitude toward the world and life, a 'spirit of the age' or *Zeitgeist*" (Hallyn, 1987: 245; see also section 4.30 on worldview). One can distinguish between different kinds of "spirit": that of a text, an author, an era (which is also the spirit of a social group in this given era), a society, a nation, a culture, a civilization, etc.

In any case, Hallyn states:

> if one abandons the conception of a *Geistesgeschichte* as outlined above, and approaches a moment in history as a node where different durations intertwine, we find that individual ideas (short duration) are situated within the framework of an ideology (medium duration) and a "mentality" (long duration). Depending on the case, the history of ideas then leads to sociocriticism [and more generally to studies of the sociality of the text] and/or to the history of mentalities.
>
> (Hallyn, 1987: 248)

See section 5.15 on history of mentalities and 5.42 on sociology of literature.

Authors: Paul Hazard, Lucien Febvre, René Pintard, Jean Ehrard, Robert Mauzi, Roland Mortier, Arthur O. Lovejoy, Friedrich and August Wilhelm Schlegel, Wilhelm Dilthey, Marc Angenot, etc.

5.15 History of mentalities

Traditional history is mainly interested in major historical events and their actors, causes, determinations, modalities, and consequences. It is particularly interested in political and economic regimes. Contemporary history also aims to grasp "a third level, that of customary attitudes and gestures" (Pelckmans, 1987: 254). The history of mentalities is concerned with precisely these phenomena. It is based on the premise that "this level of the most anodyne and unthinking acts, which their very obviousness makes us spontaneously consider as being unchangeable, changes incessantly over the centuries" (Pelckmans, 1987: 253). According to the Belgian critic Paul Pelckmans:

> the new history is less interested in individual reactions than in the stereotyped attitudes by which the average man, in each era, resembles his contemporaries and distinguishes himself from his forebears as well as from his descendants. Hence the predilection for serial sources: an isolated testimony risks being a unique case, whereas a batch of testimonies from a given period [...] informs us, through the recurrence of certain attitudes, about common preoccupations.
>
> (Pelckmans, 1987: 254)

Literature might seem to offer a particularly useful material for the history of mentalities aimed at by the new history, since "the vagaries of everyday life are, more than the arcana of high philosophy or the hidden workings of economics, the most usual material of literary fiction" (Pelckmans, 1987: 255). However, literature does not lend itself well to a serial approach: "the various [thematic] instances will never be exactly alike. It would be the most mediocre works that would lend themselves best to such enumerations: these are content to reproduce what has already been done, whereas great works of literature, which renew that which they take up from elsewhere, are by definition non-serial" (Pelckmans, 1987: 256).

Another problem is that literature is, in a broad sense, a fiction: certainly, as in real life, literature largely consists of "people talking, marrying, and dying." However, this does not necessarily mean that these events are represented in a historically accurate way, or that their meaning is the same as in real society: "For example, pastoral poetry [which presents an idealized and highly esthetic view of shepherds' lives] tells us little about the country life" of the time (Pelckmans, 1987: 256).

Yet another problem with the use of literature is that, whereas "the history of mentalities tends to take a particular interest in those who are left out of traditional historiography" (Pelckmans, 1987: 257), literature, at least until the advent of modernity, "is written, with some exceptions, in the immediate vicinity of the great and the good, whose points of view and concerns it espouses, even if only to denigrate them" (Pelckmans, 1987: 257). I would add that this problem may be even more general and fundamental: literature—at least "great literature"—is produced and consumed by the dominant in society, and ultimately represents their values, beliefs, and ethics (the three main constituents of an ideology).

However, this problem of representativeness should be put into perspective: "Being less bound to the same day-to-day tasks, these elites have the leisure to take initiatives; they thus experience most of the mental renewals, which, if successful, spread from them through the other groups" (Pelckmans, 1987: 264). I would add that the path of integration can be the other way around.

We have seen what literature can and cannot do for the history of mentalities. But what can the history of mentalities do for literary criticism?

> Let us say, then, by extending to literature a well-known definition of the fact of style, that (great) literature is deviation from the norm: the value of literary works lies not in their departure from reality, but in what they add to it [and suppress in it], how they enrich everyday life with new resonances. To understand this type of performance, it is important to also understand the norm from which it deviates; the history of mentalities provides insights into common attitudes of the past, matters that were so obvious as to be passed over in silence, which varied over the course of the centuries, and from which literary language had to dissociate itself. It sheds light on the successive points of departure.
>
> (Pelckmans, 1987: 258)

The history of mentalities therefore allows us to avoid interpretive anachronisms. Moreover, although fiction is not always made up of plausible accounts of reality:

it sometimes provides something better: insofar as they espouse the imagination of their readers, the most far-fetched plots sometimes allow us to glimpse the psychological roots of mentalities, which rarely appear through the drier notations of administrative registers or household records.

(Pelckmans, 1987: 260)

I would add that any text—and in fact any product, whether semiotic or not— provides clues (and sometimes direct information) regarding its producer, its receiver, and the society and other elements of its context.

Authors: Philippe Ariès, Emmanuel Le Roy Ladurie, etc.

5.16 Intermediality (study of)

According to Éric Méchoulan:

> The concept of intermediality operates at three different levels of analysis. It can designate, first, the relations between different media (or even between different artistic practices that are not limited to particular media): in this case intermediality appears after media. Second, it can designate the melting pot of media from which a well circumscribed medium emerges and is gradually institutionalized: in this case intermediality appears before media. Finally, it can designate the environment in general in which media take on shape and meaning: in this case intermediality is immediately present to any practice involving a medium. Intermediality will thus be analyzed with respect to "environments" and "mediations," but also with respect to "effects of immediacy," "fabrications of presence," and "modes of resistance."
>
> (Méchoulan, 2003: 22)

Intermediality can be analyzed in itself or in its impacts on signifieds and signifiers, or the content and form of semiotic products, including texts. In the latter case, the main premise of intermediality is that the medium has an impact on the signifiers and contents (signifieds) that it supports, and is not a mere neutral conduit. This premise is a particular application of a more general premise that the support, or vehicle—be it a signifier, literal meaning, form, medium, etc.—impacts on, shapes (determines, or even causes) that which is supported or conveyed—be it a signified, a figurative meaning, content or "message," etc. In reality this relation of transformation is undoubtedly highly reciprocal.

The conceptual extension of intermediality obviously depends on how we define "media." What is a medium? As Patrice Pavis notes:

> The concept is very poorly defined. The medium seems to be defined essentially by a sum of technical characteristics (possibilities and potentialities),

and by the technological way in which it is produced, transmitted, and received, such that it is infinitely reproducible. The medium is therefore not linked to a given content or thematic, but to an apparatus and to a present state of technology. And yet, this technology of mechanical reproduction and of production of the work of art implies a certain esthetic, it is only useful when it is concretized in a particular and singular work, or appreciated in an esthetic or ethical judgment.

(Pavis, 2002: 200)

In intermediality, as the name indicates, at least two media or two forms belonging to distinct media are made copresent. This copresence can be found in various degrees of intensity and various natures, ranging from a strong factual and syncretic copresence (multimedia, such as a website) to a limited borrowing (e.g., a use of cinematic lighting techniques in the theater), and from a factual copresence (e.g., if a film is projected in the course of a play) to a copresence by transposition (e.g., if an effect of cinematographic "montage" is produced in a novel) or simple thematization (e.g., characters in a novel talk about radio). Intermediality can occur not only in a given semiotic product but also within the instance of reception itself (obviously, this does not exclude a situation in which an intermedial relation is established between the product and its reception): this is what Pavis means when he suggests that the body and mind of modern man are shaped by new media. The digitization of written forms, sound, and image now produces "a new form of integration of all the traditional media on a single platform, known under the name of multimedia" (Michon and Saint-Jacques, 2002: 362). Consequently, although intermediality is in principle a transhistorical phenomenon (the papyrus scroll was already a medium), it now appears to be particularly characteristic of contemporary culture. In fact, the relation between two media can be established in the producer (e.g., in the producer's mind), in the production, in the product itself, in the reception, and in the receiver; it can also occur in the relation between any of these factors (e.g., between the mind of the author and that of the receiver). Finally, it should be noted that intermediality can occur within the same semiotic system (e.g., textual semiotics, in a case where a daily newspaper evokes a book) or between different semiotic systems (e.g., if a film is evoked within a book). On the forms that presence, and therefore also copresence, can take, see section 5.21 on literature and other arts.

The study of intermediality presupposes the study of mediation, in the sense of the setting of a semiotic product in a particular medium. For example, when several choices of medium were available to the producer, why was this particular medium chosen? And why did they opt for monomediality or polymediality? And what are the effects of these choices?

On the links between intermediality and digital media (new media) studies, see section 5.8.

Authors: Éric Méchoulan, Jurgen Müller, etc.

5.17 Intertextuality (study of)

Intertextuality is the phenomenon studied by intertextual approaches (see section 4.28). In the broadest sense, intertextuality is the relation, the process, and the result of that process, joining together at least two texts. Generally, these texts are brought together because they are identical or similar with respect to some of their properties or elements of the signifier and/or signified. However, they may also be brought together when their properties or elements are contrary to one another (e.g., if a text was written in reaction to another text) or because they are ostensibly "unattached" to one other (i.e., there is a marked absence of one work in another work, possibly suggesting a negative reaction to the source work).

Intertextual studies can include relations that may be due to chance or, on the contrary, they can be limited to those relations that are the result of presumed conscious influence (e.g., an author is consciously inspired by the Bible) or unconscious influence (e.g., an author does not realize that they are producing a work with certain similarities to *Hamlet*, although that is one of their favorite works, or is influential in general on their culture). Intertextuality can take into account all relations between a given work and others or, more commonly, only those that are significant; for example, just because a novel mentions bread, we cannot automatically assume that there is a significant intertextuality with the episode of the miracle of the loaves and fishes in the Gospel.

Transfictionality (see Saint-Gelais, 2011) is the phenomenon whereby one text extends the fictional universe of another (e.g., by relating episodes from Hamlet's childhood that are not presented in Shakespeare's play). Transfictionality is a particular form of hypertextuality (see section 4.28). When we consider a relation of intertextuality between a text and one of the variants that could theoretically have been produced if the author had followed—or were made to follow, even if this was in fact inconceivable or impossible for that author or at that time—another route that lay open at a given crossroads in the writing process, we touch upon the theory of possible texts. These crossroads present variants with respect to the signifieds and signifiers, content (what is said) and form (how it is said). When the relation of intertextuality is between the real world and the world of the text, or between the world of the text and other worlds that either may or may not have existed, or either could or could not have existed, we touch upon the theory of possible worlds (which was developed in philosophy on the basis of Leibniz's writings, and has since been applied to literature). The production of transfictionality presupposes that one writes a work that then actually exists in parallel with the source work, whereas a possible text or possible world may be evoked only in the mind of the analyst or reader, or only specified in an analytical text, without the production of any actual work existing in parallel with the source work.

Intertextuality can be understood in a narrow sense (it is then necessarily concerned with the relationship between two texts, and possibly only between literary texts) or in a broader sense (it can then be concerned with relationships between non-textual products, whether artistic or not, or between a textual product and a non-textual product, such as a film).Jean Ricardou (1975: 10–13) distinguishes between strict intertextuality (between two texts by the same author) and general intertextuality (between one text and any other, even if they are by different authors). Intertextuality, in the broad sense, can also be concerned with the relationship between a draft and another draft of the same text, or between a draft and the final text, or between a text and its various transpositions (translation, adaptation, etc.) or analyses of that text.

Intertextuality is probably the best known of the literary theoretical concepts that use the prefix "inter-." There are other well-known concepts derived from the same prefix, whether literary or not, including interdiscursivity (between two discourses), intermediality (between two media; see section 5.16), interartiality (between two arts; see section 5.21), intersemiotics or intersemioticity (between two semiotic systems, e.g., music and drama in the case of opera; we can also speak of polysemiotics or polysemioticity), interdisciplinarity (between two disciplines), and intertheoricity (between two theories). Words constructed with the prefix "inter-" often belong to a network of terms, together with words constructed with the prefixes "pluri-" or "multi-," "trans-," "meta-," "archi-," etc. For example, we can distinguish between multidisciplinarity (where two disciplines are used to study the same given object), interdisciplinarity (a theory, concept, or method is adapted from one discipline to another), and transdisciplinarity (a given element transcends two or more disciplines, etc.). When criminology and literary studies are used to analyze a detective novel, there is multidisciplinarity; when linguistic concepts are integrated into literary studies, there is interdisciplinarity.

We can distinguish between a fundamental or structural intertextuality— inasmuch as any text has a relationship with all other texts, past, present, and future, within its own culture or even across all cultures, and including texts that are possible or even impossible—and an optional or conjunctural intertextuality, which is concerned with a text's particular relation to given texts. The fundamental structuralist principle of "value" applies in these two cases, as elsewhere. According to this principle, a phenomenon (in this case a text) takes on its "meaning" (its value), according to some theorists, only in relation to all the other phenomena of the same nature (e.g., the meaning of a word is made up of how it resembles or is distinguished from all other words), or, according to other theorists, in relation to all the other phenomena in its field, its paradigm (e.g., the meaning of the word "knife" is constructed in relation to the words "fork" and "spoon" in the field of basic kitchen utensils) and this field itself takes on meaning in relation to the other fields. In short, according to the former view, the meaning of a text arises from its relation to all other texts, and according to the latter view, its meaning arises, directly, from its relation to certain texts that are close to it within the same group (e.g., in the same literary genre), and, indirectly, from the relations between its group and other groups.

Authors: Mikhail Bakhtin, Julia Kristeva, Gérard Genette, Richard Saint-Gelais, etc.

5.18 Linguistics

Linguistics is the science and study of languages (conceived as systems) and texts, whether oral or written, which are the manifestations of those systems (but texts also use systems other than language; see section 4.24 on style). Because of the very diversity of languages, linguistics is often comparative. But it can also describe a language in itself. Inasmuch as literary products are texts, they can obviously be described from a linguistic perspective. Since literary products are, as Rastier calls them, "mythical" texts (literary, religious, philosophical texts, etc.), of a different nature from what Rastier terms "practical" texts (newspaper articles, scientific articles, etc.), they must be considered with their specificities in mind (Rastier, 2016: 79–81). This may involve the use of different theoretical concepts, analytical categories, and methodologies from those that are used in the analysis of "practical" texts.

Linguistics is divided into traditional sub-disciplines which correspond to the various linguistic aspects, or at least to the particular aspects that are identified, and thereby endowed with autonomy and value (other sub-disciplines are therefore possible). Here are some of these traditional sub-disciplines (I am drawing on, and modifying, Bénac and Réauté, 1993: 135): (1) concerning sounds: phonetics (the study of linguistic sounds as physical stimuli) and phonology (the study of the minimal signifiers, phonemes, and other signifiers such as intonation); (2) concerning grammar: morphology (the study of forms) and syntax (the functions, connections, and relations of placement between elements); (3) semantics, the study of meanings (in context, in a given text) and/or significations (out of context); (4) lexicology, the study of lexicons (of morphemes, for instance the roots of words, single words, locutions or fixed word groups, and phraseologies or stereotyped sentences or phrases, such as proverbs); (5) pragmatics: "the study of language use, which deals with the adaptation of symbolic expressions to referential, situational, action-oriented, and interpersonal contexts" (Jacques, 2008: n.p.), which is particularly concerned with assumptions and presuppositions. I would add that semantics, properly conceived, must include pragmatics. I would also add that we must always consider the written, as well as the spoken, dimension of language. For example, in addition to an oral morphology we need a written morphology, and alongside phonology and phonetics we need a graphology (not in the usual sense of this word) and a graphemics.

Traditional linguistics effectively considered the sentence as its maximal unit, on the assumption that the text could be reduced to the sum of these sentences. Now, however, we must instead consider that the text is a site of interaction between units of various extents and thus of various possible segmentations, and that a complete linguistics must be able to describe morphemes (minimal linguistic signs, e.g., verb roots, prefixes), lexies (words or fixed groups of words, locutions), syntagmata (e.g., noun phrases), propositions, phraseologies (stereotyped sentences or phrases, e.g., proverbs), sentences, periods (a unit that can comprise several sentences and in which grammatical and syntactic concordance is obligatory, e.g., the replacement of nouns by pronouns is possible), sections, etc. According to Rastier (2009: vi), the global determines the local, such that the genre determines the text that belongs to it, the corpus determines the text that belongs to it, the level of the text determines the lower levels, the level of the lexis determines the level of the morpheme, etc. As I have already mentioned, the corpus, whether constructed scientifically or intuitively, determines the text. For example, the meaning of the novel *Les Misérables* necessarily changes when passing from a corpus of Victor Hugo's novels to a corpus of all the French novels of the same period.

Authors: Roman Jakobson, Émile Benveniste, Dominique Maingueneau, François Rastier, etc.

5.19 Literary genres (study of)

Generic studies are obviously faced with the problem of defining genre. As we saw in the chapter on aspects of the literary text, genre can be viewed in different ways: as a program of guidelines for the production and interpretation of texts (and other semiotic products); as a type, a model, that realizes these guidelines in an abstract form; and as a class of texts that manifest, either integrally or partially, these production guidelines and this model (see section 4.8 on deviation and norm, and section 4.11 on genre).

The main tasks of generic studies are: (1) to define genres and the various levels of sub-genres and, potentially, "super-genres" (e.g., discourses, such as literature, philosophy, or religion, which, in Rastier's view (2001: 298), encompass genres); (2) to define generic fields, in which related and competing genres are interdefined (e.g., the generic field of tragedy, comedy, and drama); (3) to observe the emergence, continuing existence, transformation (potentially begetting a derivative genre), and disappearance of genres; and (4) to classify texts into genres. The classification of a text in a literary genre is a common form of analysis in pedagogical settings. Analysis by classification is a form of comparative analysis, since it involves comparing the characteristics of the text with the characteristics of the genre to which it might belong.

Oswald Ducrot and Tzvetan Todorov rightly point out that:

> we should [...] stop identifying genres with the names of genres [...] some genres have never been given a name; others have been conflated under a single name despite having different properties. The study of genres must be based on their structural characteristics and not on their names.
>
> (Ducrot and Todorov, 1972: 193)

I would add that a single genre can be given several different names. For example, Guy de Maupassant, a French author of the nineteenth century, called some of his texts "contes" (tales), but we would generally class these works as short stories (or "nouvelles" in French). Finally, the properties of genres can vary according to the perspective in which they are viewed: with regard to the author, the immanent characteristics of the work, or the reader. Once again, we can distinguish the nominal type of analysis (that which takes as its starting point the names used, identifies their different meanings, accounts for these different meanings, or potentially conflates them by mistake) and the conceptual type of analysis (which focuses on a concept, regardless of whether it has been named or not, or named in different ways). In general, the latter type of analysis is the more relevant.

Authors: Aristotle, Jean-Marie Schaeffer, etc.

5.20 Literary history

In the broadest sense, literary history describes and interprets literary phenomena—authors, works, events, movements, forms (genres, themes, topoi, etc.), etc.—with a view to their correlations with positions in historical time.

In this sense, the first task of literary history is to identify, list, and select literary phenomena. Since a phenomenon (even a so-called "fact") is never given but is rather constructed, this step is already the result of an act of interpretation ("data [in Latin, "that which is given"] is what we give ourselves," Rastier, 2004).

Literary history is interested in three principal kinds of correlations: (1) locative correlations (the situation of a given phenomenon in time and in a temporalized series); (2) correlative, determinative, or even causal correlations (the correlative, causal, and determinative relations between the phenomenon and the contexts that exist in its own temporality, and those that immediately precede and follow it); (3) differential and comparative correlations (especially through the segmentation of the temporal continuum into periods and, correlatively, through the comparison of phenomena, whether they are temporally adjacent or not, in terms of their affinities with one another); and (4) transformational correlations (the prefiguration, emergence, growth, continuing existence, transformation, decrease, disappearance, lineage, and resurgence of literary phenomena).

> NOTE: APPROACHES TO HISTORICAL TEMPORALITY
>
> Literary history must take into account several approaches to historical temporality: (1) the linear approach (events simply follow one another without return of the same, or the identical, or the similar, or without such a return being considered); (2) the loop approach (the eternal return of the same); (3) the progressive approach (as opposed to the "regressive" or "decadence" approach); (4) the "spiral" approach, which makes it possible to reconcile the return of the similar with "progress" (but, in principle, a spiral can also be regressive and thus "descending").

Literary history defines the "internal" characteristics of the phenomenon: Who? What? When? Where? How? For whom? For what purpose? etc. It is therefore a question of dating the phenomena and thus of establishing temporal relations between them (succession, simultaneity, etc.) and sequencing them chronologically. These temporal relations can be supplemented by the addition of other types of relations, which literary history must consider: correlative relations (presupposition, mutual exclusion, positive, or direct, correlation, inverse correlation), determinative relations (those which impact on the modalities of presence of the phenomenon), causal relations (those which produce the phenomenon or suppress it), and causative relations (between the phenomenon and the effects that it produces). These "external" characteristics provide answers to questions such as: Why or because of what (causes, determinations)? For what purpose? With what effects (results, whether deliberate or not)? The causes of phenomena (and some of their effects), or at least the determinations acting on phenomena, can be found in the different contexts in which these phenomena exist (biographical, sociological, political, scientific, esthetic, etc.). See section 4.7 on context.

Generally speaking, literary history tries to restore the contemporary context of the work and to bring to light the changes that its various later contexts (or even earlier contexts, such as how such a contemporary work might have been received by the ancient Greeks) can bring to the "meaning" of the work. It also gauges and evaluates the transformations (evolutions, involutions, etc.) that the phenomenon constitutes in relation to previous, contemporary, or later phenomena.

Among the causes, determinations, and effects that literary history studies, we find, on the side of causes and determinations, the influences on and (when these exist) the sources for a given text and, on the side of effects, the texts that have been influenced by a given text or have taken it as a partial or global source (in this last case, they are hypertexts in relation to the hypotext that is the earlier text, just as Joyce's *Ulysses* is the hypertext in relation to the hypotext that is Homer's *Odyssey*).

Literary history also identifies comparative relations (identity, similarity, opposition, etc.) through its assimilation of phenomena (an interpretive operation that decreases contrasts) or dissimilation of phenomena (an interpretive operation that increases these contrasts). For example, it distinguishes, through periodization, different sectors in a given temporal continuum and thereby groups together works that it considers to be similar precisely because they belong to the same contextual period and are thus similarly influenced by it.

Literary history is also interested in the operations involved in the dynamics of the phenomenon: its prefiguration, emergence, continuing existence, transformation (growth, apogee, decline; changes in its nature and function; etc.), its possible disappearance, either with or without lineage, and its possible reemergence.

Besides demonstrating the impact (or non-impact) of contextual phenomena on a given literary phenomenon, literary history shows the particular impact that can arise from the representation (or non-representation), whether direct or indirect (e.g., by metonymy, symbol), conscious or unconscious, of historical phenomena in a literary text, corpus, or form. Indeed, any context determines the producer that is immersed in it and is therefore reflected in it, and any producer determines the product and is therefore reflected in it. These "reflections" can occur in the contents (signifieds) of a text, whether directly by thematization (e.g., the appearance of Napoleon Bonaparte as a character in a text) or indirectly (through the use of a topos that is typical of the time or, on the contrary, through reaction against the topoi that are typical of the time), and in the signifiers of a text (the forms which convey the contents, such as the use of an archaic spelling of a word, which indicates the time in which the text was produced). Any representation is produced either positively (e.g., Napoleon appears in a historical novel, represented as he was in real life), or negatively (e.g., Napoleon is presented, ironically, as a great democrat rather than the auto-crat that he was in real life), or by significant omission (e.g., a historical-political novel that discusses the beginning of the nineteenth century in France without ever mentioning Napoleon).

NOTE: IS LITERARY HISTORY A FORM OF CHRONOCRITICISM?

In the section on geocriticism, I present the three disciplines concerned with spatial analysis as follows: geopoetics (focused on production), geocriticism (focused on the product), and geoesthetics (focused on recep-tion); all three can be subsumed under the term geocriticism, used here in a broader sense. Is literary history (or, more broadly, the history of semiotic products) a chronocriticism, following the same model? No, or at least not as literary history is usually conceived, since it analyzes only or mainly real and historical time, and not other forms of time. These other forms of time are: thematized time, that is to say, the time of the fiction that is narrated, especially if it does not correspond to real historical time; and the time of arrangement of the text, created by the successive linking of units such as words, sentences; etc. Narratology is the closest thing to chronocriticism in the narrow sense (i.e., the study of time in the semiotic product), since it analyzes thematized time (in texts, but it can also be generalized to apply to any semiotic product). In order to be the exact counterpart of geocriticism (in the broad sense), literary history would therefore have to extend its object of study to include the time of the product (both its thematized time and the time of arrangement) and the time of reception (in its three basic forms: reading, analysis, criticism). Although literary history already addresses the time of production, it is mainly interested in the moment and not in that other facet of time that is duration. Duration must also be taken into account in the study of reception. Duration and temporal patterns are in fact significant even in themselves: writing a work in a single burst is not the same as writing slowly and with long intervals, etc. As for recep-tion—which always occurs after production, except for the perspective of self-reception through which an author perceives the work in progress—a work may be received and interpreted repeatedly at different temporal distances with regard to its production.

Authors: Gustave Lanson, Jacques Moisan, Luc Fraisse, Denis St-Jacques, Maurice Lemire, Robert Melançon, Claude La Charité, etc.

5.21 Literature and other arts (study of)

Literature can be included in the category of the arts, in the broad sense of the word. As such, we will consider that it shares with the other arts, to varying degrees, certain elements (or at least, for certain elements, that there is an analogical relation to the other arts, such as for the "architectural" dimension of the novel): causes, intentions, effects, natures, functions, forms (genres, themes, topoi, processes, etc.), norms, deviations, etc. We can therefore study correspondences (and non-correspondences) between literature and the other arts, which may be more or less direct, conscious, and explicit. Interartiality can be seen as a state, a relation, an operation (and its result), or a possible field of studies (e.g., in the same way as intertextuality) involving two or more different arts.

Moreover, literary texts are often found in a polyartistic context, such as when a text forms part of a comic book, a graphic novel, an illustrated book, a performance, an art installation, a play, or a film.

To the extent that an art is considered a semiotic system (e.g., sculpture) or a polysemiotic system (e.g., opera, which combines music and drama), the study of relations between arts and literature is always a polysemiotic study (but not every polysemiotic production is related to an art, e.g., a website providing medical information, with text, video, and still images). For more detail on polysemiotic analysis, see Hébert, 2020: 335–362.

The polysemiotic object being studied may correspond to a single medium (e.g., the book medium for the text and image in a comic strip) or it may involve several media at the same time (e.g., in an art installation). In the latter case, the study will also be intermedial (see section 5.16).

What are the main modalities of the copresence of literature and the (other) arts? First, this copresence can occur either in a literary element (e.g., a novel that talks about painting), in an artistic element (e.g., a painting that integrates a poem), or in an element that is neither literary nor artistic (e.g., the present text talks about arts and literature but is not a literary work). This integrating element can be a work, a content (signified), a form of expression (signifier), a sign (signifier plus signified), a type (a stereotyped form: genre, topos, stylistic rhetorical figure, etc.), a particular manifestation of a type, etc.

Second, this copresence of literature and other arts can take several forms: (1) real or factual presence: for example, the textual and the pictorial (the image) in an illustrated book; (2) a presence thematized in the signifieds: for example, a novel that talks about sculpture or art in general; (3) a presence evoked by the signifieds: for example, a literary text that talks about Venus rising from the water evokes the history of art, because this stereotyped theme is used much more frequently in the visual arts than it is in literature; and (4) a presence evoked by signifiers: for example, a poem (calligram, concrete poetry, etc.) whose spatial arrangement evokes a pictorial work. In theory, we can imagine a presence evoked by a sign as a global combination of a signifier and a signified, but this presence can undoubtedly be analyzed through the signifier and the signified separately.

It is possible to connect the relations between literature and other arts to Genette's typology of transtextual relations (see section 4.28). This relation can be intertextual, if it is between two works (e.g., a novel speaking about a particular painting that really exists). It can be hypertextual, if one work is grafted onto another (e.g., the film adaptation of a novel). It can be hetero-architextual: then, the link is not that between a work and the type to which it belongs (e.g., a given novel and the novel type, to which it belongs), which is a relation of architextuality (or, we could also say, homo-architextuality), but rather that between a work and the type to which it partly belongs (e.g., a novel written to be like a film). The relation can be metatextual (e.g., an essay by a writer or an artist that analyzes or comments on a pictorial work). We should note that there are also intra-metatextual relations (e.g., the relation between a caption painted in a painting and the thing that it describes, as we find between the text "Ceci n'est pas une pipe" ["This is not a pipe"] and the image of a pipe in Magritte's *The Treachery of Images*). Finally, the relation can be paratextual (e.g., that between a painting and its "literary" title, as we frequently find in Magritte's work).

The same producer may generate semiotic products belonging, respectively, to literature and to another art. For example, Picasso, in addition to his artistic productions (in the narrow sense), wrote, among other things, a play, *Desire Caught by the Tail*; Victor Hugo, like William Blake, both produced literary works and painted. One can then compare the skill of this producer in the two artistic domains in question (e.g., Hugo was undoubtedly a better writer than a painter).

An artistic-literary product may be produced by a single producer (e.g., Hergé writing and drawing his *Tintin* comics, or Charles M. Schulz his *Peanuts* comics), or by separate producers who are responsible, respectively, for the literary dimension and for the other artistic dimension. The second art form may be added during or after the production of the first art form (e.g., Baudelaire's *Les Fleurs du mal* was illustrated after the author's death by the painter Matisse).

As I mentioned with regard to media in section 5.16, the relation between literature and other arts (or between arts in general) can occur in the producer and the production (e.g., in the case of a writer who is also a painter, painting probably determines their writing and vice versa), in the product (by thematization or determination), or in the receiver and the reception (e.g., the reading of a novel may be influenced by the fact that the particular reader is keen on the visual arts).

Authors: Étienne Souriau, Louis Marin, Daniel Bergez, etc.

5.22 Marxism

Marxism is the "thought of Karl Marx, as it appears in his work but also through the multiplicity of appropriations and interpretations to which it has given rise" (Renault, 2006: 490).

According to Robert F. Barsky:

> Marxist literary criticism makes it possible to analyze the circumstances of production of literary works, the impact they have had [or not had] on society, and the ideology that they carry [...]. Elements drawn from Marxist theory can be found [...] integrated [...] into the theories of several other schools [such as dialogism].
>
> (Barsky, 1997: 74; see also section 5.7 on dialogism)

We can look for the determinations of Marxism in both texts and literary forms (themes, topoi, genres, processes, etc.). There are two forms of determination: by representation and otherwise. Where there is determination by representation, Marxism is integrated in the themes, the signifieds. But other forms of determination are possible. For example, a novelist's choice to use the form of the realist novel can be interpreted as indicating a Marxist posture (since Marxism traditionally favors realism) or alternatively as indicating the presence, potentially undeliberate, of a certain Marxist conception (e.g., that of the novel as being, in the view of certain analysts, a highly bourgeois genre).

In particular, we can examine how the Marxist doctrine is represented, whether positively or negatively, directly or indirectly (even by significant omission), explicitly or implicitly, consciously or unconsciously, in a text, corpus, genre, movement (e.g., Soviet socialist realism), or form (e.g., as mentioned above, the novel is viewed by some as an eminently bourgeois genre, whereas Brecht's theater was intended to be a manifestation of a Marxist ideology).

Marxism belongs to the family of forms of "ideological analysis," along with feminism, cultural studies, ecocriticism, postcolonial studies, gender studies, queer studies, etc. In each of these cases, analysts not only look for manifestations (or negations) of a given ideology, but they often also adopt the perspective of that particular ideology. Moreover, these analyses usually promote an ideology and, at least implicitly, devalue competing ideologies, often with good reason (e.g., by criticizing the racism or misogyny of a given text or author). Of course, exponents of ideological criticism will argue that even the most seemingly neutral of approaches is actually informed by ideology (since even "the private is political"). In practice, ideological analyses are often mono-ideological, seeking and, at least in their view, finding the same ideology in all semiotic products that they approach (e.g., finding that all the products of the West contain a neocolonial ideology, except for the clearly anti-colonial texts). As always, however, two approaches are possible: a top-down approach, whereby one looks for manifestations of a single ideology in several different semiotic products; or a bottom-up approach, whereby one looks for all the manifestations of different ideologies in a single semiotic product. Indeed, we can start from the premise that any text manifests several ideologies (e.g., a Marxist text will, at least implicitly, present, in a more or less distorted way, the competing ideology of capitalism). Finally, for Marxism as for any other ideology, we can consider that it may be present or at least functional in semiotic products even before its official birth. We can therefore, for example, read the Bible from a Marxist perspective.

Authors: Karl Marx, Lucien Goldmann, Jean-Paul Sartre, Theodor W. Adorno, Walter Benjamin, Louis Althusser, etc.

5.23 Mythanalysis

In the broadest sense, mythanalysis can be understood as the study of the relations between myth and literature; in an even broader sense, it is the study of myths of any kind (sociomyths, idiomyths, etc.), in any way. Myth is, then, the particular aspect of the semiotic products that is analyzed (texts, images, etc.) and mythocriticism is the approach that analyzes it.

A myth, in the narrow sense, is a socially defined narrative, whether textual (oral and/or written) or not (mental narrative, image, etc.), involving generally supernatural and/or transcendent actors (gods, forces, the Cosmos, etc.), which often explains a state or element of the past, present, or future world as a consequence of a past, present, or future event, and which either was, or still is (or has never been) considered to be non-fictional. However, mythocriticism is not limited to myth in this narrow sense. It can include forms that, although socially defined as myths in the narrow sense, do not correspond to the definition provided above (e.g., the "myth" of Snow White, or of Hamlet), or even individually defined forms (personal myths, such as those analyzed in the psychocriticism practiced by Charles Mauron). More generally, myth, at least in the narrow sense of the term, belongs to the forms that mediate between transcendence and immanence. The mediating form makes it possible to aim for, reach, think, know, represent, or experience transcendence, and to unite, cause to interact, or mediate between immanence and transcendence.

We must distinguish between the myth as a type—the abstract model, for example that of the mermaid—and the particular manifestations, in more or less altered forms, of those models—such as the different particular mermaids that appear in different texts. Among these manifestations, there may be one particularly prominent instance that plays a dominant role in the constitution of the type or in its transformation (in which case the type is constituted by taking on the form of this manifestation almost completely); for example, the particular mermaid in the Disney film version of *The Little Mermaid* has come to define the type of the mermaid in the contemporary and popular imaginary.

On the basis of the distinction between type and individual manifestation (or "token"), we can define the myth in four ways: as a type, as a given manifestation, as the set of manifestations, or as the sum of the type and its manifestations. Whereas the type contains the "obligatory" (or optional but frequently occurring) features of the myth, the set of manifestations of the myth also includes all the features of each manifestation. The different manifestations are variations or variants of each other. They are also variations with regard to the type to which they belong. The main operations targeted by mythanalysis are therefore the generation of the manifestation from the type, the typicization (constitution of the type) arising from manifestations, and the various possible comparisons between type and type, manifestation and manifestation, type and manifestation. The comparison may also be between a type and itself, a manifestation and itself, over either historical time or semiotic time (e.g., the time of the story told or the sequence of units, such as words). In all these operations, we compare forms to see what is preserved, transformed, deleted, added, etc.

Using my typology of semiotic systems, we can establish a typology of myths consisting of: (1) anthropomyths (shared by all cultures), such as the myths of creation and destruction of the universe by the elements; (2) culturomyths (common to one culture); (3) sociomyths (common to a given social group, down to a theoretical minimum of two individuals), such as the celestial origin myths shared by some large families in Tibet; (4) idiomyths (common to a given individual, personal myths); (5) textomyths (common only to a single text); and (6) amyths (a non-mythical form). If we distinguish between the overlying (apparent) enunciator and the underlying enunciator, we can show that a given overlying enunciator (e.g., Disney, in the case of the mermaid) is merely taking over the myth from an enunciator of a higher system (e.g., the mermaid in the Western culturolect); but this overlying enunciator can modify the preexisting myth, for example, by adding elements of their own (as Hans Christian Andersen did, and then Disney after him).

Mythocriticism studies the causes, modalities, and effects of the presence of mythical forms in a text, corpus, or abstract literary form (e.g., a genre, a topos). Logically, it must also do the same for the absence of a given mythical form (especially if its presence was expected), or of any mythical form.

In the analysis of a particular literary text, mythocriticism identifies the mythemes, that is to say, both the signifieds (thematized elements including characters, spaces, objects, events, situations, etc.) and signifiers (e.g., the conventional use of a given word, wordplay, or phrase) that are constitutive of one or several myths. These myths may be, to varying extents, explicit or implicit, direct or indirect, and conscious or unconscious. Indeed, although the myth is generally considered as a content, it can also be considered as a sign, and can therefore consist of both signifiers and signifieds.

I would say that mythocriticism, when applied to the content of a work, is a specific form of thematic analysis (in the broad sense), since it focuses on a particular kind of theme, and that it is also intertextual, since it generally compares different forms of a theme in different texts (even if only between the text under analysis and another text containing the identified myth). Since every myth is a stereotyped theme, that is to say, a topos (even if it is a personal topos, or idiotopos), mythocriticism belongs to that sector of thematic analysis that we can call topical analysis; however, not every topos is necessarily a myth (e.g., betrayal between lovers). However, the border between topos and myth can be unclear (e.g., impossible love can be seen as a myth and/or as a topos). If the analysis relates to several cultures, it is then also comparativist, in the narrow sense, and also obviously intercultural.

Authors: Pierre Brunel, Gilbert Durand, Joseph Campbell, Georges Dumézil, etc.

5.24 Narratology

The words "story," "narrative," and "narration" are highly polysemous, so it is important to understand the particular way in which I use these terms here and elsewhere in this book. Narratology is concerned with the structure of the story told in texts, and thus with the structure of the narrative—that is, the narration of the story—and the dynamic interactions between these two structures. The story is understood as the logical and chronological sequence of states and processes (actions). States and processes involve actors (including, but not limited to characters, e.g., a magic sword) and circumstantial elements (elements that do not play a role in the action, as agents or patients do, although they are copresent in the action; e.g., the clouds that are present or absent when a murder takes place). In other words, the narrative is the result of the shaping of the story by the process of narration, or more schematically: narrative = story + its shaping by narration. Narratology takes a particular interest in the instances between which the transmission of the story takes place: the narrator (the instance that tells the story), the narratee (the instance to whom the story is told), their characteristics (natures and functions), and their interactions. We should recall that the narrator is not the author and the narratee is not the reader; they are both internal functions of the text.

In narratological analysis, "we therefore try to see the possible relations between the elements of the triad narrative / story / narration. These relations can be described, in particular, with reference to four analytical categories." In brief, these categories are: narrative mode (the distance between the narrator and the events narrated, the functions of the narrator, etc.), narrative instance (the narrative voice, the grammatical person of narration, the narrative perspective, the time of the act of narration, whether later, earlier, or simultaneous, etc.), narrative level (nested narratives, metalepsis, such as when characters address their author, etc.), and narrative time (order—flashback, anticipation, etc.—narrative speed, the frequency and number of occurrence of events, etc.) (Guillemette and Lévesque, in Hébert, 2019).

Insofar as narratology is concerned with the structure of the story, action-oriented analysis—for example, the forms of action-oriented analysis within semiotics, including the actantial model, the narrative program, the canonical narrative schema, etc.—overlaps with narratology. On the forms of action-oriented analysis mentioned above, see Hébert, 2019: chapters 6, 7, and 8).

Authors: Gérard Genette, Claude Bremond, Philippe Hamon, Gerald Joseph Prince, Seymour Chatman, Mieke Bal, Shlomith Rimmon-Kenan, etc.

5.25 New Criticism

New Criticism was an influential formalist movement in North American literary theory from the 1930s to '50s which emphasized the close reading of literary texts and the self-sufficiency of the literary object. New Criticism rejected the tenets of literary historicism, according to which a work must be understood through acknowledgment of its historical context, the situation of the author, etc. In contrast, New Criticism emphasized the closed esthetic unity of the poetical text as one that transcends or circumvents social and biographical influence. The opposition to historicism is summed up by John Crowe Ransom in a 1937 article, where he argues that "the students of the future must be permitted to study literature, and not merely about literature" (Ransom, 1937: 588). For Ransom, whose 1941 collection *The New Criticism* gave its name to the movement, "criticism must become more scientific, or precise and systematic, and this means that it must be developed by the collective and sustained effort of learned persons" (Ransom, 1937: 587). New Critical close reading involves sustained, intensive attention to a short work, usually a poem; emphasis is placed on detailed analysis of individual words, syntax, and related formal elements. The group of early New Critics— including Ransom, Robert Penn Warren, and Allen Tate—"saw themselves as champions of rigorous literary criticism focused on esthetics, which they opposed to approaches to literary study that emphasized historically-focused scholarly research, morally-oriented readings like those of New Humanists such as Irving Babbitt, and Marxist sociological analysis" (Hickman 2012: 6). New Criticism was famously influenced by the writing of T.S. Eliot, who asserted that poetry was "ontologically separate from other forms of expression and accordingly, merited a criticism equipped to do justice to its distinctness and autonomy" (Hickman, 2012: 12).

While New Criticism is generally held to have been eclipsed by European post-structuralist theory in the 1960s and '70s, some significant recent scholarship has emphasized "the value of revisiting a movement that was crucial to the foundation of the discipline as we know it now, especially to the development of 'close reading'" (Hickman and McIntyre, 2012: vii). Indeed, the New Critical championing of "close reading" has been argued to represent a crucial precursor for contemporary critical practice (Hickman 2012: 3), traces of which can in fact be seen in post-structuralist movements such as deconstruction. Although New Criticism is no longer part of modern literary critical practice, recent resistance to caricatures of New Criticism as a conservative, ahistorical, and elitist critical practice have proved important for allowing a greater

understanding of New Criticism's unacknowledged influence in the development of modern criticism, especially to considerations of what we understand
as "the text itself."

NOTE: NEW CRITICISM, RUSSIAN FORMALISM, AND CULTURAL STUDIES

Although New Criticism appears not to have been directly inspired by
Russian Formalism, the two approaches have major similarities:

> The New Critics categorically refused to paraphrase the literary
> work [...] or to reduce it to a hypothetical "authorial intention"
> [including the author's so-called "message"]. They strongly proclaimed
> the importance of purely literary studies, in preference to approaches
> marked by psychology, sociology, or traces of historicism. In the eyes
> of the New Critics, literature was a unique phenomenon, and only a
> careful reading that took into consideration the grammatical, syntac-
> tical, lexical, and phonetic aspects of the works could reveal their full
> value.
>
> (Barsky, 1997: 87)

The study of poetry suited the aims of both the Russian Formalists and the
New Critics. But "while the [Russian] Formalists sought to identify the
techniques and processes used by the author, the New Critics, with a philosophical bent, were primarily interested in the ambiguities and tensions
operating within the work" (Barsky, 1997: 97). Formalists' and New Critics'
restriction of their corpus to poetry is problematic:

> the New Critics confine their field of study to a corpus of canonical
> works, thus seeming to reduce literature to poetry alone, which con-
> siderably limits the scope of their approach. Moreover, the theory's
> questionable, to say the least, political underpinnings, which insist on a
> clear-cut, even elitist distinction between the literary and the non-lit-
> erary, remain problematic.
>
> (Barsky, 1997: 98)

Moreover, "New Criticism can easily lead its adherents to believe that
poetic language constitutes a language distinct from and superior to all
others, since it allows for the enunciation of quasi-religious truths" (Barsky,
1997: 99). Cultural studies played a role in overturning such a hierarchy,
not without raising new problems in turn: popular literature then became
the superior literature, since great literature and canonical literature were
suspected of elitism and therefore of producing harmful effects on readers
and society. The attention paid by New Criticism to the ambiguities of the
text would later, in a sense, come to be radicalized in deconstruction.

Authors: Ivor Armstrong Richard, Cleanth Brooks, T.S. Eliot, John Crowe Ransom, Allen Tate, Robert Penn Warren, etc.

Sam Gormley and Louis Hébert

5.26 Onomastics

Literary onomastics is the study of the modalities (including possible natures and structures), causes, and effects (both the voluntary and involuntary functions) of the presence (or absence) of proper nouns in a literary work or corpus, or even a literary form (e.g., a genre). Onomasticians generally consider that the proper noun is the type of word that lends itself most readily to literary analysis (for several reasons: the use of neologisms, their etymological motivation, their evocations or connotations, etc.); it is rare, for example, to produce an analysis focused exclusively on the use of adverbs or prepositions in a text.

The main elements of the methodology of onomastic analysis are as follows:

1. Compile an onomastic inventory, that is, a list of all the proper nouns directly present in the text. If the search is carried out in a digitized text, one can begin by searching for all capitalized words (although not all capitalized words are proper nouns). This step assumes that you have settled on a definition of proper nouns and established criteria for identifying them. You may then wish to eliminate certain kinds of proper nouns from the inventory (e.g., by retaining only the names of people).

2. Establish links between proper nouns in the text on the basis of the signifier (e.g., "Godot," "Godin," "Godet" in Beckett's *Waiting for Godot*) and/or the signified (e.g., "Mr. Faithful" and "Mr. Unfaithful").

3. Establish links, on the basis of the signifier (at least initially), between the proper nouns in the text under analysis and identical proper nouns (e.g., "Miranda" in Beckett and Shakespeare) or similar proper nouns in other literary texts or texts of other sorts (historical, religious, etc.). Sometimes the link is not with an individual text but rather with a nebulous group of oral and/or written texts (which are part of the "social discourse"); e.g., "Napoleon" (the name of a dog, given in reference to the historical figure) → "Napoleon" (first Emperor of the French, a name present in many texts, speeches, films, etc.).

4. Establish links on the basis of other phenomena. There are cases without either homonyms or paronyms (e.g., in the phrase "the name of the first Emperor of the French," the proper noun "Napoleon" is absent but evoked). Note that words other than proper nouns can also be evoked by means other than homonymy or paronymy (e.g., in the autonymic periphrase "the f-word"). The evoked word, whether it is a proper noun or not, is then present only in the "mental text" constituted by the act of interpretation. In the terms of Rastier's theory, we would say that this evoked word belongs solely to the "reading" of the text, understood here as the result of the interpretation of the

text (see Rastier, 2009: 276). Others use the term "infratext" to refer to the text that is made up of words or passages that are not manifest in a text but are nevertheless presupposed by it.

5. Establish links on the basis of the signifier (e.g., "Ernest" and "earnest" in Oscar Wilde's play, *The Importance of Being Earnest*) and/or signified (e.g., from Molière, "This Mister Loyal's a disloyal sort!") between proper nouns in the text and units in the text that are not proper nouns (which may be morphemes, words, expressions, passages, etc.). In particular, links should be established between a proper noun and other units (other proper nouns, pronouns, definite descriptions, etc.) that relate to the same "label," that is to say, those that designate the same actor (e.g., "Napoleon," "Bonaparte," "the first Emperor of the French," "him," "the small general," etc., all designating Napoleon Bonaparte). The non-proper-noun unit may be present in the text (e.g., "Ernest" and "earnest" in Wilde's play), or it may be absent from the text but present in language in general (e.g., a text may include a character called "Ernest," whose name is linked to the common noun "earnest," even though the latter does not appear in that text and does not form a significant link to another text), or it may be present in another particular text (e.g., the proper noun "Ptyx" in works by Victor Hugo then Alfred Jarry, and the common noun "ptyx" in a sonnet by Mallarmé).

6. In general, establish the contribution of proper nouns to the meaning of the text, which may involve: the actualization (integration) of new content; a change in the intensity of presence (salient, normal, attenuated) of content that is already present; or the virtualization (neutralization) of content that is already present. Conversely, one can note the impact of the other units of the text on the meaning of the proper nouns.

7. Check whether direct links are established, on the one hand, between phonemes (or phonemic features) and/or graphemes (or graphemic features) and, on the other hand, any sort of semantic contents. By "direct links" I mean links that are not made by passing from the signifier to its signified (morphosemantic assimilation) but by passing directly between the signifier and semantic contents. For example, consonants are often associated with semantics of intensity, even violence, whereas vowels are often associated with semantics of softness, etc.

8. In addition, it is possible to analyze the properties of the signifier, in terms of phonemes (or phonemic features) and/or graphemes (or graphemic features), without reference to the direct or indirect semantic impact of those properties. For example, one might observe assonance or alliteration in a proper noun, the paronymy of a proper noun with an adverb (but without any semantic impact), an abnormally high frequency of a given phoneme or phonemic feature in the onomastic network of a text, etc.

On onomastics, see Hébert and Trudel, forthcoming.

Authors: François Rigolot, Yves Baudelle, Jean-Louis Vaxelaire, etc.

5.27 Philosophy

The term "philosophy" is used with several distinct meanings: (1) a discipline that produces scholarly systems explaining the meaning of existence and our world, and that, on this basis, indicates how to lead a "good" (happy, meaningful) life (I am drawing here on Ferry, 2014). These systems constitute a particular form of scholarly ideology (an ideology is made up of beliefs, values, and ethical precepts). (2) One of the subdivisions of that discipline: the philosophy of art, the philosophy of literary creation, the philosophy of science, etc. (3) One or a group of those explanatory-prescriptive systems: idealist philosophies, Spinoza's philosophy, etc. (4) A philosophical form, which may be, to varying degrees, personal, consciously held, scholarly, explicit, and systematic: a philosophy of life, a philosophy of work, the philosophy of a novelist, of a novel, etc. (5) A system of beliefs, values, and ethical precepts (e.g., "good business practices") specific to an institution, an organization, an establishment, or a company: the philosophy of a particular company, etc. I would add that a philosophy of life is not necessarily a form of wisdom (e.g., a dictator also has a philosophy of life). With regard to the second meaning, I would add that all the intersections between philosophy and one of the disciplines (e.g., the philosophy of psychoanalysis, or of science) or fields of activity or interest (e.g., the philosophy of sex, or of literature) are in fact possible.

Existing philosophies can be used as a method for analyzing literary texts (e.g., by applying Marxism or existentialism to the analysis of texts). One can also study the influences (through their determinations on the signifieds or signifiers, the content or the form) of these philosophies on literary texts and/or the representation of these philosophies in literary texts. These influences and representations will be, to varying degrees, either conscious or unconscious, direct or indirect (possibly by significant omission, or the presence of their opposite), and explicit or implicit. A work may contain representations of or determinations from earlier and contemporary philosophies, as well as philosophies that are specific to the author, whether the latter are rudimentary or sophisticated, and either consciously or unconsciously held. A work can also be ahead of its time and present, in its own way, a philosophy that is still to come or still to be widely established. For philosophy, as in principle for any approach or form, we can distinguish between a top-down strategy (one that seeks a given philosophy in several works), and a bottom-up strategy (one that identifies all the philosophies that are present in a given work). We can also distinguish between an emic approach, which uses the analytic categories inherent in the work and/or the culture to which the work belongs (e.g., if one draws out the philosophy of a given text), or an etic approach, which uses analytic categories external to the work or the culture in question (e.g., if one uses Marxist philosophy to analyze a medieval or capitalist text). For more on emic and etic approaches, see section 6.3 on the corpus.

We can place individual producers on a spectrum ranging from "pure" philosophers to "pure" writers, with the intermediate terms "writer-philosophers" (e.g., Rousseau, Sartre, Beauvoir) and "philosopher-writers" (e.g., Shakespeare, Balzac, Beckett). See also section 5.10 on feminism, 5.22 on Marxism, and other ideological approaches.

Authors: Aristotle, Simone de Beauvoir, Albert Camus, Jean-Paul Sartre, Jacques Derrida, Michel Foucault, etc.

5.28 Poetics

In a broad sense, poetics is the study of semiotic products (artistic or not), forms (genres, themes, topoi, etc.), and processes (signification, etc.) in and for themselves, that is to say, in a way that is methodologically separated from other instances: from the author of the product, the process of production, receiver of the product, the process of reception and, more generally, from the context of the product. In a narrow sense, poetics is concerned only with literary texts. The separation of the object of study from other instances is obviously only relative, as it is impossible to analyze a product well without taking into account the other instances to some degree. The reverse is also true: it is impossible fully to understand a work, or even its context, without a good internal analysis.

Poetics is thus "opposed" to non-immanentist approaches, which deal directly and extensively with the five other instances mentioned above. Poetics in the narrow sense shares the immanentist perspective with other approaches such as structuralism, semiotics in general, and several linguistic theories. It differs from them in that it is applied exclusively to literary texts (and not to other kinds of texts or other semiotic products, such as images, films, etc.). In Western culture, poetics was initiated by Aristotle, but the whole field of rhetoric was already situated in the field of poetics (at least for the most part; see section 5.37).

Narratology can be considered as a branch of poetics. In fact, any approach that, by nature or in a given analysis, methodologically excludes the other instances of a semiotic product can be considered as belonging to poetics: for example, even traditional thematic analysis can be considered as such when it remains internal to the work. See also sections 5.18 on linguistics, 5.24 on narratology, 5.43 on structuralism, and 5.41 on Semiotics.

Authors: Aristotle, Gérard Genette, Tzvetan Todorov, etc.

5.29 Postcolonial studies

Postcolonial Studies is a loosely grouped field that examines: "the making of colonies and empires in history" (Nayar, 2015: x); the cultural, political, and artistic legacies of colonization; and the remaining structures of neocolonial oppression and exploitation in formerly colonized and colonizing states. Its central concerns are "racialized power relations, subjectivity, identity, belonging, the role of the nation-state, cultural imperialism and resistance" (Nayar, 2015: x), all of which postcolonial theorists bring to bear on analyses of a range of texts. It should be noted that the modern use of the term "postcolonial" is not necessarily temporal or historical (i.e., in reference to a period after colonialism, which is generally how it was used before the 1990s), but rather refers to "an engagement with, and contestation of, colonialism's discourses, power structures, and social hierarchies" (Gilbert and Tompkins, 1996: 2) in an ongoing manner. A focus on the deconstruction of colonial structures of dominance combined with detailed discourse analysis gives postcolonial studies a post-structuralist (Foucauldian) flavor, though more recently postcolonial critics have turned their attention to the material conditions of colonialism and its embodied effects on native/indigenous subjects of colonial rule.

Adopting the interdisciplinary attitude of comparable recent critical fields, postcolonial criticism searches for the traces and structures of engrained colonial assumptions and mentalities in a wide range of cultural and artistic texts. The work of Edward Said (1978) continues to exert influence in the field, particularly for its deconstructive approach to such oppositional binaries as Occident/Orient, developed/underdeveloped, colonizer/colonized, etc. In the 1990s, Dipesh Chakrabarty introduced a Marxist element to postcolonial studies of India, bringing the voices of peasants, laborers, women, and other "subalterns" to the fore and in so doing reversing a critical tendency to focus on the testimonies of literate elites. The practice of "decolonization" is one visible result of the impact of postcolonial studies, referring to pragmatic, politically oriented attempts to dismantle traces of colonial logic at the personal, collective, and institutional levels (including the material legacies of colonialism on university campuses).

Authors: Frantz Fanon, Gayatri Spivak, Edward Said, Homi Bhabha, Dipesh Chakrabarty, etc.

Sam Gormley

5.30 Posthumanism

We can broadly distinguish between two versions of posthumanism: (1) a technological posthumanism and (2) a cultural-theoretical posthumanism. The first version emphasizes the intertwinement of humanity and technology as a path toward a new evolutionary stage (hence it is *post*human). Cyborgs and clones are two key manifestations of the popular posthuman imaginary in literature and cinema. The second version, related to the first but often at odds with it, is a field of critical inquiry that seeks to challenge the founding tenets of humanist thought, especially as it was developed by figures such as Descartes (hence it is post*humanist*). Posthumanist thought adopts an anti-anthropocentric position, contesting assumptions about human essentialism and human separation from the nonhuman world. Neil Badmington describes it as follows:

> Posthumanism [...] emerges from a recognition that "Man" is not the privileged and protected center, because humans are no longer—and perhaps never were—utterly distinct from animals, machines, and other forms of the "inhuman"; are the products of historical and cultural differences

that invalidate any appeal to a universal, transhistorical human essence; are constituted as subjects by a linguistic system that pre-exists and transcends them; and are unable to direct the course of world history toward a uniquely human goal.

(Badmington, 2010: 374)

Posthumanist criticism therefore takes as its starting point the internal instability of humanism in order to show how the human has always been enmeshed within networks of other beings and things. As such, posthumanist analysis often (but not exclusively) focuses on texts that decenter the human in favor of non-hierarchical webs of relations. Critical posthumanist approaches to texts are noted for their deconstructive attitude toward commonplace ideas about humanity and demonstrates a so-called post-structuralist awareness of how "the human" has been historically and institutionally constructed.

Posthumanism belongs to no particular discipline and is regularly deployed in the fields of geography, history, social sciences, politics, and architecture, as well as in analyses of literature and film. It dialogues freely with feminism, philosophy, ecological criticism, and media studies among many others.

NOTE: IS TECHNOLOGICAL POSTHUMANISM STILL A HUMANISM?

There has been considerable effort within critical posthumanism to show how "technological posthumanism" is just a more intense form of traditional humanism (and by extension a radical form of *transhumanism*). The politics of these two forms are therefore quite different: technological posthumanism takes a techno-optimistic approach to posthumanism, arguing that we should welcome the posthuman era in utopian terms. The critical variety, on the whole, is more rigorous, takes a more methodical approach to the question of the human, is more attuned to factors of race, gender, and sexuality, and is more comfortable drawing on figures such as Derrida. It is worth noting that certain leading theorists, in particular Donna Haraway and Cary Wolfe, have moved away from using the term "posthumanism" in recent years.

The relativism (in the neutral sense of the word) of posthumanism—insofar as the human is only one ontological category among others—leads both to a fragmentation of the world (each ontological category sees the world in its own way and none is the "right way," or, for that matter, the "wrong way") and to the question of transcendence (I will leave aside the matter of spiritual transcendence), i.e., the overcoming—whether possible or impossible—of a given relative position by an attempt to encompass all relative positions, or alternatively the elimination of all relative positions by accessing the noumenon (things in themselves), insofar as it exists. It should be noted that only humans are able to put themselves, or try to put themselves, in the skin of other ontological categories and thereby transcend their "species subjectivity" (see Von Uexküll, 2010). This fact is sufficient to relativize the relativity of the human, or at least to attenuate this relativity with respect to that of the other ontological categories.

The prefix "post-" implies the end, and in particular the overcoming of something, which thereby becomes obsolete. However, the use of the label "post-" does not guarantee that the approach or situation it describes is actually beyond that which is supposedly outdated, or even dead. Indeed, it is often argued that one of these "post-" phenomena (e.g., postmodernity) is merely a continuation—but in a different form, which explains the error of categorization—of what preceded it (e.g., modernity). The label is some-times applied abusively, wrongly implying that the new, "post-" phenom-enon makes the "old" approach obsolete, especially when it is motivated by intellectual-professional considerations (e.g., the vigorous promotion of a new approach, supposedly better than the old one, which violently suppresses the old one with an ideology of "disruption"); for example, the birth of post-structuralism followed almost immediately after that of struc-turalism, an approach that is still very much alive (when it is not presented as a caricatured image of a discipline frozen in time) and, probably, timeless.

Authors: Donna Haraway, Cary Wolfe, Neil Badmington, N. Katherine Hayles, Rosi Braidotti, etc.

Sam Gormley and Louis Hébert

5.31 Pragmatics

Pragmatics has been considered either as a part of linguistics, insofar as it is interested, traditionally at least, in the language system, or as an independent discipline, insofar as it is interested in speech, that is to say, the concrete manifestations of the language system in particular utterances. It has variously been considered either as belonging to semantics or as being separate from it (Neveu, 2004: 236).

Moeschler and Reboul define pragmatics as follows:

> In a very general way, we will define pragmatics as the study of the use of language, as opposed to the study of the linguistic system, which is strictly speaking the domain of linguistics. If we speak of the use of language, it is because this use is not neutral in its effects either on the process of com-munication or on the linguistic system itself. It is a commonplace, in fact, to note that a certain number of words (the deictics of time, place, and person such as "now," "here," and "I," for example) can be interpreted only in the context of their enunciation. It is somewhat less common to recall that, in verbal exchange, we communicate far more than that which our words signify. It is even less commonly observed that the use of linguistic forms produces, in return, an inscription of that use in the system itself: the

meaning of the utterance consists in a commentary on its conditions of use, that is to say, its enunciation.

(Moeschler and Reboul, 1994: 17)

Pragmatics is particularly interested in presuppositions (e.g., the question "How's your wife?" presupposes that the addressee is married) and assumptions or implied meanings (e.g., "It's cold" may actually mean "Close the window").

In my view, a fully-formed linguistics—one that analyzes both the language system and speech, and both conversation and the literary text, at every level, from the morpheme to the whole text or even the corpus—necessarily incorporates pragmatics. Furthermore, pragmatics necessarily depends on an understanding of linguistic systems (in the plural, since there are other systems than that which pertains to speech) in order to understand the contextual meaning that is "derived" from them and, in this respect, it depends on linguistics in the narrow sense.

Authors: Émile Benveniste, Paul Grice, Dan Sperber, Oswald Ducrot, John Langshaw Austin, John R. Searle, etc.

5.32 Psychology, psychoanalysis, and psychocriticism

Psychology is the discipline and study that analyzes the human (and animal) psyche. The psychology of a particular person or character is the particular configuration of their psyche (e.g., the psychology of Madame Bovary, Hamlet, or Lennie from *Of Mice and Men*). There are many different broad strands of psychology (humanistic, behaviorist, cognitive, etc.), and although psychoanalysis is probably the one that has been most used in literary studies, in principle each of these strands can be used, either with or without adaptations (ideally with adaptations), to study the literary object. A psychological analysis may also be "naive" (whether deliberately or not) and not refer to a particular psychological theory, but rather to popular psychology.

Like many disciplines (sociology, linguistics, philosophy, etc.) that have been transposed, in a modified form, to describe literature (e.g., sociocriticism), or applied directly to literary objects, psychology can be conceived and applied in relation to the three general dimensions of the literary object: the producer and the production (the emotions, lived experience, pathology, motivations, writing lapsus, etc., of the author); the product itself (the psychology or psychoanalysis of the text, of the characters, etc.); and the receiver and reception of the product (the emotions, experience, pathology, motivation, interpretive lapsus, unconscious, etc., of the reader, the critic, the analyst, etc.).

The direct application of a psychological theory or method is usually problematic. For example, whereas the discourse of a clinical patient is oral and, in principle, spontaneous and free, the novel is a highly reworked and rewritten object structured by generic rules. An analysis must take account of the distinction, and interface, between the empirical, real author (e.g., the real Herman Melville) and the constructed author (e.g., the image of the author provided by the work—in this case, *Moby Dick*). Finally, the characters (including the narrator and the narratee), being textual phenomena, are endowed only with a "paper" psyche, which may not function like the psyche of a real person.

As we have seen, a theory or approach can be used to understand texts, and conversely texts can be used to constitute, validate or invalidate, modify, or illustrate a theory or approach. For example, Freud used Sophocles's play *Oedipus Rex* to illustrate (almost too perfectly) his theory of the Oedipus complex. As always, one can use an emic approach by looking for the psychological conception at work in a text and/or an etic approach, "applying" an approach that is "alien" to the text, but relevant (as Freud did with *Oedipus Rex*).

Authors: Sigmund Freud, Jacques Lacan, Jean Bellemin-Noël, Julia Kristeva, Charles Mauron, etc.

5.33 Queer studies, queer theory

Queer studies is a branch of sociocultural and literary studies that attends to the history, representation, and practice of LGBTQ+ or otherwise non-normative identities and sexualities. As an umbrella term, "queer" encompasses a larger spectrum of sexual identities than that covered by Women's Studies and Gay and Lesbian Studies, though it is closely related to these disciplines in its commitment to excavating unexamined and/or countercultural queer histories and communities, as well as to questioning "why society should allocate resources and grant privileges according to sexual orientation" (Buchanan, 2018: n.p.). Queer studies is informed by an activist politics of liberation and can be considered alongside other interdisciplinary fields—including postcolonial studies, feminism, and race studies—that seek to challenge the validity of existing labels and definitions, here pertaining to the norms governing sexual identities and the social and political expression thereof.

Queer approaches to texts focus on "authors, characters, or formal aspects of various texts" that demonstrate (explicit or implicit) elements of queerness or resistance to normative sexualities; this approach also asks, "what difference the gendered sexuality of the reader or spectator—a 'queer eye,' perhaps—makes to the meaning and significance of any particular text" (Somerville, 2020: 4), and as such draws on a critical tradition of reception studies (see section 5.36).

Queer theory grew out of queer studies and is defined as a "post-structuralist approach to the analysis, documenting, history, and understanding of human sexuality" that serves to raise "definitional and ontological questions concerning what it means to be bisexual, gay, lesbian, or straight" (Buchanan, 2018). Eve Kosofsky Sedgwick's *The Epistemology of the Closet* (1990), a founding text of queer theory, draws on the thought of Michel Foucault and Friedrich Nietzsche in its critical analysis and contestation of the hetero/homosexual binary in modern literature and film. Modern queer theory closely analyses the social, racial, and gendered construction of sexualities that fall outside the norms of heterosexuality in Western, and more rarely non-Western, contexts. It has become common in recent years to speak of "queering" as a critical practice of re-reading texts or historical communities to throw into relief queer elements that had previously received little attention (e.g., "queering the Renaissance").

Queer studies and queer theory, while closely related, have distinct histories and differing influences. In general, queer theory is associated with textual and cultural criticism whereas queer studies is a larger, more historically oriented field of inquiry that includes cultural history, political history, and activism.

Authors: Eve Kosofsky Sedgwick, Lauren Berlant, Judith Butler, Jack Halberstam, Lee Edelman, José Esteban Muñoz, etc.

Sam Gormley

5.34 Race and ethnicity studies, critical race theory

The construction and experience of race and its role in contemporary and historical societies has become a central theme for critics in all major academic disciplines, particularly literary and film studies, cultural theory, sociology, and history. The ongoing legacy of slavery, civil rights movements, apartheid, and countless recent examples of police brutality against people of color have shaped the current scope of research on race, which combines theoretical and empirical study of structural inequality with an engaged, activist ethic. In the field of literary analysis, recognition of the ways race is constituted and represented through language and within texts—and, just as importantly, omitted from language and texts—has inspired numerous re-readings of the (white) Western canon with an eye to revealing the logic of race and racial bias, even when not addressed explicitly. Insights from race and ethnicity studies are thus invaluable for understanding how Black, Asian, indigenous, and other ethnic minority voices have been obscured or marginalized in Western literary culture. Such readings are often combined with nuanced analyses of gender, sexuality, class, and disability to show how combinations of factors relating to individual and communal identity are inextricable from forms of racial discrimination. This "intersectional" mode of analysis—which takes into account the interactions between and mutual reinforcement of race, ethnicity, gender, and sexuality—is inspired chiefly by the insights of third-wave feminism.

The academic study of race and racial inequality emerged in the field of sociology, particularly in the wake of civil rights and Black power movements in the 1950s and 1960s. Early studies of race and ethnicity in the US used emerging empirical data to highlight structural issues of inequality and discrimination (Murji and Solomos, 2014: 3). In the UK, the growth of research into race and ethnicity revolved around longstanding questions of empire, migration, and (post)colonialism, and intersected with the emergence of cultural studies. Critical race theory, a recent development of race and ethnicity studies, has its roots in critical legal studies, which aims to show "how the law operates to constitute race and maintain hierarchy" (Capers, 2015: 26). The field subsequently developed through close contact with radical feminism in the 1980s. Delgado and colleagues thus distinguish critical race theory from earlier political movements:

> The movement considers many of the same issues that conventional civil rights and ethnic studies discourses take up but places them in a broader perspective that includes economics, history, setting, group and self-interest, and emotions and the unconscious. Unlike traditional civil rights discourse, which stresses incrementalism and step-by-step progress, critical race theory questions the very foundations of the liberal order, including equality theory, legal reasoning, Enlightenment rationalism, and neutral principles of constitutional law.
>
> (Delgado et al., 2017: 3)

As a wide-ranging critical method for understanding how racism operates within society at both individual and structural levels, critical race theory "insists on progressive race consciousness, on systemic analysis of the structures of subordination, on the inclusion of counter-accounts of social reality, and on a critique of power relationships that is attentive to the multiple dimensions on which subordination exists" (Capers, 2015: 26).

NOTE: RACISM AND DISCRIMINATION

Although the principle of equality between all humans is widely accepted in theory, in reality it is far from being achieved. Racism—individual, social, and institutional—belongs to a wider set of discriminations, in the sense of: (1) differentiations made between humans on the basis of relatively objective factors (e.g., skin color) or supposedly objective, but actually constructed factors; and (2) the attribution of negative qualities and (therefore) disadvantages to one or more groups, and of positive qualities and (therefore) privileges to one or more other groups. Reactions against racism have led to a focus on self-representation (e.g., African Americans talking about the experience and history of African Americans). However, "heterorepresentations" and "heterohistories" (in the sense of representations and histories produced by people who do not belong to the groups in question) should not, on this basis, be rejected in principle, but should instead be judged according to their merit. Studies of racism must show how, why, and with what effects the concept of race has been invented, used, and represented, and how, why, and with what effects it can be deconstructed and/or used against itself.

Authors: Derrick Bell, Kimberlé Crenshaw, Richard Delgado, Patricia Williams, Angela Onwuachi-Willig, etc.

Sam Gormley and Louis Hébert

5.35 Reading (theories of)

We can distinguish between three main forms of reception of a text: normative criticism (which says whether the work is good or bad, relevant or not, etc.), analysis (or descriptive criticism), and reading. We can consider that the normative criticism of works presupposes at least a minimal degree of analysis, and that the latter presupposes at least one reading. Theories of reading are devoted to this last operation, and they can therefore be considered as a subdivision of the theories of reception. That being said, even the most "naive" reading involves at least a minimal degree of analysis and, of course, some normative criticism, even if this takes place only unconsciously and involuntarily.

Literary reading, as an operation, involves not only recognizing the signifiers (the forms that convey the contents) and their relations and interactions, but also enjoying them from an esthetic point of view; similarly, it involves not only recognizing or identifying the signifieds (the contents) and their relations and interactions, but also enjoying these from an esthetic point of view. One might think that reading proceeds in a linear way from a signifier (e.g., that of a word) to its signified, then to the next signifier, and so on. But this fails to take into account the fact that the signifier and the signified can select each other mutually, through successive hypotheses and validations, and that effects of anticipation—which are sometimes mistaken, such as if the reader commits a reading lapsus in the course of their interpretation—can occur leading from signifiers to signifieds and vice versa.

One of the tasks of theories of reading is to define typologies of readers and readings, in addition to being able to describe a particular reading of a given work. With regard to readings, we can distinguish between (some categories partially overlap): a naive reading (carried out by people with no particular scholarly training) and expert or scholarly reading; an initial reading and possible successive readings; reading in progress and a completed reading; linear reading (which proceeds from one unit to the next) and tabular reading (which can move from one unit to any other, even if it is earlier; see the chapter on the plan of the analytical text); a comprehension reading (one simply decodes the signifiers and signifieds on a basic level) and an interpretive reading (one finds more diffuse meanings); in Rastier's theory, reading under the regime of clarity—faster, with simpler and clearer interpretive paths (when the text is simple and clear)—and reading under the regime of obscurity—slower, with more complex and more tenuous interpretive paths (when the text is richer, more difficult, or even hermetic); in Rastier again (2001: 299),[3] methodologically reductive reading (which deliberately neglects certain contents), non-methodologically reductive reading (which involuntarily neglects certain contents,

---

3 In Rastier's theory, the word "reading" often takes on a technical meaning, as the result of an interpretation. This is the case for his typology of "readings." Nevertheless, the typology is also valid for reading in the usual sense of the word.

through under-interpretation), descriptive reading (which takes account of all the contents), and productive reading (which adds, whether consciously or not, contents that are not present, by over-interpretation). The reductive and productive readings constitute "erroneous" or "erratic" readings, at least when they are not relevant to the objectives of the analysis. An erratic reading can nevertheless be interesting or revealing (of the reader, if not of the text itself).

With regard to readers, we can distinguish between: empirical (real) readers and constructed readers (the image that, for example, the text gives of the expected, non-expected, desired, non-desired readers, etc.); model readers (who behave perfectly according to the expectations of the text, making the right deductions, interpretations, or, in a detective story, the expected mistakes, etc.) and non-model readers; sub-competent readers (e.g., a child reading adult literature), competent readers, optimally competent readers (corresponding to the model reader), over-competent readers (e.g., an adult reading a children's detective story); average and marginal readers; actual and non-actual readers (those who will never actually read the work), whether desired, non-desired, expected (but not necessarily desired), or non-expected; individual readers and collective readers (e.g., how a given social class or culture has read a given work overall); types of readers (e.g., young women) and actual, empirical (token) readers (a specific young woman). See also section 5.36 on reception.

The various permutations of one/several works and one/several readings allow us to envisage: intensive reading (only one book is read, an unlimited number of times, e.g., the Bible, for many believers in former times); extensive reading (an unlimited number of books, read only once); and mixed reading (a mixture of intensive and extensive reading depending on the books in question). On these concepts, which were brought to my attention by Claude La Charité, see Hall, 1983 and Chartier, 1996.

Obviously, as for production, reception (including reading) can be analyzed *for* the work or *within* the work (thematized production and reception, e.g., the narrator as writer or reader, or the reading and writing carried out by characters).

Authors: Bertrand Gervais, Richard Saint-Gelais, Vincent Jouve, Umberto Eco, etc.

5.36 Reception (theories of)

The term "reception theories" refers to a group of theories that share a focus on the reception of works (reader, analyst, interpreter, and the reception process) rather than on the other two major dimensions of the work, namely that of production (the author and the writing process) and that of the semiotic product itself (the immanent study of the text itself, e.g., in stylistics, narratology). However, according to Molino (2018: 59), such an approach is reductive if it is not complemented by these other two facets of the literary. In other words, a literary text is necessarily constituted by these three inseparable facets, and any study of only one of these facets must be a methodological reduction (i.e., conscious, explicit, and relevant to the objectives of the analysis). The main contribution of the theories of reception has been to counterbalance the former dominance of analyses based on studies of production (biographical criticism, literary history, etc.) with analyses based on studies of reception, on the principle that the receiver is, in a sense, the co-author of the text.

One might think that there are three overall approaches to analysis (focused on production, text, or reception), or perhaps five (author, production, text, reception, reader). In fact, there are at least 21 overall situations of analysis (see Hébert, 2014: 299–304, where I present the typology of analytic situations that was created by Nattiez [1997], himself drawing on Molino). For example, we could start from a study of reception in order to produce hypotheses about who the author is and how the writing took place; we could also start from a study of the writing process to consider how the work could be received and by whom.

Reading and analysis (comprehension, description, interpretation, etc.) are the two main processes described by the theories of reception. More precisely, the (evaluative) criticism of a work presupposes a stage of analysis (which may be more or less superficial, and more or less conscious), and the analysis of the work presupposes reading. Reading itself is treated in greater depth in the theories of reading (see section 5.35).

We can consider that the theories of reception appeared as both a reaction and a complement to approaches based on the author and production, and, more generally, contextual approaches (literary history, etc.) and approaches based on the product itself (immanent approaches, such as linguistics).

In short, within the broad range of theories and methods devoted to reception that exist, there is a somewhat nebulous group of theories and methods that are referred to as "theories of reception," which are associated with the names of the authors below.

Authors: Roman Ingarden, Hans Robert Jauss, Wolfgang Iser, Stanley Fish, Umberto Eco, etc.

5.37 Rhetoric

Rhetoric can be defined as "an art and theory of the construction of discourses" (Neveu, 2004: 256) and, to precisely the same extent, it can be used to "deconstruct" discourses, that is, to analyze them. Some people limit rhetoric to the art of persuasion, which obviously excludes the non-argumentative parts of semiotic products (images, films, etc.), including literary texts, not to mention the fact that the main function of most artistic works is not, strictly speaking, to persuade, but to produce an esthetic effect (even if they use persuasive devices to do so). Since it is undoubtedly more common for people to continue in their established opinions than it is for them to be persuaded, we can instead speak of the art of trying to persuade (Angenot, 2007: 57), rather than the art of persuading.

Traditionally, rhetoric is divided into: (1) invention (gathering ideas), (2) arrangement (putting ideas and words in order), (3) style (gathering stylistic figures), (4) delivery (the study of gestures and diction), and (5) memory (Bénac and Réauté, 1993: 204). For a classification of the main rhetorical stylistic figures, see section 4.24. The division pertaining to "delivery" is conceived with only oral textual products in mind. This is therefore obviously irrelevant for the analysis of written texts, whether literary or not (although there are literary texts that are entirely or partially oral), unless we consider that aspects such as typography, page layout, and the construction of the book are the written counterparts of the delivery of an oral textual product.

In Western culture, rhetoric is probably the oldest of the internal approaches, that is, of those that focus on the semiotic product itself and not on the other aspects of semiotic communication (author, receiver, context, etc.). Indeed, even when, as a theory and method of discourse analysis (pertaining to oral and/ or written texts, and even other semiotic products), it focuses on seemingly external elements—authorial phenomena such as gestures, diction, or ethos (the moral credibility of the author)—these can nevertheless be considered as being internal to the overall rhetorical semiotic performance.

Authors: the ancient rhetoricians, the μ Group, Chaïm Perelman, Michel Meyer, Marc Angenot, etc.

5.38 Rhythm (study of)

Rhythm could be defined as a way of flowing. I would say, more specifically, that this means: a way of making elements appear, remain, transform, and disappear, and a way of arranging those elements in time and/or space. Indeed, any semiotic product (and any phenomenon, even the human body and mind) can be considered as a flow of processes rather than as a static entity.

In the broadest sense, rhythm is the configuration (and its effect) of at least two elements (it can be the same element repeated) arranged in at least two different temporal and/or spatial positions. In principle, for there to be rhythm, the elements forming the rhythm must belong to the same class of phenomena (e.g., phonemes) without necessarily being of the same kind (e.g., different phonemes).

Rhythms are not limited to the (often fairly basic) phenomena studied in traditional versification, nor are they limited to poetry, literature, or artistic productions: any product, whether semiotic or not (e.g., the rhythm of a blacksmith's hammering), human or natural, includes rhythms as long as it is either inherently deployed over time (as in a film) or effectively deployed over time in the way that it is perceived (as in the successive "reading" of the parts of a painting, even though the object is in itself static). Rhythms can involve signifiers (e.g., the phonemes of words) and/or signifieds (e.g., the content of words); in these two cases we can speak of semiotic rhythms. One might ask whether rhythm can be produced in the spatial substrate itself or only insofar as the spatial substrate is correlated with the temporal substrate. This remains an open question. It is certain, however, that one can temporalize space by considering successively different portions of space (e.g., the three parts of a pictorial triptych).

It is surprising, given the proliferation (or even omnipresence) and importance of rhythmic phenomena, that rhythmology has not developed more widely as an independent discipline (let alone becoming institutionalized in university departments, courses, etc.). For my own part, I have tried to make a modest contribution to this discipline (see section 4.17 and Hébert, 2019: chapter 15).

Authors: Henri Meschonnic, Lucie Bourrassa, Claude Zilberberg, Pascal Michon, etc.

5.39 Russian Formalism

Russian Formalism is:

> [a] current of thought that emerged in the USSR between 1915 and 1930, then later became known in France through Tzvetan Todorov's translation (*Théorie de la littérature*, 1965). As Stéphane Mallarmé and Paul Valéry had already claimed, and in agreement with structuralist criticism, formalism considers the literary text as an autonomous [...] formal totality; the study of the text requires the search for formal criteria, and not historical or biographical clues [or causes].
>
> (Bénac and Réauté, 1993: 97)

Russian Formalism therefore focuses on the work itself, in its immanence, rather than on the two other main dimensions of literary communication, namely those of production (whose main agent is the author) and reception (of which the reader is one of the agents); it also reduces to a minimum the study of other elements of context (since the author and the reader are contextual elements), or at least these other elements become means rather than ends. In these respects, Russian Formalism and New Criticism (see section 5.25) are similar. Russian Formalism is an immanent, internal approach, and in this respect it resembles all other such approaches (semiotics, narratology, etc.).

Roman Jakobson's well-known model of the functions of language (see Hébert, 2019: chapter 16) is an example of this approach, and the analysis of Baudelaire's sonnet "The Cats" by Jakobson (the best known work of analysis by the best known of the Russian Formalists) and Claude Lévi-Strauss (a famous French anthropologist, the founder of structural anthropology) is probably the most famous work of analysis issuing from this school of thought (Jakobson and Lévi-Strauss, 1962). I would say that this type of analysis consists in: (1) establishing, for each word or for each group of words, certain characterizing criteria, such as morphological (the nature of words: noun, verb, etc.), grammatical (gender: feminine, masculine, neuter; number: singular, plural; etc.), syntactic (function: subject, complement, etc.), or semantic (contents), etc.; (2) identifying the correlations between characterizing criteria (e.g., singular words in a given text convey a certain theme); (3) identifying the correlations of the characterizing criteria with positions in the text (e.g., words at the beginning or the end of sentences, or of the text), as distinguished through various complementary segmentations of the text (e.g., segmentation of the text by words, syntagmata, propositions, sentences, verses, paragraphs, stanzas, etc.).

Another important contribution of Russian Formalism comes from Vladimir Propp, whose work would provide the foundation for the famous semiotician Algirdas Julien Greimas to create the actantial model (see Hébert, 2019: chapter 6), a simple and rigorous device that makes it possible to analyze all actions efficiently (for a definition of the actantial model, see section 8.3.1).

Authors: Roman Jakobson, Yuri Tynyanov, Vladimir Propp, etc.

5.40 Semantics

In its broadest sense, semantics is the study of semiotic contents: whether these contents are types (e.g., the signification of words in the language system) or actual occurrences, or tokens (e.g., the meaning of words in the context of the text in which they occur); and whether these contents are associated with textual signs (e.g., words) or non-textual signs (e.g., images).

In this sense, semantics is a sub-discipline of semiotics, since the latter studies both signifiers and signifieds (semiotic contents). To avoid confusion between semantics in the narrow sense (limited to linguistic contents) and the semantics of cognitive contents (mental images, etc.), we can refer to semantics in the broad sense as semiosemantics.

In the narrow sense, semantics is the study of the content of textual units (whether oral or written)—morphemes (e.g., "agri-"), groups of morphemes or lexies (e.g., "water," "agriculture"), phraseologies (stereotyped parts of phrases or whole phrases, e.g., proverbs)—and of their combinations and dynamics of meaning in oral and/or written texts. It is therefore a sub-discipline of linguistics. Linguistic semantics was initially concerned with the meaning of lexical units and the meaning of sentences (the meaning of the text was then seen as being merely the sum of the individual meanings of its sentences). It now also studies meaning beyond the level of the sentence, and notably the meaning of the whole text. Consequently, the meaning of the text, in many domains of contemporary linguistics, is no longer seen as the simple sum of its constituent units: the meaning of the text determines the meaning of sentences, and the meaning of sentences determines the meaning of the lexies (individual words or expressions), etc. Indeed, there is a general "holistic principle" (as opposed to the "compositionalist principle") that the global determines the local: the context determines the text; the corpus determines the text; the genre determines the text; the text determines its sentences; etc.

As the study of semantic contents (there are also mental or cognitive contents), semantics is the study of signifieds, and as such, it can use the technical concepts related to signifieds in order to describe them: semes (parts of a signified), isotopies (repetition of a given seme), semic molecules (repeated groups of semes), the actualization of semes (their activation, e.g., the seme /luminosity/ in "sun" is actualized in the expression "bright sun"), and the virtualization of semes (their neutralization, e.g., the seme /luminosity/ in "sun" is virtualized in the expression "black sun").

Semantics is therefore interdefined with morphology, in the broader sense, or semiomorphology (to avoid confusion with morphology in the narrower sense, as the exclusive study of textual signifiers), which refers to the study of signifiers, whether textual or otherwise (see section 4.19 on sign, signifier, signified).

Authors: Algirdas Julien Greimas, François Rastier, etc.

5.41 Semiotics

In the broadest sense, semiotics is the discipline—founded independently by both Charles Sanders Peirce in the US and Ferdinand de Saussure in Europe between the end of the nineteenth and the beginning of the twentieth centuries—that studies the production, the internal dynamics (as an immanent approach), and the interpretation of semiotic products (textual, pictorial, etc.). Like many disciplines, semiotics is made up of three domains: theories, methods, and applications. And like many disciplines, semiotics studies both an empirical, concrete object (semiotic products) and a constructed object that is abstracted from empirical objects (the sign, semiosis, "semioticity," meaning, signification, etc.).

The field of semiotics has a greater or lesser extension depending on the theory in question. It can be immense, or even infinite: according to Peirce, everything can be seen as a sign (without being reduced to the nature of a sign), including the universe, the human being, etc., provided, as Jean-Marie Klinkenberg (1996: 3) would say, that a "semiotic decision" occurs, which chooses to see or to create a sign in something that was not necessarily in principle a sign.

Semiotics is the most general of the disciplines that study signifieds (meaning, semiotic content) and signifiers (the container or vehicle of signifieds). Literary studies, for example, also study signifieds and signifiers, but only in the context of literary texts. It should be noted that, although in principle signifiers and signifieds are of equal interest, in practice the study of content dominates, and signifiers are essentially considered only as a means of grasping the contents that they convey or of noting correlations with those contents. Some disciplines, which can be called the sciences of meaning, specialize in the study of contents (e.g., hermeneutics, semantics), while others, which can be called morphological sciences, specialize in the study of signifiers (in linguistics, phonology and morphology). Peirce's semiotics uses a tripartite sign, made up of a representamen (which sometimes, but not always, corresponds to the signifier), an interpretant (which sometimes, but not always, corresponds to the signified), and an object (a referent, the thing that the interpretant "speaks" about and to which the representamen refers). We can therefore consider that there exist—in addition to the sciences of meaning and the morphological sciences—referential sciences, which are focused on the referent. The referential sciences could be seen as corresponding to the natural sciences, including psychology and the cognitive sciences (since some referents, such as the referent of "glory," do not correspond to material objects). However, referents may also correspond to individual or multiple imaginary objects (e.g., the referent of the game of "quidditch" from the world of the *Harry Potter* novels, and the referent of "unicorn").

In addition to the concepts of the signifier (e.g., the phonemes of a word) and the signified (e.g., the semantic content of a word), several other semiotic concepts are widely known and used: the referent (what the signified points toward, what is spoken of; e.g., the actual apple or apples referred to by the signified "apple"), the seme (the parts that make up the signified), isotopy (the repetition of a given seme), the semiotic square (the analysis of a given opposition by means of ten subcategories), the actantial model (the analysis of an action in terms of six facets or actants), the symbol (a conventional sign, e.g., a pair of weighing scales is the symbol of justice for those who know the convention), the index (e.g., smoke as an index of fire), the icon (e.g., a photograph of a person as an icon of that person), etc. (see section 4.19). For an introduction to semiotics, see Hébert, 2019.

Authors: Ferdinand de Saussure, Charles Sanders Peirce, Charles W. Morris, Louis Hjelmslev, Roland Barthes, Joseph Courtés, Algirdas Julie Greimas, Umberto Eco, Thomas A. Sebeok, Jacques Fontanille, Claude Zilberberg, François Rastier, Jean-Marie Klinkenberg, etc.

5.42 Sociology of literature

Following Paul Dirkx (2000: 7), I will use the term "sociology of literature" in a broad sense to encompass all the relations between sociology and literature, and thus everything that is covered by the terms "sociology of literature" (in the narrow sense), "literary sociology," "sociology of literary facts," "sociology of the text," and "sociocriticism."

Sociology is the discipline that studies, as an empirical object, social phenomena and, as a constructed, abstract object, sociality. The same principle applies to literary studies, where the empirical object is the literary text and the constructed object is literarity (and the many ways of conceiving it, under this name or another). When the social phenomena being analyzed are literary, we can speak of the sociology of literature, in the broad sense.

The sociology of literature is interested in five social phenomena in particular: (1) social classes (sex, gender, profession, age, socioeconomic class, etc.), (2) social institutions (the state, justice, the church, education, literature, etc.), (3) ideologies (these are necessarily social because they are collectively shared or even constituted; we can use the term "idioideology" to refer to an individually held ideology), (4) sociolect (the establishment of the abstract language of an ideology before it is deployed in an actual text; e.g., the typical vocabulary, metaphors, etc., of a particular ideology), and (5) social discourse (everything that is said, written, filmed, etc., within a society, including on the society itself and on other societies; Angenot, 1989: 13). Social classes can be based on any criterion that makes it possible to construct a system of interdefined social classes, and not only on the traditional socioeconomic criteria (categories such as the bourgeoisie, workers, etc.). Abstract institutions (e.g., literature) are manifested by empirical institutions (e.g., literary societies, writers' associations, publishers, etc.). Institutions manage the production, circulation, and distribution of material capital (money, goods, etc.) and symbolic capital (awards, fame, etc.). An ideology is a system—which may be either more or less consciously held, structured, rigorous, and complex—made up of three subsystems: beliefs (true/false/undecidable, etc.); values (positive/negative/neutral/undecidable, etc.); and ethical precepts (things to be done/things not to be done/optional/undecidable, etc.).

The first four major social phenomena are considered with regard to their determining effects on the analyzed literary text—its signifiers and signifieds, or its form and content (which is not exactly the same thing)—and/or with regard to the reflection of those phenomena in the literary text, or representation in it as a theme, whether directly or indirectly, explicitly or implicitly. The main modalities of reflection are direct (e.g., reflecting the emperor Napoleon as he was), indirect (a character who exercises authoritarian power in his family is named Napolito), negative (e.g., ironic: Napolito is presented as a great democrat), or by significant omission (e.g., a royalist historical novel set in France at the beginning of the nineteenth century that does not even mention Napoleon, the sworn enemy of royalty). Sociological analysis can obviously be applied to other literary phenomena than texts themselves (genres, rhetorical stylistic figures, themes, processes, movements, events, etc.).

The sociology of literature can obviously focus on any of the three main dimensions of literary analysis: production (the author, writing, etc.), the work itself, and its reception (the reader, reading, criticism, analysis, etc.). In the approach to the work itself, the focus is on identifying and characterizing the "society of the text" and its various instances (individual, collective, and institutional actors; institutions; ideologies; sociolects; etc.), relationships, and processes.

Authors: Pierre Bourdieu, Claude Duchet, Marc Angenot, etc.

5.43 Structuralism

The word "structure" is highly polysemous (see section 4.23 on structure, relation, operation). In the broadest sense, a structure is an entity made up of terms and relations between these terms (one can add operations to this list, notably those that create, modify, or suppress terms, relations, or operations). From a structuralist perspective, relations are more fundamental than terms, and it is relations that "create" and define terms (e.g., the meaning of a word in a language is produced entirely by its relations, notably of difference, and especially opposition, with other words). Since relations are produced, operations are ultimately more fundamental than both relations and terms.

Structure can be assimilated to a system, in the two main senses of the word: (1) in that it is produced and governed by norms, and also produces norms (e.g., type, or model units, rules, and programs for combining units, such as syntax); (2) in that its constituents are interdefined and interdependent: since a system is underpinned by a holistic, rather than compositionalist, dynamic, it is more than the sum of its parts, and if you alter one of its parts, you affect all the other parts and the whole.

Structuralism, as a family of approaches, is a rough grouping of theories that appeared in the 1960s (with the important exception of Saussure, who was a precursor of this group) and that have a shared emphasis on perspectives that are synchronic (rather than diachronic, historical), immanent (rather than external, and methodologically excluding the context and the producing and receiving subjects), and systemic (rather than compositional, in that the parts are considered to form a dynamic whole). They are also alike in favoring analyses of a technical or even formalized nature (as, for example, algebraic mathematical analyses are to an even greater extent).

Structuralism, despite the fact that it was quickly followed by a "post-structuralism" (Foucault, Derrida, etc., which the Anglophone world refers to as "French Theory") that supposedly surpassed it, is still very much alive and constitutes a theoretical and methodological asset not only for semiotics but also for other approaches in literary studies and, more generally, in the humanities and sciences of culture. Although structuralism might seem to be a predominantly Francophone phenomenon, its principles appear to be universal, and have been adopted—sometimes unknowingly—by other approaches, whether earlier, contemporary, or later. It has also been taken as a reference point to kick against, for example, in analyses that are supposedly non-technical, without metalanguage, or even with an assumed anti-rationalism and uncritical relativism.

Rastier has reservations about the amalgamation of various theories under the term "structuralism." This is how Rastier (forthcoming) defines structuralism:

> In the narrow sense, it is the current of historical and comparative linguistics aimed at systematizing descriptions, in the tradition of Saussure, Hjelmslev, Coseriu, and Greimas, among others. In a broad sense, it is a theoretical trend in the sciences of culture in the twentieth century aimed at a systematic description of the semiotic world: see in particular Cassirer in philosophy, Dumézil in the history of religions, and Lévi-Strauss in anthropology. It should not be confused with the structuralism (or distributionalism) of the North American syntacticians of the 1940s, nor with the vague federation [of theories of the sixties that critics group together, on the basis of a historiographic fallacy—that is to say, by grouping together different currents on the sole basis that they are contemporary with each other and not

traditional—which would include the work of Foucault, Lacan, Althusser, Barthes, Greimas, etc.]

(Rastier, forthcoming)

Authors: Ferdinand de Saussure, Louis Hjelmslev, Claude Lévi-Strauss, Nikolai Sergeyevich Trubetzkoy, Louis Martinet, Roman Jakobson, Roland Barthes, Algirdas Julien Greimas, Jacques Lacan, Louis Althusser, etc.

5.44 Stylistics

Let us take the following definition to begin with: "Stylistics is the linguistic study of style, that is, of the idiolectal regularities [specific to a producer] observed in literary works" (Neveu, 2004: 272).

In this definition, stylistics is seen as a branch of linguistics, or at least as a discipline using (exclusively) concepts and methodologies from linguistics. One might well disagree with this, at least in part. Moreover, it is possible, and probably legitimate, to extend the field of stylistics to apply to all texts, whether oral, written, or both oral and written (websites, etc.), whether literary or non-literary, and more broadly to all semiotic products, artistic or not, and even to non-semiotic products (e.g., the style of a blacksmith's hammering). We are then faced with a general stylistics and a series of more specific stylistics (textual, filmic, pictorial, etc.). In each case, style is defined relative to the idiolect. My own typology of the systems at work in texts (and possibly in other semiotic products) comprises the following types: (1) anthropolect (universal regularities), (2) culturolect (regularities common to a culture), (3) sociolect in a general sense (regularities common to a society) and sociolect in Rastier's sense (regularities defined according to the genres of texts, etc.), (4) idiolect (regularities common to an author), (5) textolect (regularities common to a text), and (6) alect (the non-systemic part of a text). However, the idiolect reuses, either with or without modifications (qualitative and/or quantitative), the units and rules of all the higher-level systems (those of the sociolect and above). In fact, each lower-level system does the same with the higher-level system(s). Style is therefore a matter of the differential between a higher level and its immediately lower level, or between the higher levels and a given lower level. In other words, style is not found only in the idiolect, but in all the systemic levels, or more precisely in the relation between them. In fact, the word "style" reflects this double nature: we speak of the style of a given writer (an individual phenomenon), but also of a generic style (a social, sociolectal phenomenon, such as the Romanesque or Gothic architectural styles). The same typology of systems can be used as a criterion to produce typologies of other phenomena: genre (culturogenre, idiogenre, etc.), symbol (anthroposymbol, textosymbol, etc.), myth (anthropomyth, idiomyth), topos (sociotopos, idiotopos, etc.), ideologies (anthropoideology, idioideology, etc.), etc.

The opposition norm/deviation is often used in the study of style. In this case, the system obviously represents the norm. The use of this system by a lower-level system will then realize the norm of the higher system with regard to some units, but will also produce deviations from the higher system with regard to other units. Consequently, style is not (only) deviation. In other words, style is not (only) deviation from the expected degree, and stylistics cannot be defined (only) as the study of deviations, let alone as the study (only) of individual deviations.

Like many other approaches (e.g., literary history, rhetoric, semiotics) and phenomena (e.g., God, according to Nietzsche, and the literary author, according to Barthes), stylistics was once decreed "dead," or at least outdated. It is obviously still both alive and relevant.

Authors: Charles Bally, Leo Spitzer, Michael Riffaterre, Georges Molinié, Étienne Karabétian, etc.

5.45 Textual statistics and computer text analysis

A given phenomenon can be described qualitatively and/or quantitatively; similarly, between two or more phenomena, the relation of identity or alterity can be characterized qualitatively (in terms of its nature) and/or quantitatively (in terms of its degree). Any university student can see that qualitative studies largely dominate in literary studies. In general, more "intuitive" and "artisanal" approaches prevail over more "technical" and "formal" approaches. With the emergence of easily accessible textual databases, computers, and simple and powerful text analysis software, the field of literary studies no longer has any pretext not to venture into the realm of quantitative analysis.

Textual statistics, or textometry, measures the absolute and relative occurrences of textual forms within a text, a corpus of texts, or a textual type (e.g., a genre). It studies, from a statistical perspective, the regularities and irregularities of these textual forms.

In fact, the production and interpretation of statistical data can be done "by hand" or with the help of computer-aided text analysis (CATA) software. The measures, regularities and irregularities mentioned can be connected to "raw" data (e.g., a count of each specified word) or to codings that have been applied to the data. For example, one can count the words that have been coded according to their nature (e.g., noun, verb, etc.) or their theme (e.g., as being related to humans or to animals). The codings may be carried out entirely or mostly by hand, or automatically (with or without a subsequent stage of manual validation) with the use of thesauri (pre-existing lists of words belonging to a given category or semantic field); for example, a thesaurus will automatically identify "man," "woman," "child," etc., as belonging to the "human" field or theme, and "fox," "octopus," "zooplankton," etc., as belonging to the "animal" field or theme.

The analysis of texts by computer makes it possible to characterize phenomena of different extents (words, groups of words, phrases, texts, etc.) and to compare the values associated with them. To take a simple example, one can compare the average number of words (or syllables) per sentence within a single text, but also between two different texts. The various data produced by the computer must generally be interpreted by a "human" analyst to make the best use of it, even if this interpretation consists in reprocessing the data using a different algorithm.

The three main advantages of computerized text analysis are, first, and most obviously, that of speeding up the analysis (which is all the more useful for a larger text or corpus), but also increasing the standardization of the analysis (since the computer does not make mistakes), and, above all, bringing to light "new observables" (Rastier, 2004), which are either difficult or impossible to perceive by means of a "manual" analysis (except by re-performing the computer-generated analysis by hand).

Obviously, the identification, qualification, and quantification of a phenomenon can be followed by a demonstration of the causes and effects of this phenomenon and of (non-causal) correlations between it and other phenomena. These causes, effects, and simple correlations can be internal (e.g., related to the text itself), external (e.g., related to the author or the social context), or intermediate (e.g., related to an abstract form connected to the text, such as a genre to which the text belongs).

Authors: Charles Muller, Étienne Brunet, etc.

5.46 Thematics and symbolism (analysis)

In the broad sense, thematics is the approach that studies the contents or signifieds of a text or corpus; it would then coincide with semantics (in the narrow sense, as a subdivision of linguistics), if it were not for the fact that its analyses are not necessarily as formalized ("technical," "mathematical") as those of semantics, and for the fact that semantics also (or especially) describes contents out of context (in the language system, "in the dictionary") and not only in context (see section 5.40). It would also coincide with the semiosemantics subdivision of semiotics, which studies the contents of signs, if it were not for the fact that it is not as formalized and that it applies only to texts (or only to written texts, or even only to literary written texts), whereas semiotics describes all kinds of semiotic products (texts, images, etc.) (see section 5.41).

Traditional thematic analysis is often limited, whether consciously or not, to the study of what we could call the "big themes," especially existential ones (love, death, freedom, creation, sexuality, etc.); it then excludes grammatical contents (singular, plural, use of tenses, etc.) and trivial or secondary contents (e.g., tobacco in *Madame Bovary*). Although all thematic contents are, in principle, of equal importance, thematic analyses generally favor the "big themes," which are necessarily strongly recurrent from one work to another, or alternatively the "small themes" that are connected, either more or less directly, with the big themes of the work, or with literature in general, and which thereby constitute concrete symbols of the big themes. Understood in a broad sense, thematics studies all contents and therefore includes all the aspects linked to the content, especially the characters and action of the text. This content, understood in the broad sense (that of "what is said"), is then interdefined with form ("how it is said"). See section 4.6 on content and form.

A theme can be seen in a more synthetic way (e.g., love as a whole) or more analytically (e.g., love broken down into three parts: X loves Y). A theme is either stereotyped or not. If it is stereotyped, it must appear in more than one work (e.g., love, the unfaithful lover). If it is not stereotyped, it will constitute either a nullax (a phenomenon of which there are no occurrences), such as the theme of a one-legged bacterium that loves downhill skiing, or a hapax (a phenomenon that appears only once), starting from the (perhaps debatable) principle that a theme that appears in two different works is already stereotyped, even if only weakly. Some stereotyped themes are considered to be topoi, in the sense of stereotypes of content (e.g., love is not generally considered a topos, but impossible love and unfaithful lover are); see section 4.27 on topos.

Thematic criticism, as a specific critical current (espoused in the Francophone world by Blin, Poulet, Richard, Starobinski, Rousset) rather than the general analysis of textual themes ...

> bases its analysis on an existential conception of writing: it is then a question of elucidating the relationship between the "living" and "saying" of an author [...]. Thematicians therefore study these themes in order to produce insights into the structure of the work or of the author's universe.
> (Bénac and Réauté, 1993: 236)

The author's life then elucidates the themes, just as the themes elucidate the author's life.

The term "thematic analysis" (or figurative, thematic, and axiological analysis) is used to refer to a semiotic analysis that distinguishes between three kinds of content, and in which Joseph Courtés is the major specialist: figures are contents that directly evoke one or more of the five senses (e.g., "chocolate" [taste], "hard" [touch], "night" [sight], etc.); themes are contents that do not directly evoke any of the five senses ("glory," "hope," etc.); axiological analysis consists in attributing a thymic value or modality (euphoric or positive, dysphoric or negative, etc.) to a theme or a figure (e.g., in the expression "I hate apple pie," the figure "apple pie" is marked as negative, dysphoric).

Symbolic analysis is the study of symbols, which are ultimately a particular type of theme. If topical analysis is the study of topoi, in the sense of stereotyped themes, symbolic analysis is a subdivision of it, although symbols may not be stereotyped in all systems or in any particular system (see section 4.27 on topos, and for a typology of systems, see section 5.44 on stylistics). The symbol has two sides: the symbolizer (e.g., weighing scales) and the symbolized (e.g., justice). In symbolic analysis, as in any form of analysis, there are certain traps to be avoided, and in this case the greatest risks are those of listing and anaculturalism. In the case of listing, one reads a work, without nuance, by applying a pre-established and universal grid such as a dictionary of symbols, just as one might "analyze" a dream using a dictionary of dreams, such that every pointed object is interpreted as a phallus, etc. In the case of anaculturalism (which is to culture as anachronism is to time), one interprets a work by applying symbolic systems from an outside culture (e.g., given that, in certain tribes, the big toe is a symbol of fertility, one views any appearance of a toe in any text as a symbolic of fertility, even if the text does not come from that culture). The emic approach, which uses the internal categories of the culture associated with the object under analysis, is necessarily, barring errors in the analysis itself, non-anachronistic and non-anaculturalistic. On the other hand, the etic approach, which uses categories external to the culture associated with the object being analyzed, is often anaculturalistic and sometimes also anachronistic, but it can also still be relevant and productive. For example, Freud uses an etic approach that is relevant (at least from a psychoanalytic perspective) when he sees in *Oedipus Rex*, a play from Greek Antiquity, the perfect symbolization of the concept of the Oedipus complex, which he had just invented or discovered.

For a typology of symbols, see section 5.44 on stylistics.

Authors: Gaston Bachelard, Georges Blin, Georges Poulet, Jean-Pierre Richard, Joseph Courtés, Tzvetan Todorov, etc.

5.47 Versification (study of)

Versification, as an object of study, is a set of more or less codified textual aspects that are specific to texts that are (1) versified (in the sense of being divided into verses, either by line breaks on the written page, or by means of the verbal delivery of the speaker); and/or (2) follow a rhyme scheme; and/or (3) follow a scheme of syllabic measurement and arrangement (such as schemes of metric feet or of fixed syllabic verse lengths); as well as some aspects that are in some cases shared with other textual forms (e.g., alliteration and assonance, rhythm). These three elements must be distinguished from one another, since there are, for example, texts with a rhyme scheme and fixed verse lengths but no metric feet, texts with metric feet but no rhyme scheme, etc. In fact, all combinations of these three elements are possible.

Versification is:

> traditionally, the set of rules that govern the teaching and practice of writing in verse—rules that obviously vary according to time and culture. It is also, in modern literary analysis, the set of phenomena that constitute the specificity of verse.
>
> (Demougin, 1992: 1692)

I would add that the same rules that guide the production of texts also guide the reception of those same texts. I would also add that the study of the specificity of versified texts presupposes the study of the specificity of non-versified texts, and these two studies must obviously also identify the things that are common to both types of texts (e.g., rhythm is found in both classes of texts, although to varying extents in non-versified texts such as prose, concrete poetry, visual poetry, etc.). As always, the differences between phenomena can be of nature (qualitative) and/or of degree (quantitative).

The study of versification can be carried out independently, or alternatively in combination with the identification of non-versified elements, such as the contents (signifieds, themes, etc.) of a versified text. The well-known analysis of Baudelaire's sonnet "The Cats" by Lévi-Strauss and Jakobson (1962) is an example of a combined analysis of versification and contents (including grammatical contents), linked to an analysis of matters of arrangement (which take into account the linear position of phenomena in the text).

Authors: Maurice Grammont, Jean-Michel Gouvard, Jean Mazaleyrat, Michael D. Hurley and Michael O'Neill, John Hollander, etc.

5.48 World literature

The term *Weltliteratur* was first coined by Johann Wolfgang von Goethe, who declared in 1827 that "the epoch of world literature is at hand" (quoted in Damrosch, 2003: 1). Since then, the study of world literature has become a major field within literary studies. World literature approaches transcend national understandings of literature in favor of a global perspective of the broader evolutions of genre and form in order to gain new insights into contested relationships between center and periphery, high and low literature, and canonical and popular texts. David Damrosch defines world literature as encompassing "all literary works that circulate beyond their culture of origin, either in translation or in their original language" (Damrosch, 2003: 4). The political and cultural aspects of the translation and localized reading practices of foreign literatures are closely related to this approach. World literature theorists work with a huge corpus of texts to track formal changes across a defined historical period. World literature can thus be understood as an alternative or supplement to, and critique of, the "close reading" methodology adopted by most literary scholarship. As with the global capitalist system, a world literature approach understands the literary sphere as a united but unequal system: "like the political world and the world market, world literature is seen as one system, albeit one that is characterized by difference and unequal conditions for exercising influence" (Thomsen, 2011: 138).

Franco Moretti is the most important theorist of world literature and its related methodological tools. Moretti proposes a "distant reading" model for the study of world literature that allows readers to "focus on units that are much smaller or much larger than the text: devices, themes, tropes—or genres and systems" (Moretti, 2000: n.p.). Moretti's distant reading entails dramatically altering the scale at which literary criticism takes place in order to understand the systems and patterns emerging at the global level. This is the case for his study of the novel, which bypasses the Anglo-French influence to show how the novel arose after 1750 "just about everywhere as a compromise between West European patterns and local reality" (Moretti, 2000: n.p.). Moretti's process is described as follows: "you define a unit of analysis [...] and then follow its metamorphoses in a variety of environments—until, ideally, *all* of literary history becomes a long chain of related experiments."

Authors: Franco Moretti, David Damrosch, Pascale Casanova, Gisèle Sapiro, Christopher Prendergast, etc.

Sam Gormley

6 Corpus

6.1 Introduction

A corpus, in the broad sense, consists of: (1) one or more semiotic products (e.g., written texts) that are preferably complete (i.e., not just extracts from a complete product); chosen either on the basis of (2) personal taste or inclination (a self-selected corpus); or on the basis of (3) specific criteria (a constructed corpus) that are objective (or at least objectivated), conscious, explicit (they are presented to the reader), rigorous, respected (they are applied correctly and consistently), and relevant to the desired application; and (4) that are the object of an analysis.[1]

In principle, when a group of semiotic products are analyzed together, it is considered that they constitute, in one way or another, a corpus.

Objective and rigorous criteria: a group of products can be chosen simply out of personal preference, in the case of a self-selected corpus. This personal preference can of course be paralleled by conscious, explicit, rigorous, and relevant criteria. Note that a random sampling is an objective and rigorous criterion of selection, but it is then necessary to check that the resulting selection is relevant to the desired application.

NOTE: CORPORA WITH A SINGLE SEMIOTIC PRODUCT

The analysis of a constructed corpus (with specific criteria) consisting of a single product is not the same thing as the analysis of a single product chosen out of personal preference. It can happen that the particular combination of the selected criteria leads to the construction of a corpus with a single product. This is not the same thing as deciding, on the basis of

---

1 Rastier narrows the definition further by adding that the corpus must be homogeneous in terms of discourse (literary, philosophical, theological, etc.) and genre (detective novel, serious novel, etc.). This is how he defines the corpus: "A corpus is a structured grouping of complete texts, documented, possibly enriched by [digital] labeling, and assembled: (1) in a theoretically self-reflexive way that takes account of discourse and genre, and (2) in a way that is practically oriented toward a range of applications" (Rastier, 2011: 33–34).

DOI: 10.4324/9781003179795-9

criteria that are extraneous to the intended analysis (such as the analyst's liking for a particular work, or their curiosity about it), to focus the analysis on this one work.

Relevant criteria: "The novels on my bookshelf" is an example of a criterion that is objective, conscious, explicit (if it is presented to the reader), rigorous, and respected (if it is properly applied), but not relevant to academic analysis in general.

Conscious, explicit, and respected criteria: the criteria used to construct the corpus must be consciously conceived by the analyst, clearly shared with the reader of the analysis, and consistently respected at the time of the actual constitution of the corpus. The criteria must not only be presented to the reader but also justified and discussed: Why these criteria? What other criteria were possible? Why were they rejected? What are the possible positive or negative effects (especially the introduction of undesirable biases) of the selected criteria on the results of the analysis?

Complete products: sometimes the term "corpus" is used to refer to a collection of parts taken from complete semiotic products (individual words or extracts from a text, etc.) or even units isolated from almost any context (e.g., the individual words of a language, not taken from any specific text). However, these are not corpora in the strict sense. To take the example of written or oral texts, "the text is, for an evolved linguistics [one that addresses phenomena larger than the sentence], the *minimal* unit, and the corpus is the whole in which this unit takes on its meaning" (Rastier, 2011: 33). That said, "*working sub-corpora* in individual studies vary according to the particular stage of the study and may contain only relevant passages from the text or texts being studied" (Rastier, 2001: 36). I will return to the subject of working sub-corpora later.

The meaning of a product depends on the corpus in which it is situated, by virtue of the principle that the global (in this case the corpus) determines the local (in this case a particular semiotic product in this corpus). If we change the corpus in which the product is situated, the product necessarily changes its nature and meaning. Thus, the maximal unit of analysis is not the text, but the corpus in which the analyzed text is situated, even if the existence of the corpus remains implicit.

When studying a corpus of texts, one must address the edition of the text that is to be used. In most cases the text has already been published, often in several different editions with different publishers, and it is then advisable to present the list of possible editions, and the strengths and weaknesses of each edition in general and in relation to the research being undertaken, especially with regard to their effects on the results (and especially the introduction of biases). The choice of a particular edition is then presented and justified. Usually, if an established reference edition exists, this will be chosen, and ideally this will be a scholarly edition with a critical apparatus of notes, textual variants, etc.

The main aspects of the corpus are its typological forms, its epistemological nature, its objectives, the stages of its initial treatment, its representativeness, and its homogeneity.[2]

6.2 Typology

We can first distinguish between a corpus of application and a corpus of illustration. These two cases correspond to two ways of using an approach (e.g., semiotics, narratology) with respect to the corpus. In the first case, an approach is used to analyze a semiotic product or group of products (e.g., a group of literary texts); the approach is then a means to an end, where the end is the analysis of the semiotic product. In the second case, the semiotic product or products can be used to illustrate, complete, modify, validate, or invalidate an approach, or even, if the approach has not yet been fully constituted, to establish it; it is then the semiotic product itself that is a means to an end, and the end concerns the treatment of the approach.

Rastier distinguishes—in relation to texts, but this can be generalized to any semiotic product—four levels of definition for the corpus:

> (1) The archive gathers all the documents accessible for a task of description or analysis. It is not a corpus, because it is not constituted for a specific research project. (2) The reference corpus is constituted by [the] set of texts with which the study corpus will be contrasted. (3) The study corpus is delimited by the needs of the research project. (4) Finally, working sub-corpora vary depending on the particular stage of the study and may contain only relevant passages of the text or texts being studied. For example, in *L'analyse thématique des données textuelles: l'exemple des sentiments* [an analysis produced by Rastier and collaborators][,] the archive is the Frantext database [a textual bank containing thousands of French texts], the reference corpus is made up of 350 novels published between 1830 and 1970, the study corpus is made up of passages containing nouns denoting feelings, and the sub-corpora contain the contexts [i.e., the surrounding words] for particular feelings [e.g., love, ambition].
>
> (Rastier, 2011: 36)

I would extend this list to distinguish between the following levels of definition for the corpus:

1. the study corpus (or primary corpus, that is, the corpus of primary texts): the text or texts studied in the edition or editions chosen;
2. the reference corpus: the texts with which the study corpus is contrasted (in particular, by establishing comparative relations, observing operations of transformation, identifying norms, deviations, etc.);

---

2 I would like to thank Éric Trudel for drawing my attention to the texts by Mayaffre (2002) and Habert (2005).

3. the metacorpus: the corpus of earlier analytical texts devoted to the texts in the study corpus and those in the reference corpus (the corpus of analytical texts devoted to the study corpus—and in a broader sense, also to the reference corpus—can be termed the secondary corpus, that is, the corpus of secondary texts);
4. the aspect corpus: theoretical texts on the aspect or aspects under study (e.g., texts devoted to the concept of the theme in general);
5. the approach corpus: theoretical texts on the selected approach or approaches (e.g., texts on thematic analysis).

We could also add the following categories of corpus to this list:

6. the configuration corpus (e.g., texts on the theme of love);
7. the proposition corpus (e.g., texts on the proposition that Hamlet is really in love with Ophelia).

For the distinction between aspect, approach, configuration, and proposition see Chapter 2 on the components of analysis.

6.3 Epistemological nature: a corpus is a relative and determining object

A corpus is not a set of raw "data" (in the etymological sense of things that have been "given"), since its data are not "given" but always constructed: "as always in the sciences of culture, data are made up of what one 'gives' oneself [...], and the perspective with which the corpus is constituted inevitably conditions the subsequent research" (Rastier, 2001: 86).

A corpus (or a theory, approach, or concept) can be treated from an etic perspective and/or from an emic perspective. The emic approach uses the analytic categories inherent in the work and/or the culture to which the work belongs, whereas the etic approach uses analytic categories external to the work and/or the culture to which the work belongs. In principle, an emic approach can be sufficient in itself, but an etic approach must be accompanied by an emic approach; in fact, a combination of the two approaches is generally preferable. For example, if in a novel a tomato is considered a vegetable: from an emic perspective, this tomato must be considered a vegetable and placed in the "vegetable" theme together with cucumbers and celery; from an etic perspective, we know that it is in fact a fruit and it will therefore be placed (in addition) in the "fruit" theme, together with apples and oranges (since most readers, and probably the author of the work, also know that tomatoes are scientifically classified as fruit). Another example: if we analyze the underlying ideology of a novel, we must in principle identify the ideology of this novel and not simply superimpose an ideology that is external or even anachronistic and/or anaculturalistic (even if the latter is held to be more accurate, or even the only true way of seeing things); for example, we should avoid analyzing a medieval text using

Marxist (or postcolonial, etc.) analytic categories, at least without also taking into account the feudal ideology that is necessarily at work in this text.

6.4 Objectives

The main objectives relating to the corpus are, according to Rastier:

> testing and improving its homogeneity, its representativeness, its coding (e.g., by indicating the genre of each text); producing relevant subsets of the corpus for a particular category of inquiry [i.e., analysis]; using it as a means for the semantic analysis [or other type of analysis] of textual structures.
>
> (Rastier, 2001: 87)

6.5 The stages of the treatment of the corpus

According to Rastier (2001: 87), "the process of validating a corpus consists of the following stages: an initial assumption of coherence [the analyst assumes that a coherent collection can be established using the selected criteria]; establishment; enrichment; annotation; commentary; and use."

6.6 The representativeness of the corpus is relative

As Rastier (2001: 86) puts it, "The *representativeness* [of the corpus] is not objective and depends on the types of use that are intended for it." A corpus is representative if it corresponds to the "legitimate" needs and scope of the research being undertaken:

> The corpus is a heuristic object [that contributes to the discovery of new knowledge]. It is an arbitrary [i.e., ad hoc] construction, a relative composition that has meaning, value, and relevance only in relation to the particular questions that we are addressing, the answers that we seek, and the results that we find. It is the researcher's intention that is important here and gives the corpus its meaning.
>
> (Mayaffre, 2002: 55)

This being said, the nature of this initial intention is constrained by rational principles: there are research aims that are questionable in themselves, such as those that are frivolous or based on inaccurate presuppositions, and there are corpora that are inadequate for the aims set by the research project being undertaken, or inadequate for the interpretation that is drawn from them. I will return to the subject of possible errors relating to the corpus in section 6.8.

Since a corpus is used on the basis that it is representative, it is necessary to explain precisely what it is representative of. This oversight is particularly a problem in linguistics: "Curiously, the expression *representative corpus* is sometimes used without specifying which linguistic population the corpus in question is supposed to represent: French [or any other language] as a whole, literary language, colloquial language, specialized language ..." (Habert, 2005: 17).

If a corpus is used on the basis that it is representative of a *population* (in the technical sense of a set of elements that are the object of a statistical study), there are two particular errors to avoid:

> From a statistical point of view, we can consider a corpus to be a sample of a population (of language events). Like any sample, a corpus is subject to two types of statistical errors that risk undermining any generalizations from it [...]: "uncertainty" (*random error*) and "deformation" (*bias error*). Uncertainty occurs when a sample is too small to represent the true population with sufficient accuracy. Deformation occurs when the characteristics of a sample are systematically different from those of the population that the sample is intended to reflect.
>
> (Habert, 2005: 17)

6.7 Homogeneity is relative

In textual analyses, the generic status of the texts is generally the most important criterion of homogeneity, but this is not always the case:

> Generic homogeneity should be the default choice, even for stylistic research [...]. As a general rule, semantic studies of texts should focus on corpora that are as homogeneous as possible in terms of their genre [e.g., serious novel, funeral oration], or at least in terms of their type of discourse [e.g., literary, religious]: indeed, a text can "lose" its meaning if it is placed among inappropriate texts, since comparison with them does not allow for the selection of relevant contrasts. The need for homogeneity is not, however, absolute, since philological criticism can lead to the problematization of variations in the corpus.
>
> (Rastier, 2001: 86)

If the corpus is judged to be insufficiently homogeneous, it is because the criteria that led to its constitution were too broad. If the corpus is insufficiently heterogeneous, internal contrasts will be more difficult to find.

6.8 The main problems relating to the corpus

We have already encountered, both directly and implicitly, some possible errors in the constitution and use of a corpus. In particular, a constructed (rather than self-selected) corpus may not be based, as it should be, on (sufficiently) objective, rigorous, explicit, relevant, and respected criteria. I shall now summarize, without claiming to be exhaustive, the possible errors or problems encountered in relation to constructed corpora (some points also apply to self-selected corpora):

1. There is no corpus of "literary texts" (in the narrow sense of poems, novels, etc.), such as in a study that is focused on a text of literary theory and that does not refer to a corpus of illustration composed of straightforwardly "literary texts." Some literary critics do not approve of such a practice, and their objections should be anticipated through counter-argumentation. These critics do not consider texts concerned with literary approaches or theories to be literary works. Obviously, this view is open to criticism.

2. The corpus is not a corpus of application (where the analysis of the corpus is an end in itself) but only a corpus of illustration (e.g., serving to illustrate, constitute, validate, invalidate, nuance, transform, or complete an approach). Some critics do not approve of such a practice and consider that an analysis should also feature a corpus of application. Their objections should be anticipated through counter-argumentation.

3. There is no literary corpus, even in a broad sense, such as in a study of texts, concepts, or theories that are not literary or do not address literature. The inventory of what is or is not a literary product, in either a narrow or a broad sense, varies depending on the person, institution, etc. Where there is ambiguity, anticipate objections through counter-argumentation.

4. The criteria for the construction of the corpus are not appropriate (insufficiently objective, rigorous, or relevant).

5. The criteria for the construction of the corpus are not applied properly or consistently.

6. The editions of texts to be analyzed are poorly selected, either because the chosen editions contain errors or simply because other editions would be preferable. Another error of this sort consists in using an earlier version of the text in question, unless there is a particular reason for doing so.

7. The corpus is not sufficiently homogeneous (e.g., it contains both recipes and novels by different authors). In principle, a corpus is made up of works of the same genre. If it consists of texts belonging to different genres, one can analyze the texts belonging to each genre together, as separate sub-corpora, then compare the results produced from the different genres.

8. The corpus is not representative of the elements that it is supposed to represent (e.g., if one makes generalizations concerning all the novels written by a particular author on the basis of just one novel that happens to be very different from the others). This problem is more likely to occur when the analysis is of the sampling type. The same principle of representativeness applies to the internal analysis of each text in the corpus (e.g., if one analyzes a single chapter of a novel on the basis of its presumed representativeness of all the chapters).

9. The corpus is too small. This problem may appear in one of three ways: (1) the analysis of a small corpus, such as a single short poem, may not provide enough material for the required size of the analysis (e.g., the requirement for a

doctoral dissertation to be of a sufficient length, corresponding to a substantial work of analysis); (2) even if a small corpus provides a significant amount of material for analysis, some evaluators may consider that the scope of the analysis is too small; (3) finally, the corpus may be too small to support the generalizations that the researcher wishes to draw from it. In fact, with the exception of the third case mentioned here, the problem of an excessively small corpus is rarely encountered in the analyses undertaken in a pedagogical setting. The problem is usually the opposite, owing to the limitations on time and word count faced by, for example, a doctoral student in writing their dissertation.

10. The corpus is too large. Most projects for a work of literary analysis begin by envisaging a corpus that is too large and/or a subject matter that is too broad (too many aspects are targeted, too many approaches are used, too many propositions, including hypotheses, are put forward, etc.).

11. A corpus is selected that has already been analyzed too much in the past (e.g., Shakespeare's best known plays). The problem can be circumvented if a new proposition (e.g., a novel hypothesis), approach, and/or aspect is used. The fact remains, however, that in these cases establishing the state of the question (the literature review)—surveying what has been said about these known works—is a long and complex process, and finding an original angle can be difficult. In short, a corpus may have been over-analyzed or under-analyzed in terms of its signifieds (semantic contents), and over-analyzed or under-analyzed in terms of its signifiers. It may also be over-analyzed or under-analyzed with regard to phenomena other than the signifiers and signifieds, such as the author's life or the artistic context of its time.

12. The corpus is uninteresting (it contains bad or mediocre works). Obviously, whether the corpus is considered interesting or not depends on the particular readers, institutions, approaches, etc. However, the analysis of bad or mediocre works can allow a better understanding, by contrast, of the qualities of works that are considered to be acceptable, good, excellent, or exceptional. Furthermore, mediocre works, which are inevitably more numerous, are more representative of the genre in question or of the society in which they were produced compared with excellent works, and especially compared with those considered to be masterpieces.

13. The approach is inappropriate for the corpus, such as the use of a criminological approach for novels in which there is little or no reference to crime. However, in general, any approach can be applied to any corpus. In short, one should not limit oneself to the approaches that are most clearly called for by the corpus (e.g., a psychoanalytical approach for a text that talks about psychoanalysis), especially as these more obvious ways of treating the text are more likely to have already been used. Moreover, even when the approach does not work well for the analyzed text, or even fails to produce convincing results, these problems can be interesting in themselves for the understanding both of the approach and of the work, just as, in the natural sciences, we can say that "no result is a result."

7 Aspects of theater

7.1 Definitions of literature and its main genres

As a rough guide, let us define the major traditional genres of literature, starting with the broad category of the literary text. In fact, the major traditional genres can be described as "super-genres," since it seems that genres in the strict sense are constituted at a more specific level (e.g., not at the level of narrative or the novel, but rather that of the detective novel, or even a narrower category such as the noir detective novel).

7.1.1 The literary text

- A text (oral and/or written) that is primarily intended to produce an esthetic effect.

An esthetic effect, by and large, is manifested in the body (goose bumps, increased heart rate, etc.), in the "heart" (affects, emotions, etc.), and/or in the "head" (admiration for formal complexity, the creation of a new idea, etc.). A literary text is supposed to produce an esthetic effect, but this does not necessarily mean that it will actually produce an effect in a given reader.

The literary text is defined in opposition to the non-literary text. The difference can be viewed as qualitative and/or quantitative, and it can relate to what is said (the content) and/or how it is said (the form). For example, should we characterize the literary text by its greater use of stylistic rhetorical figures (a quantitative difference) and/or by the presence of specific stylistic rhetorical figures (a qualitative difference), while acknowledging that any text, whether literary or non-literary, contains some stylistic rhetorical figures? We can ask the same question regarding the distinction between poetic literary texts and non-poetic literary texts; thus, we can consider that, compared to literary texts in general, poetic literary texts contain more rhetorical figures (in quantity and/or in variety) and/or specific rhetorical figures.

The defining, or at least characteristic feature of literature is its literarity, which can obviously be conceived in different ways. One of these conceptions of literarity uses the criterion of stylistic rhetorical figures (which may be

DOI: 10.4324/9781003179795-10

specifically literary or merely characteristically literary, since stylistic rhetorical figures are used outside literary texts, and indeed outside texts). One can also speak of a specifically (or characteristically) literary esthetic effect.

7.1.2 The essay

- An argumentative literary text in prose (with some exceptions);
- containing totally or partially subjective argumentation (e.g., an intuition, an opinion);
- generally written in the first person;
- on a topic that may be literary, philosophical, social, scientific (non-specialist), etc.;
- generally not very technical (using few or simplified technical terms);
- written in a literary style (as opposed to, for example, the style of a scientific article).

7.1.3 Poetry

- A generally non-argumentative literary text;
- generally not very narrative;
- either fictional or not (e.g., relating lived experience);
- generally short (in the case of modern poetry);
- in verse (traditional poetry is generally in verse, using meter and rhyme), in prose, or some other form (e.g., pictorial poetry);
- presents a characteristically literary density of signifiers (rhythms, sonorities, metaplasms, etc.);
- presents a characteristically literary density of signifieds (images, etc.; it offers the reader more numerous, more complex, and subtler interpretive pathways).

7.1.4 Literary narrative discourse (the novel, short story, tale, etc.)

- A literary text that is generally non-argumentative (with some exceptions, such as the *roman à thèse*, i.e., a novel intended to promote or defend an idea);
- written in prose (in its modern manifestations);
- short (e.g., the short story) or long (e.g., the novel);
- relating a real (e.g., autobiography) or fictional (e.g., the novel) story, or one with a mixed or ambiguous truth status (e.g., autofiction).

7.1.5 Theater

- A bimodal genre, consisting of a script (the published or unpublished text of a play) and performance;

- considered either as literary, or partially literary (in the case of the script), or as outside literature;
- the script is considered either as literary or paraliterary (such as a television or film screenplay), and underlies in principle an actual theatrical perform-ance (which has been performed or is still to be performed);
- the performance is considered as being non-literary, except as an expres-sion of the written text;
- the script consists of the lines to be spoken by actors and stage directions (e.g., instructions for the actors);
- generally non-argumentative (except for *théâtre à thèse*, by analogy with the *roman à thèse*);
- it depicts either a true story (a historical figure or real but unknown people), fictional events, or a mixture of the two;
- it features at least one character (usually embodied in the performance by an actor), who speaks and participates in actions (movement, conflict, etc.);
- the performance involves several semiotic codes other than the textual, some of which are essential and some optional: make-up, costume, hairstyle, facial expression, movement, action accompanied by music, sound effects, lighting, stage sets, props, etc.;
- the text may be in verse (e.g., classical French theater) or prose (e.g., modern theater) or both (e.g., *Hamlet*).

7.2 Text and performance

The aspects of the literary text (in general) discussed in Chapter 4 can be applied to theater, with some adjustments in certain cases. However, there are obviously some aspects that are unique to theater, and that are not found (except possibly as a theme) in non-theatrical literary texts. Let us consider some of these aspects.

To begin with, we can examine the written text of a play (the script) and/ or the theatrical performance. The status of the text in relation to the perform-ance is like that of a musical score in relation to the musical performance based on that score. The text may precede the performance, as is usually the case, or it may be the transcription of a particular performance (if, for example, one creates a transcription of a theatrical improvisation).

7.2.1 The two main aspects of the theatrical text

The theatrical text (excluding any images that might accompany it, etc.) consists of lines (to be spoken by the actors) and stage directions. There are several kinds of stage directions (see diagram in Figure 7.1). The theatrical text should be distinguished from the actual enunciation of the words during a performance, which is here referred to as "speech," and which constitutes a text of its own, made up of physical auditory linguistic stimuli, signifiers, and signifieds. It must

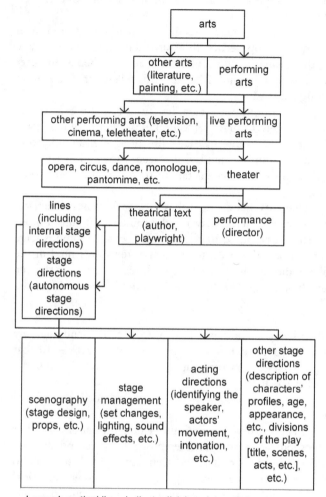

Legend: vertical lines indicate divisions into sub-types, horizontal lines indicate parts of a whole.

Figure 7.1 Arts, theater, and stage directions

also be distinguished from any written text that appears in the performance, for example, if text is projected onto a screen behind the stage.

We can arrange theatrical texts along a spectrum ranging from, at one end, texts without any stage directions at all (or almost none, since it is difficult to avoid indicating divisions in the performance or the names of speakers, which also count as stage directions) and, at the other end, texts made up only of stage directions (such as Beckett's *Act Without Words*). This is complicated by the fact that in some avant-garde plays the stage directions, or at least some of them, are meant to be spoken (e.g., by a narrator).

Often the lines contain implicit stage directions, which are referred to as "internal stage directions" (as opposed to the unspoken "autonomous stage directions," of the sort that I mentioned above). For example, when a character speaks the line "You are coughing hard, Madam," this tells us that the other character must have coughed hard.

In theory, all the types of autonomous stage directions can also exist in the form of internal stage directions. In practice, some kinds of autonomous stage directions are difficult to produce as internal stage directions (e.g., an indication of the speaker's name, the division of the play into scenes, etc.). However, in a non-realist play it is quite possible for characters to state which act and scene they find themselves in.

Formally, one of the elements that distinguishes theater from non-theatrical literary forms (but not from film screenplays) is the presence of autonomous stage directions. But it should be noted that some forms of autonomous stage directions can be found in non-theatrical texts, such as texts presented in the form of dialogue, which indicate who is speaking in the same way as in theater. For example, in Diderot's philosophical dialogue *Rameau's Nephew* we find the following exchange:

> ME—No, but when I've got nothing better to do, I enjoy spending a few moments watching other people doing a good job of it. HIM—In that case, you don't enjoy yourself very often; apart from Legal and Philidor, the rest of them don't have a clue.
>
> (Diderot, 2019: 17–18)

Finally, some stage directions have equivalents in non-theatrical texts. For example, in a novel, the subdivisions into numbered or titled parts and chapters are the equivalent of the indications of acts and scenes in a play. It should also be noted that a blank page or other significant space can act as a stage direction, both in a theatrical text (e.g., indicating a change of act in a play) and in a non-theatrical literary text (e.g., indicating the beginning of a new part of a novel).

7.3 The performance and the imagined performance

Let us use the term "imagined performance" to refer to the idea that one has in mind, while reading the theatrical text and with the help of the autonomous and internal stage directions, of what the actual performance could be (or what it may have been in the past). In other words, the terminology relating to theatrical performances, which is summarized in Figure 7.1 (p. 155), can be used not only to study "real" performances, but also imagined performances created using the theatrical text.

Other forms of literary texts similarly give rise to mental representations of the characters and events (we read a novel and imagine "the scene" in our minds), but these mental representations have a different status and undoubtedly take on different forms: while reading a theatrical text, we may create in our minds a mental representation of the action, as if these events were really taking place before our eyes; alternatively, we may create in our minds an imagined performance, as if we were watching the events performed on a stage by actors. In theory, throughout a reading of a play, one could experience only "realist" mental representations without any imagined performance, or on the contrary, one could exclusively experience an imagined performance. In practice, we undoubtedly oscillate between "realist" mental representations and imagined performances. Even in cases where a reader would not fully visualize an imagined performance, surely their "realist" mental representations of the events would still be marked by an awareness that the theatrical text is ultimately intended as the basis for a real performance. Conversely, when attending a real theatrical performance, spectators can form an idea of the theatrical text, with its lines and stage directions (especially if the spectator has a good knowledge of theater). They may also imagine the scene being played out before them as if it were happening in real life.

Among these mental representations or images, we can distinguish those that are, in theory, obligatory (if we are told that a certain female character has brown hair, for example, we *must* visualize her with brown hair) and those that are optional (e.g., if we are not told anything about the color of a certain character's hair). Our mental images may or may not conform to what the text asks or allows us to imagine, and may therefore be said to be adequate or inadequate (e.g., if someone sees a blonde-haired woman where the text has mentioned a woman with red hair, they are failing to conform to an obligatory representation). Fortunately, there is no "representation police" to sanction such "errors" in our representations, whether they are made deliberately or not.

7.4 Aspects of performance: the languages of theater

Figure 7.2, adapted from Kowzan (1992, 49), presents the semiotic codes or languages (broadly conceived) of theater, describes them, and classifies them according to several different criteria. It should be noted that some performances use, in addition to sight and hearing, the senses of touch (e.g., if actors touch the spectators, or if pieces of velvet are distributed to the spectators), taste (e.g., if bread is distributed), or smell (e.g., the smell of cigarette smoke). Other sensory experiences other than the five standard senses may also come into play (e.g., kinesthetic or somesthetic experience).

Let us consider these languages in more detail.

In theory, each of these languages can be manifested in a dynamic form (which changes over time) and in a static form (because it appears only for a moment, or because the phenomenon remains the same over a period of time). For example, a prop—apparently a static element—can enter or leave the stage, or be transformed, whereas music—apparently a dynamic element—can be static if a single note is sustained relentlessly throughout a whole play.

No.	Language	Family of languages	Language support	Space or Time	Type of signs
	LINGUISTIC				
1	verbal language (speech)	words spoken on the basis of the theatrical text	actor	time	auditory signs (produced by the actor)
2	phonic verbal language	phonic aspects of expression (tone, accent, etc.)			
3	textual language	text depicted on stage	outside the actor	space	visual signs (scripto-visual) (outside the actor)
4	graphic textual language	graphic aspects of the text (font style, size, etc.)			
	NON-LINGUISTIC				
5	facial expression	bodily expression	actor	space and time	visual signs (produced by the actor)
6	gesture				
7	movement				
8	make-up	external appearance of the actor		space	
9	masks				
10	hairstyle				
11	costume				
12	props	appearance of the stage area	outside the actor		visual signs (outside the actor)
13	stage design			space and time	
14	lighting				
15	music	non-linguistic sound effects		time	auditory signs (produced by the actor, e.g., singing, or outside the actor)
16	sound effects				auditory signs (produced by the actor, e.g., footsteps, or outside the actor)

Figure 7.2 The languages of theatrical performance

In theory, each of these languages has a visible/invisible version, and an audible/inaudible version. For example, an actor, a mask, or a facial expression may be invisible if the actor performs with their back to the audience, if a curtain or panel obscures the view, or if the play is conducted in absolute darkness. The same applies to audible phenomena (speech, music, sound effects), which may be drowned out by other audible phenomena or may be of such a low volume that they are only barely heard or not at all (even though the spectators are aware that the sounds have occurred). Each of these languages also exist in negative, minimalist, normal, and maximalist versions. For example, full nudity can be conceived as a negative version of the language of costume, a fig leaf would be a minimalist version, a suit and tie a normal version, and a costume of architectural proportions, almost a set in itself, would be a maximalist version. There are also literal/metaphorical versions of these languages: lighting may be used to indicate on the ground where the walls of a house are situated, the head of one actor may act as a toothbrush for another actor, etc.

In relation to all these possible versions (and others), the manifestation of these languages in a particular play can correspond to a form that is expected (the norm), or to a form that is unexpected (a deviation from the norm). The fact that it is "expected" does not necessarily mean that it is desired and positive. The expected form varies according to the generic levels in question, and the instance of these genres constituted by a particular performance. Here is an example of the generic levels involved in a given performance: theater in general > expressionist theater > theater by this expressionist author > this particular expressionist play. For example, the expected form of make-up in an expressionist play is a strongly accentuated, stylized make-up, which is opposed to the expected form of make-up in theater in general, or at least in mainstream theater, in which make-up is typically moderate and realist.

Phonic verbal language includes (some elements may overlap): intonation, volume, articulation, rhythm (pauses, speed, acceleration/deceleration, silences, flow), rhythmic accents, accent, pronunciation, timbre, pitch, etc.

Graphic textual language includes font (Times, Arial, etc.), size, forms of emphasis (bold, italics, underlining, etc.), color, layout, etc.

Gesture here refers to any bodily positioning, especially of the limbs. Gesture can be dynamic or static (posture).

Movement is related to the position ("static" movement) or the change in position ("dynamic" movement) of an element in the three spatial axes (up/down, left/right, forward/back). A distinction can be made between the movement of an actor and the movement of other elements (props, light, etc.).

Make-up may not be limited to the face (e.g., in the case of a painted nude body) and includes the use of prostheses (e.g., a fake nose). Make-up can be dynamic (e.g., it can run down the face).

A prop is usually a small, movable object that is handled by an actor. A gun that stays in one place throughout the play is more a part of the stage set than it is a prop. On the other hand, a gigantic staircase, which would normally be a part of the set, but which is moved, can be considered a prop at least in part.

Elements that usually belong to another language can become a prop if they are handled. For example, a sword that remains in its scabbard throughout the play is an item of costume, but if it is drawn it becomes (also) a prop. Thus, in theory, it is the function of an element of the performance that determines which language it belongs to, and not that element's ontological status. Accordingly, an actor can very well become a prop, such as a bench.

Music, in the broad sense, is an intentional arrangement of sounds that are necessarily structured for esthetic purposes. By comparison, noises are sounds—single or multiple, intentional or not—which are generally not arranged, and are not produced for esthetic purposes.

Other languages (aspects of theater) or sub-languages (sub-aspects) may be considered: the languages of acting (e.g., naturalistic, symbolist, external acting, internal/method acting), staging (e.g., polished, rough), scenography (the organization of the stage space), etc.

7.4.1 Signifier, signified, stimulus, mental image

Each language can be subdivided into signifieds (semantic contents) and signifiers (the forms that convey the contents). For example, a red light (signifier) can signify love, desire, violence, or danger (signifieds).

In verbal language the signifiers are phonemes (or in the case of written text, graphemes, which roughly correspond to letters), punctemes (the signifiers of punctuation marks), and certain suprasegmental features (which develop over the course of several smaller units, such as over a series of words, as in the case of intonation).

Signifiers, as a type (as abstract models), are necessarily manifested in actual practice by physical perisemiotic stimuli (physical, because stimuli can also be mental; perisemiotic, because they are not strictly part of the sign but are associated with it). For example, phonemes (analyzed in phonetics), as abstract models, are manifested in practice by phones (analyzed in phonology). Thus, whether the phoneme *i* is concretely manifested in the phone *i* by a woman's or a man's speaking voice, with the corresponding differences in pitch and timbre, its value as a phoneme (which allows it to constitute the word "illusion," for example) does not change from one instance to another, and the signified associated with it will be the same each time (roughly speaking, the signified of the word "illusion" is: "that which does not conform to reality"). In general, many theorists confuse the signifier and the perisemiotic physical stimulus, or do not wish to make a distinction between the two. Similarly, they confuse the signified and the concept (the mental image) or do not wish to distinguish them. However, although a person who has been blind since birth may understand and use the signified "white" perfectly (and know, for example, that it is the opposite of the signified "black"), the mental image that they associate with it must necessarily be very different from the mental image experienced by a sighted person.

However, perisemiotic stimuli can produce other signifiers beside strictly linguistic ones. For example, the word "illusion" spoken with a particular accent may indicate the geographical origin of the speaker, for example, New York or the Southern United States. A very deep voice may indicate that the speaker is the villain in this particular play.

The same principles apply to graphemes. Graphemes are signifiers (abstract models), and are manifested by physical perisemiotic stimuli that can be called "graphs." For example, the *i* in the written word "illusion" projected above the stage may be formed in Times New Roman or in a Gothic font, but in either case its value as a grapheme remains the same. On the other hand, it is known that websites presenting racist content often use Gothic fonts. This means that, for the authors of these sites, a Gothic font conveys some meaning related to their ideology, or in other words, that a Gothic font has a signified and is therefore a signifier.

7.4.2 Dynamic and static languages

Some languages are generally dynamic, except in special cases: speech, gesture, movement, facial expression, music, sound effects, lighting. Others are generally or often static, and may not even change over the course of the whole play: masks, costume, make-up, stage design, props (when these are not moved, handled, or transformed).

If a language is dynamic, it can change at a key moment of the plot or the performance, thereby overdetermining its "meaning": for example, a character may have new make-up after an intermission, or wear a new costume for a new entrance on stage.

A generally dynamic language may have static moments or aspects. For example, gesture includes both the motionless position of a limb (e.g., arms hanging to the side of the body) and the change from one position to another. The same principle applies to movement, which relates both to a position in space and the change of position in space. We can even extend this static/dynamic distinction to other languages: make-up, hairstyle, clothing, etc.

7.4.3 The analysis of polysemiotic products

Theater is a polysemiotic product: that is, it combines several semiotic codes and languages. There are a number of different ways of characterizing polysemiotic products (films, websites, songs, plays, illustrated books, etc.). We can thus specify:

1. the inventory of coexisting semiotic codes (e.g., text and image in comics);
2. essential and optional semiotic codes (e.g., speech is essential in theater in its strict sense);
3. the type of presence of the semiotic codes: a factual presence (e.g., a film is projected during a play), thematic presence (the characters talk about a film), implied presence (a "montage" effect in the play brings to mind a cinematic montage), etc.;
4. the expected form (the norm) and the unexpected form (producing a deviation from the norm) of semiotic codes;

5. the comparative relations between semiotic codes: identity, similarity, opposition, alterity, analogy, etc. (e.g., between gestures of love and music associated with love, or, on the contrary, military music);
6. the logical relationship governing the copresence of semiotic codes: pre-supposition, mutual exclusion, etc.;
7. the temporal relations between semiotic codes: simultaneity, succession, etc.;
8. the effect of the copresence of semiotic codes (ranging from compositionality—the whole is equal to the sum of its parts—to holism—the whole is greater than the sum of its parts, or the parts are affected by the other copresent parts);
9. the degree of presence and the mixing of semiotic codes (the relative strength of each semiotic code, e.g., does the music remain in the back-ground or does it almost constitute a character?). The structure of the work may even tend toward an equivalence of each semiotic code, thereby pro-ducing a kind of neutral structure in which no semiotic code really stands out overall (even if a particular semiotic code is more prevalent at certain moments);
10. the prevalence and intensity of the mixing and unmixing (separations) of semiotic codes: separation, contiguity, intermingling, fusion, etc.; for example, is the music overlaid on the action (separation) or does it merge with it (fusion)?

For a more detailed treatment of these issues, see Hébert, 2020: 335–362.

7.5 Mixing of languages and the predominant language

I mentioned the mixing of languages and the degree of prevalence of these languages. Michel Vinaver (1993) distinguishes between plays where speech is an instrument of action (e.g., *Hamlet*) and those where speech is itself action (e.g., psychological or language-based plays, such as the plays of Chekhov or Beckett's *Waiting for Godot*). In other words, in the first case, action is the driving force of the play; in the second, speech is. However, in theory, each of the types of language present in theater can be the driving force of a play. For example, in prop-based theater—where, for example, a suitcase may become a house, then a boat, then a computer—it is the objects that are the driving force of the play, by means of their potential uses and meanings.

Part III

Components of the analytical text

8 The general structure of analysis

8.1 Introduction

This chapter presents the general model for an analytical text, consisting of: (1) the three classic parts of the introduction (the *topic lead-in*, the *topic statement*, and the *topic division*); (2) the three parts that I suggest using for the development (presentation of the *method*, *description* of the text, and *interpretation* of the data produced by the description); and (3) the two classic parts of the conclusion (*summary* and *opening up of the question*). I then provide an example of an analysis that follows this model.

8.2 General presentation

The term "analysis" refers to both a cognitive operation and a textual genre. This chapter provides a general method for producing an analytical text, or in other words, the textual manifestation of the cognitive operation of analysis.

A standard analytical text, like most argumentative essays, generally consists of three parts: the introduction, the development, and the conclusion.

Schematically, these three parts can be presented as follows: in the introduction you say what you are going to say, in the development you say it, and in the conclusion you say what you said.

The three operations to be carried out in order to produce an argumentative essay are as follows:

1. Write the development;
2. Write the introduction;
3. Write the conclusion.

Clearly, the order of composition does not correspond to the order of the parts in the final text. In practice, after writing the development, it becomes much easier to write an introduction that states precisely what the development is going to say, and a conclusion that is fully relevant.

DOI: 10.4324/9781003179795-12

8.3 The introduction and conclusion

The introduction (topic lead-in + topic statement + topic division) and conclusion (summary + opening up of the question) each account for about 10 percent of the text. For example, a 500-word text will have an introduction and a conclusion of about 50 words each. However, it may be less than 10 percent in a longer text, for instance less than 10 pages for a 100-page text.

> NOTE: THE SIZE OF THE INTRODUCTION
>
> In general, the shorter the text, the larger the introduction and conclusion will be as a proportion of the text's total length. For a 500-word text, the introduction may well be more than 50 words, whereas for a 100-page text, the introduction may take up fewer than 10 pages.

In situations where there is a limit on the total length of the text (which is common in educational contexts and for texts written for publication), the more words you use in the introduction, the fewer words you have available for the development, which is the real heart of the text. You should therefore avoid drawing out the introduction or conclusion unnecessarily.

In particular, the introduction should not contain any in-depth analysis of the main object of the analysis. The same applies to the conclusion, which should not contain any new arguments relating to the main object (the summary contained in the conclusion should not tell the reader anything new).

8.3.1 The introduction

An introduction generally consists of three parts: the topic lead-in, the topic statement, and the topic division. Only the first of these three parts can be considered optional.

8.3.1.1 The topic lead-in

The topic lead-in, as its name suggests, serves to lead to and introduce the topic statement, which generally involves a movement from the general to the particular. For literary analyses there are many possible approaches for the topic lead-in, but they can be divided into the following main types (on approach, aspect, configuration, and proposition, see Chapter 2 on the components of analysis):

1. Through the author: "Victor Hugo is often considered the greatest French writer of the nineteenth century. I will analyze here his most famous work ..."
2. Through the corpus: "*Les Misérables* is probably the mostly widely known work by Victor Hugo. In my view, it is also the best. I will show here the stylistic qualities of this work."

3. Through the approach (that is to be used in the analysis): "Geocriticism is the study of the relationship between spaces and literary works. I shall undertake, for the first time, a geocritical analysis of Victor Hugo's *Les Misérables*."

4. Through the aspect (that is to be analyzed): "An ideology can be defined as a structure of beliefs, values, and ethical precepts. I shall here analyze the implicit and explicit humanistic ideology found in Victor Hugo's *Les Misérables*."

5. Through the configuration (that is to be analyzed): "The theme of thwarted love is frequent in literature. I shall consider the traditional and innovative dimensions of the use of this theme in Victor Hugo's *Les Misérables*."

6. Through a proposition: "One may ask whether Superman is a saint or simply a hero. The same question can be asked of the character Jean Valjean in *Les Misérables*, as we shall see."

7. Through a generic classification (genre, period, movement, etc.): "In nineteenth-century France, authors generally sought to make a name for themselves in the theater, yet Victor Hugo became famous through poetry and the novel. We analyze here Hugo's novel *Les Misérables*."

8. Through a sociocultural event, or one that had a sociocultural impact: "The performance of Victor Hugo's play *Hernani* in 1830 gave rise to fierce clashes on social and esthetic issues, yet the publication of *Les Misérables* in 1862 did not cause such disputes. I shall undertake an analysis of the social and esthetic issues raised by this novel."

9. Through current events (the example here is made up): "Recently, a manuscript of Victor Hugo's *Notre Dame de Paris* was found that was thought to have been lost forever. But we shall focus our attention on another famous novel by the same author."

10. Through a personal connection: "From an early age I have been fascinated by Hugo's work, which always seemed so rich and monumental, especially his novel *Les Misérables*. I undertake here an analysis of that novel."

The topic lead-in must be (1) relevant and (2) closely and explicitly related to the subject statement. It should also be (3) appealing. Here are a few further clarifications:

With regard to the relation of the topic lead-in to the topic statement, you should avoid approaching the topic from a vantage point that is too far removed from it, and also failing to make an explicit connection with the topic.

Here is an example of a topic lead-in that starts too far from the topic: "As soon as humans developed language, they turned it to esthetic uses, giving rise to songs, poems, novels, and plays. I undertake here an analysis of one of these esthetic productions, namely a poem by ...."

Here is an example of topic lead-in that fails to make the connection with the topic explicit: "Novels can be divided into, on the one hand, novels in the strict sense, and on the other hand, poetic novels. I consider here whether Hubert Aquin's novel *Next Episode* presents a pessimistic vision of Quebec nationalism." If the reader does not know that this work is considered to be a poetic novel, the link will not be clear, and so the reader must be provided with this information. In some cases, where the connection will be obvious to some readers but not to others, it may be appropriate to qualify this information with a phrase such as "as is well known."

Here is another example where the topic lead-in fails to make an explicit connection with the topic: "[*topic lead-in*] Humans are creative. [*topic statement*] But can literature created specifically for the internet truly be considered literature?" Here, the lack of an explicit connection could be corrected through an additional explanation: "[*topic lead-in*] Humans are creative. Because of this creativity, whenever a new technology appears, they try to make literary use of it. [*topic statement*] But can literature created specifically for the internet truly be considered literature?"

Finally, it is essential for the topic lead-in to be appealing, since it is the path that leads the reader toward the full text. It should whet the reader's appetite, and make them want to continue reading. Here is an example of a banal, and therefore unappealing opening: "Since the dawn of time, humans have sought new esthetic forms." The phrase "since the dawn of time" is a cliché, and furthermore, the idea that is introduced here is too vague and uninformative. You should avoid clichés and commonplace ideas.

8.3.1.2 The topic statement

The topic statement presents the main topic of the analysis clearly, precisely, and completely.

When one is analyzing one or more texts, the topic statement explicitly or implicitly presents: (1) the corpus being studied (e.g., *Les Misérables*); (2) the aspect of the text being studied (e.g., affects); (3) the approach used to study it (e.g., traditional psychological analysis); potentially (4) the configuration that has been selected for study (e.g., the feeling of love); and (5) the proposition to be defended and developed (e.g., because Jean Valjean is unable to pursue his love for Fantine, he transfers it, sometimes awkwardly and excessively, to her orphaned daughter, Cosette). On these five elements, see Chapter 2 on the components of analysis.

In a pedagogical essay it is possible to repeat, word for word, the terms of the essay question or writing instruction. However, it is preferable to rephrase it in your own words, while taking care not to change the meaning. One way of doing this is to transform what was a direct question in the writing instruction into an indirect question, or vice versa. For example, the writing instruction "Are you for or against violence in literature?" (a direct question) can be transformed into the following phrase (which is a sort of indirect question): "We must consider whether violence is acceptable in literature." Avoid mechanical, formulaic phrases such as "We are therefore led to consider the following question: ...."

The topic statement can be used as an opportunity to define the limits of the topic, possibly by briefly identifying the elements that you will not be addressing. This task can also be carried out, or pursued at greater length, in the method section (I shall come back to this later).

8.3.1.3 The topic division

The topic division lists the different parts, or sections, that will be found in the development, generally in the order in which they will appear.

The following errors should be avoided: (1) listing the sections of the development in the wrong order; (2) including the conclusion in the list of parts; (3) presenting an organization that does not correspond to the sections of the development, but is instead a logical organization that is not present in the analysis, or one that is present but at a lower level of organization than that of the sections of the development. For example, in a comparative text, the topic division might state that the development will consider "similarities," then "differences," whereas in fact the development itself does not contain a section devoted to "similarities" followed by a section devoted to "differences," but instead considers a similarity, then a difference, then another similarity, etc. Finally, one must avoid—while taking care not to enter into the argumentation prematurely—(4) giving an overly general and abstract outline of the development, such as in this example: "First, I consider the arguments that support the thesis; next, I consider those that invalidate it; finally, I decide between them." This can be remedied as follows: "First, I consider the biographical and historical arguments that support the thesis; next, I consider the themes addressed in the text itself that are opposed to the thesis; finally, I decide between the two possible positions."

8.3.2 The conclusion

A conclusion consists of two parts: first, a synthesis or summary of the development, and second, an opening up of the question.[1]

NOTE: HOW NECESSARY IS THE CONCLUSION?

The second part of the conclusion, the opening up of the question, is sometimes considered to be optional. The same applies to the summary, or even to the conclusion in its entirety. The summary is most useful in longer texts, where it serves to remind the reader of content that they may have forgotten by this point.

---

1 I prefer to speak of an opening up of the question rather than a contextualization, because an opening up does not necessarily involve contextualization. One might, for example, propose that the analysis that has just been carried out could be complemented by a different approach to the same literary work.

The first part of the conclusion, the summary, consists of three parts: (1) a reminder of the topic of each section of the development; (2) a reminder of the precise content of each section of the development (obviously it is not possible to refer to every element of each section, but at least one element from each section each is needed); and (3) where appropriate, a statement or reminder of the judgment that has been reached (e.g., "as I demonstrated, the poem analyzed here is indeed symbolist"). The summary found in the conclusion therefore repeats the elements that were listed in the topic division, but in the light of the clarifications that have been added to those elements over the course of the development. For example, if the topic division states that the analysis will examine the positive qualities of the poet (in the view of the author of the analyzed text), followed by a treatment of the poet's flaws, the summary should specify the main qualities and flaws that have been identified in the development. Just as for the topic division, a synthesis that is too general or abstract should be avoided ("We have seen, first, the arguments in favor of our hypothesis; second, those that invalidate it."). Other errors to avoid include that of repeating too closely the words of the introduction (particularly from the topic division), and that of producing an excessively long summary, or one that fails to mention whole sections of the development (it is particularly common to forget to mention the method section from the development). As a rule of thumb, for the summary part of the conclusion, one can ask oneself: if a reader were to read only this, would they have an overall understanding of what I have argued in this text?

The opening up of the question is similar to the topic lead–in found in the introduction: "It opens up the subject in relation to aspects that have not been dealt with in the development; it places the topic in a wider context, in a broader perspective" (Goulet, 1987: 99). Indeed, this final part can draw attention to other facets of the object of analysis that would be worth considering, in the form of a question for the reader to reflect on, or as a possible further line of analysis to be pursued. These suggested lines of inquiry should of course be relevant to the topic, rich, and appealing. Just as with the topic lead–in, the opening up of the question must be interesting and precise. Indeed, whereas the topic lead–in is responsible for producing the reader's first impression, the final opening up of the question found in the conclusion often determines the memory of the text that will stay with the reader.

To avoid producing a weak opening up of the subject, the following model can be used (although others can be used successfully). This simple and effective model possesses three characteristics: (1) it leads toward the discussion of another topic; (2) it is closely connected to the topic that has just been addressed and supports the analysis that has just been undertaken; and (3) it demonstrates the interest of this new line of inquiry, suggests an approach that could be used, and/or provides some initial elements of analysis (some answers to the question being posed, a problematization, the method to be used, an underlying hypothesis, etc.). Obviously, one should avoid introducing a topic that should have been dealt with in the current analysis.

8.4 The development

8.4.1 Introduction

The development part of an analysis generally comprises the following three dimensions, whose presence may be implicit or explicit to varying degrees, and which—in terms of the actual arrangement of the text—may either be placed in three separate sections or combined with each other: (1) method (addressing the means that will be used for the analysis), (2) description of the object (with justification), and (3) interpretation (deriving "meaning" from the characterization produced by the description of the object, with justification). I suggest using a structure that makes these dimensions explicit. As I see it, this structure is not a new approach, but rather systematizes, explicitly and meticulously, what I believe every analyst does, whether consciously or unconsciously. Thus, even a traditional thematic analysis that lacks an explicit method section is implicitly based on a method (it uses a certain definition of the concept of the "theme" and applies certain ideas of how to find themes, handle them, connect them, make use of them, etc.).

Let us use the analogy of a machine for carrying out analysis. The text is a raw material that the analyst must transform into a finished object. To do this, the analyst must first construct a machine (a method), and describe its parts and functioning. The analyst then sets the machine to work, which it does by processing the text, for example, by cutting it up into small pieces which fall into different trays according to their different natures. Finally, once the text is processed, the analyst considers the results of the processing, examines the contents of the trays, and offers an interpretation of these results.

We can apply this scheme to the concrete example of conducting a survey. To do so, we must first address the method to be used. What is a survey? What do we want to know and, consequently, what questions should we ask? In what order? What are the possible answers? And so on. Next, we proceed with the survey by classifying the answers according to defined criteria (e.g., "yes," "no," "don't know," "prefer not to say"). Finally, we interpret the raw data of the survey beyond the level of merely stating quantitative findings (so many respondents say "yes," so many say "no," etc.). Why did people give these responses? Can the categories of responses be correlated with other categories, such as education, income, region, gender? How do our results compare with those produced by similar surveys, and how can we explain the differences or similarities? Did the survey introduce biases that were not perceived at the time of its design? etc.

Now for a more literary example: suppose that you want to describe the action of a novel using Greimas's actantial model (see Hébert, 2019: chapter 6). In the *method* section you would present the actantial model (in its general form, or with improvements or adaptations to the task at hand). This model breaks down an action into six mandatory facets. The subject (1) and the desired object (2) (or object to be disposed of) form the quest. The person who asks for the quest to be performed is the sender (3), while the one for whose benefit the performed is the receiver (4). A helper (5) helps in the performance of st and an opponent (6) hinders it. In the *description* section, you would the selected elements of the novel and classify them (with justification, ᵥ.ᵤ ₑplanation, citation, argumentation) into one or other of the six analytical classes (plus a seventh class for irrelevant elements). In the *interpretation* section, you would extract "meaning" from the results of the description. For example, if you discover a correlation whereby all the opponents are female and all the helpers are male, you might consider whether this is a sexist fictional world.

In other words, the method section presents the analysis machine, the description section operates the machine to process the text, and the interpretation section gives meaning to the results of the machine's processing of the text.

Throughout the analysis, but especially in the development, the process of argumentation consists in making a logical proposition (formulated either positively or negatively) and by justifying the truth value (true, false, undecidable) that one assigns to it (in general, if you are asserting that the truth value is "false," this usually relates to someone else's proposition). The quality and quantity of the argumentation should be inversely proportional to the obviousness of the proposition (e.g., there is little need to demonstrate that Hamlet is the main character of Shakespeare's play of the same name, whereas it would require very extensive argumentation to make the opposite claim). See Chapter 12 on argumentation for more detail.

8.4.2 The method section

The elements of method presented in the method section may relate to the parts or stages of the description of the analyzed object and/or to those of the interpretation. They may also apply, exclusively or additionally, to stages to be completed prior to the description, such as the principles to be used for constructing the corpus or for selecting the editions of the texts to be analyzed.

The method section presents and justifies the approach (e.g., a traditional thematic approach) that will be used, as well as the aspect(s) (e.g., themes), configuration(s) (e.g., the theme of revenge), and proposition(s) that have been selected (e.g., those who exact revenge harm themselves more than they redeem themselves). It also presents and justifies any criteria that have been used to delimit the corpus. It may mention other methodological elements, such as the successive stages of the description and the interpretation (whether these steps are integral to the chosen approach, or are used only in the current analysis). These elements of method may be specific to the cultural sciences in general (sociology, literary studies, etc.) or to literary studies alone.

The method section should not be disproportionately long relative to the other sections of the development. However, the more rigorous and meticulous the analysis, the longer this section needs to be, and it can sometimes exceed the length of the other two sections combined. In this case, even if less space is devoted to the analysis itself, the resulting descriptive data will be all the more valid and convincing. Just as when building a house, the foundation must be sound for everything else to function well. It obviously follows from this that the method section should not be too short.

8.4.2.1 Approach

One or more approaches may be used for a given analysis. These approaches can be pre-existing ones, or they may be the result of a combination of pre-existing approaches, or they may even be newly invented by the analyst. A combination of terminologies, theories, approaches, and methods can be used, as long as the different elements are compatible, any necessary modifications to the elements are made, and the combination is explained and justified.

It is possible to present not only the chosen approach, but also the other possible approaches that have been rejected, while explaining the reasons (i.e., the causes) and the consequences of this choice (e.g., their advantages, disadvantages, impacts on the results, etc.). For example, if I want to analyze the plot of a literary text, several models are available to me, including a traditional non-formal approach, a formal approach such as Greimas's actantial model, Joseph Campbell's mythic model, etc. Which approach should I choose, and why? What are the advantages, disadvantages, limitations, presuppositions, etc., of this approach? What will be the possible or inevitable qualitative or quantitative consequences of this choice on the results of the analysis, their validity, etc.?

8.4.2.2 Definitions

Generally, a definition should contribute directly to the analysis: it serves to clarify a central concept that will be used. In the method section (possibly in a "definitions" sub-section), only the main definitions relating to the descriptive or interpretive method are included. In addition to these fundamental definitions, it may be useful to introduce an incidental definition at the appropriate moment in the course of the description or the interpretation. This helps to avoid producing an overly heterogeneous, long, or boring "definitions" section within the method section. However, it is also possible to include (possibly in a shortened form) definitions which are not used directly in the analysis, but which allow for an exhaustive presentation of the approach used. It can be useful to illustrate definitions with a simple, concise example of the concept in question (drawn from something other than the text being analyzed). In the case of longer texts, it is sometimes necessary to provide the reader with a brief reminder of the definition at a later point. In all cases, you should avoid presenting a simple sequence of definitions that do not relate to one other and are not used explicitly in the analysis (except to produce a complete presentation of the approach, as mentioned above).

What should be defined? All terms, whether technical or not, should be defined if they are likely to be unfamiliar to the intended reader of the analysis (e.g., a specialized concept such as that of isotopy), if they are polysemous (e.g., the various definitions of style), and/or if they are being used with a different meaning than the most commonly used meaning. Let us consider which terms should be defined in the following example: "The French literary movement of Parnassianism is characterized, among other things, by pessimism, naturalism, misogyny, and agnosticism." At the very least, "Parnassianism," "naturalism" (which can be given several definitions), and "agnosticism" (which is a more specialized term) should be defined.

8.4.2.3 The corpus and establishing the text

If the corpus for analysis has been chosen on the basis of personal preference (e.g., you have selected these novels only because you like them), you do not necessarily have to justify this choice. However, if you have constructed the corpus on the basis of objective principles, you must present it and justify the criteria used to make this selection (e.g., you have selected only novels written in Texas between 1950 and 1960). You may also mention the other possible criteria that could have been used for selection, and the impact that this might have had on the corpus and, consequently, on the analysis and its results (see Chapter 6).

In any work of textual analysis, the stage of establishing the text for analysis is crucial. Using a poor-quality edition of the text will undermine the validity of the results. In general, therefore, you should choose reference editions, ideally scholarly critical editions, rather than cheap reading editions or hastily digitized editions found on the internet. One should therefore take stock of the high-quality editions that are available and explain the reasons (justifications, causes) and consequences (advantages and disadvantages, impacts on the results) of the specific choice of edition for the analysis.

8.4.2.4 Limiting criteria

There are three ways of limiting the scope of the analysis in relation to the object of study: (1) spatial (or dispositional) limitation (e.g., only a particular page or chapter), (2) conceptual limitation (applying only a particular part of the approach, or treating only a particular aspect, configuration, etc., but across the whole text), and (3) spatial and conceptual limitation (e.g., treating only a particular aspect in a particular chapter or section). For example, in an actantial analysis, the analysis may be limited to character actants (thereby excluding object actants, animals, concepts, etc.); this limitation is then applied to the approach (reducing its scope) and to the corpus, from which the analysis draws fewer elements than it might otherwise have done. To take another example, it would be impractical to study repetition in general in a given work (most texts include countless forms of repetition, both of signifiers and signifieds), but one could limit an analysis to one or several forms of repetition (e.g., the repetition of words denoting affects). Ideally, one would present a general typology of the phenomena being studied (e.g., the different kinds of love), then identify the specific forms that will be studied (e.g., only parental love). Alternatively, one may study all of those forms, or a number of them, but only enter into detail on one or a small number of them.

Obviously, one should avoid conceptually excluding what should be included (e.g., it would be strange to exclude the character actants). However, spatial limitation also has its pitfalls, such as the risk of selecting a part of the object that is less relevant than another for the purpose (e.g., less representative of the work or of the phenomenon being studied), or that of failing to make a connection in the analysis between the selected parts and the other parts of the object, so that the selected parts appear to exist in isolation.

The limiting criteria, like any (acceptable) methodological reduction, must be consciously chosen, explicitly stated, appropriate for the analysis, and respected in the implementation of the analysis. For example, the following situation should be avoided: someone claims to be studying only female characters, yet in the analysis female characters are overlooked and male characters are described instead. In short, the stated criteria must accurately reflect the materials and parts that are actually selected and rejected in the analysis. When establishing the limiting criteria, you should state their advantages and disadvantages, and their impact on the results of the analysis. You may also mention other possible limiting criteria, and the reasons why these were not adopted.

8.4.2.5 Problems encountered

The method section can also include a statement of the general methodological choices that have been made in response to the particular difficulties encountered in the analysis. More specific choices can also be indicated at the appropriate time in the course of the description or interpretation section.

For example, in a thematic analysis, it may be necessary to explain the different possible ways of understanding metaphors thematically and symbolically (e.g., for the expression "this man is an angel"): in one understanding, the compared item takes on the nature of the comparator (the human becomes an angel); or the comparator takes on the nature of the compared item (the angel becomes human); or both of these are true at the same time; or neither is true (the human remains a human and the angel remains an angel). The choice that is made between these options should be stated and justified.

In principle, one should indicate the nature of the problem, its undesirable effects, the possible causes of the problem, the possible solutions, the chosen solution, the justification for this choice, and the impacts of this choice on the analysis.

Obviously, there is no need to mention the problems that are inherent in any analysis (e.g., the need to look up obscure terms from the text in the dictionary).

8.4.3 The description section

The nature of the description depends on all the parameters of the analysis: the corpus (e.g., *Hamlet*), the aspect to analyzed (e.g., themes), the approach (e.g., traditional thematic analysis), the configuration to be analyzed (e.g., the themes of love and death), the proposition (e.g., "love causes death"), the limiting criteria (e.g., only the final scene), etc.

8.4.4 The interpretation section

In general, description of the analyzed object is not enough on its own, and interpretations are needed to find "meaning" in the "raw data" produced by the description. The interpretation is the culmination of the analysis, and it is often therefore both the most important part of the analysis and the most difficult to produce. The interpretations provided must be numerous, deep, meaningful, relevant, applicable both locally and globally, etc.

In the same way that the method section constitutes the foundation of the description section (although the interpretation also involves methodological elements), the latter constitutes the foundation of the interpretation section (or the interpretation stage of the analysis). Indeed, if the description is flawed, the interpretation, which is based on the data provided by the description, will necessarily be flawed as well. Unlike the everyday usage of "interpretation," which suggests a way of seeing that may be purely personal and subjective, in analysis the interpretation must be supported by rational arguments that are, if not incontrovertible, at least plausible. An interpretation is generally subjective in that its starting point is the perspective of the subject producing the analysis, but it then becomes objective with the help of valid rational arguments presented in an explicit way.

The interpretation section does not merely involve a deepening of the description, and in particular it should not contain the explanation, argumentation, or justification of the logical propositions presented in the description (in any case, any interpretation, in so far as it contains logical propositions, must also be justified). This stage of the analysis has a different nature of its own. Thus, it would not be the task of the interpretation section, for example, to justify the specific form of the actantial model extracted from the analyzed text or the network of themes that one has observed in the work.

It is not enough that the description and the interpretation concern the same object (the same work); it is also essential that the specific claims made in the interpretation follow directly from the data presented in the description. In principle, in the interpretation section you should not interpret the object directly, thereby bypassing the description, but instead interpret only the data presented in the description section. In short, the interpretation presupposes the description, which presupposes the method. It is necessary to avoid producing an interpretation section detached from the description section, and similarly a description section detached from the method section. A detached description might not, for example, make explicit and sustained reference to the concepts defined in the method section. In principle, there should be a dynamic relationship between the method section and the whole "application" stage of the analysis (i.e., description + interpretation): they should "talk" to each other. In particular, the concepts defined in the method section must be reused (with rare exceptions) in the application stage of the analysis.

The three most common errors in analysis (whether through laziness, ignorance, or carelessness) are: (1) under-explaining one's meaning (while assuming that the meaning of one's words is self-evident); (2) under-arguing or insufficiently justifying one's case, including providing insufficient counter-arguments (failing to prove that what one sees is actually present, addressing only the evidence that supports one's case, or not attending to potential objections); and (3) under-commenting or making insufficient use of the evidence presented (not seeing or making full use of the interpretive possibilities opened up by a descriptive discovery). If one looks only for arguments that validate a thesis (e.g., that Hamlet is mad) without looking for arguments that support the opposite claim (that Hamlet is not mad), or while ignoring them or even hiding them from the reader, one commits the error of "confirmation bias."

We can use two criteria to distinguish between different forms that the interpretation can take on. The "spatial" criterion concerns the place in the analytical text where the interpretation appears. Depending on this criterion, the interpretation will be either alternating or consecutive. In the case of alternating interpretation, one finds an element of description, then its interpretation, followed by another element of description and its interpretation, etc. A consecutive interpretation appears (as a distinct interpretation section) only once the whole task of description is complete. It then takes up again all the elements presented in the description and provides an interpretation of them. An alternating interpretation is generally more effective, since it is not necessary to restate the element of description (first to introduce it, then a second time to remind the reader of it and add the interpretation).

The second criterion concerns the scope of the interpretation, which can be local (dealing with a single element of description) or global (dealing with several or all elements of description). Global interpretation should aim to encompass as many elements of the description as possible, therefore leaving as little as possible beyond its scope. This does not mean that this interpretation will be unitary; it may include several distinct stages and forms which, together, make it possible to account for most or all of the elements of the description. A global interpretation may come at the end of the development part of the essay, just before the conclusion, but it is also possible that there will be several global interpretations, placed at different points in the analysis.

In light of these two criteria, errors in the interpretation may include: (1) failing to interpret each of the elements of the description, either out of forgetfulness or an inability to distinguish between the stages of description and interpretation; and (2) failing to produce, where appropriate, a global interpretation that accounts for the overall structure of the elements identified by the description (and instead providing only the individual interpretive "meaning" of each element).

In general, describing or interpreting a literary text from an academic or at least rational perspective requires establishing with a reasonable degree of certainty (not necessarily beyond all doubt) and with the use of rational arguments (not just opinions or impressions), the presence (or absence) of a given phenomenon in the text at the time of its creation and/or publication (which avoids anachronisms), whether the author was aware of it or not.

In interpretation, as in description, a certain dialectical attitude must be maintained. In literature (and more generally in the cultural sciences), two opposing or even contradictory interpretations are not necessarily mutually exclusive: a matter may be neither black nor white, but both, in varying proportions, and either in the same or in different respects. In some cases, there may be a hierarchy of interpretations (e.g., hypothesis A is more strongly supported in the text or more plausible than hypothesis B). For example, when Hamlet kills Polonius with his sword in the belief that he is killing his mother's husband, he symbolically kills: (1) his mother (he had just been expressing his anger to her, and she complained that his words were daggers in her ears), (2) his father (through a form of Oedipus complex, killing his mother's second husband amounts to symbolically killing his father, and furthermore his uncle addresses Hamlet as his son), (3) his uncle (who sent Polonius there), whom he wishes to kill and actually believes himself to be killing, in an instance of tragic misunderstanding, (4) himself (like Polonius, he is "mad" and similarly eavesdrops in the scene of the uncle's prayer, and, above all, he entertains the idea of suicide and more or less consciously goes to his death by accepting the duel in spite of his premonitions), etc. Too often we imagine that a single interpretation is the only one possible. We must always check whether an opposing interpretation also has some value, otherwise we are engaging in selective argumentation and suffering from confirmation bias. We should not only assume that our favored interpretation is not the only possible interpretation, but also study the other interpretations, take them into account, and tell the reader about them.

The following is an extensive, but probably not exhaustive, typology of possible interpretations (as distinct from the possible forms of the interpretation discussed above). It is based on two criteria: the kind of textuality involved and the kind of relation involved. On the basis of the first criterion, and with reference to mainly comparative examples, we can distinguish between (1) intratextual interpretations (e.g., comparison between two characters in the text), (2) intertextual interpretations (e.g., comparison between two characters in different texts, or between a text and a film), (3) architextual interpretations (comparison between a text and an abstract form, e.g., between a text and its genre, or a text and the thematic stereotypes it uses, possibly transforming them in the process), and (4) extratextual interpretations (comparison between text and world, e.g., between a character and a real historical person, or the study of the way the text was determined by the author's biography).

Let us now turn to the second criterion, that of the relations involved (and for each of these types of relations there is a corresponding operation). Several of the types of interpretation defined on the basis of this criterion can take on an intratextual, intertextual, architextual, and/or extratextual modality.

1. Comparative relation: this type of interpretation uses comparative relations: identity, similarity, opposition, metaphorical or non-metaphorical analogy, homologation, alterity, etc. (see section 4.23 on structure, relation, operation). Examples of the possible content of this kind of interpretation are similarities/differences with other elements of the same work, with a stereotypical form (e.g., a cliché, a topos), with the genre to which the work is supposed to belong, with works from the same/different eras, from the same/different authors, from the same/different periods, from the same/different genres, etc.

2. Causal relation: this type of interpretation uses the relations and operations connected to causality: causes (including those initiated either with or without any conscious intention), effects, and determinations. To take a crude example, the causes of a tree include the initial seed, moisture, light, heat, and nutrients. Broadly speaking, causes relate to the presence/absence of the phenomenon, in this case the presence of the tree. A constant wind that makes the tree lean to one side determines the tree. Broadly speaking, determinations affect the quantitative (intensity, etc.) and qualitative modalities of the presence/absence of the phenomenon. Like comparisons, causes can be either internal (e.g., characters' actions may be explained by their own inclinations), external (e.g., the socio-political state or life of the author, the influence of a given text, etc.) or archi-internal (the influence of a given architextual phenomenon such as a genre or topos). Similarly, effects can be internal (e.g., the impact of one theme on another, of one character on another, etc.), external (e.g., the impact of a given textual phenomenon on society), or archi-internal (e.g., the constitution of a new architextual phenomenon such as a genre or topos). The same principle applies to determinations. For example, internally, one might ask which of Hamlet's actions cause Ophelia to go mad, or what internal esthetic reasons explain it; externally, one might ask what elements of Shakespeare's psychology caused him to make Ophelia go mad rather than producing another outcome. In addition to this typology of causal factors, we can add the instigator (the spark that initiates causation or determination) and the catalyst (an element that facilitates causation or determination). On closer examination, instigators and catalysts are essentially causes of causes or causes of determination, and can therefore broadly be considered as causes of the phenomenon concerned.

From this perspective, the analysis consists in proposing, then proving: the absence/presence of a phenomenon; the modalities of this absence/presence (both quantitative and qualitative modalities: intensity, constituent parts, functioning, functions, categories to which the phenomenon belongs, etc.); the potential or proven causes of this presence/absence and/or its modalities; and the effects of this presence/absence and its modalities on the "meaning" attributed to the phenomenon, that is, on the interpretation that can be made of it.

3. Correlation: two types of correlations can be distinguished: the first are categorical correlations (without any gradation), which simply note the absence/presence of two phenomena relative to each other; the second are gradual correlations, which note the effect of the increase/decrease of one phenomenon on the increase/decrease of another phenomenon.

Let us take the first type of correlation. We speak of simple presupposition if A presupposes B, but not vice versa (e.g., in a given text, when the theme of night [A] is present, the theme of death [B] will also be present, but sometimes death is present without night). We speak of a reciprocal presupposition if A presupposes B and B presupposes A (e.g., if the theme of night and death are always copresent and therefore always co-absent). Finally, we speak of mutual exclusion if the presence of A presupposes the absence of B and the presence of B presupposes the absence of A (e.g., in *Hamlet,* when the ghost is present, Claudius is absent, and vice versa). Let us consider another example: all those whom Hamlet loves, die (his father, his mother, Ophelia, but with the notable exception of Horatio, who wants to commit suicide but is prevented from doing so by Hamlet) but not all those who die are necessarily loved by Hamlet (Claudius, Polonius, Rosencrantz and Guildenstern, etc.). In other words, this is a simple presupposition: being loved by Hamlet presupposes dying (roughly speaking), but dying does not presuppose being loved by Hamlet. In the example of the survey discussed on p. 171, if a respondent answers "yes" to a given question, this will generally presuppose that they belong to a certain sociological category (age, profession, etc.) rather than another. Finally, let us take an example from the actantial model: the fact of an actant being a "helper" may presuppose belonging to a particular analytical category (e.g., all "helpers" may be female). Correlations may be established in relation to the spatial dimensions of the text: for example, is a given theme concentrated in one or more parts of the text, or is it spread throughout the text (e.g., a given part may presuppose a given theme, and vice versa)?

We can distinguish two kinds of gradual correlations. In the case of positive (or direct) correlations, the more A increases, the more B increases, and the more A decreases, the more B decreases, and vice versa (e.g., in *Hamlet,* the more time passes, the more the number of deaths increases). In the case of inverse correlations, the more A increases, the more B decreases, and the more A decreases, the more B increases, and vice versa (e.g., in a tragedy, the more time passes, the fewer light or happy moments occur).

Correlation is not necessarily causation (but all causation is also correlation). For example, there is a correlation between the level of ice cream sales and the number of deaths by drowning, but it cannot be said that ice cream causes drowning. There is actually a third underlying factor, that of the weather: when it is hot, people both consume more ice cream and swim more.

4. Relation to another approach: a common type of interpretation consists in applying a second approach, usually substantially different from the one used in the description, to provide an additional layer of meaning to the data produced by the first approach. For example, one might apply a psychoanalytical, feminist, or sociological approach in order to reprocess the results produced by an initial stage of traditional thematic description. In other words, approach-1 produces data-1 (descriptions and their initial interpretation), which are then reprocessed by approach-2, which produces data-2. Therefore, data-2 constitute interpretations relative to data-1.

5. Relation between the results and the method—including the theory that the method presupposes—used to obtain them: in this type of interpretation, the results of the analysis are brought to bear on the particular theory and/or method used. The interpretation does not focus on the data of the description, but on the means that were used to obtain them. Here are some of the questions that one might ask in this regard: Did the method work, and if so, how well? Can or should it be modified? If it failed to produce results, or produced only limited results, is this a consequence of the approach itself, or of the particular way it was used, or of the aspect, configuration, proposition, or corpus to which it was applied? Is it a consequence of the theory that is present, at least implicitly, in the approach? Do the results (or lack of results, or limited results) of the analysis lead us to validate, invalidate, add, remove, qualify, etc., one or several elements of the theory or method (or even the whole theory or method)?

8.5 Other possible parts of the analysis

In more extensive works of research, such as master's dissertations and PhD theses, other elements may be added to the overall structure of the analysis. These elements may also be addressed briefly in a shorter analysis. These include, but are not limited to, the following elements: (1) issues and/or a problematic, (2) a hypothesis (or principal research question), (3) aims and objectives, (4) the current state of the question, (5) the originality of the analysis being undertaken, (6) possible outcomes of the analysis, (7) presentation of the author(s) of the works in the corpus, (8) presentation of the corpus (criteria for selection, summary or overview of the works, etc.), and (9) presentation of the editions chosen, when more than one edition is available.

1. An "issues" section presents the general and specific context in which the research takes place. When the issue is a problem to be solved, we can speak of a "problematic" in the narrow sense of the term. A research question based on a problematic can be formulated schematically as follows: is there a problem X? How can problem X be solved? Would Y be a solution? A problem consists here in the absence, incompleteness, or uncertainty of knowledge of a subject and/or situation, which leads in turn to other problems than those related to knowledge. One will then generally present the problem; the moment when it appeared or was discovered; its different manifestations and the modalities of its manifestation (its constituent parts, typologies, functioning, etc.); its evolution; its possible causes; its possible or proven negative effects; the solutions (either unsatisfactory or partially satisfactory) that have been used up to now; the solution that one is now proposing, and how to implement it; the benefits (complete or partial) of the proposed solution.

2. For any given research question, we can say either that it has been asked before, or that it has never been asked before, or that it has been asked in the wrong way. We can also say either that it has been answered before, or that it has not yet been answered, or that it has been answered incorrectly or incompletely. A given research question is either problem-based or not (e.g., "What

is the theme of *Hamlet*?" is not strictly speaking problem-based). We should recall here that some analyses have a (central) hypothesis, while others have a (principal) research question or purely descriptive aims. Examples of the first type would include: "Hamlet is indeed mad" (here the answer to the problem is already indicated) or "Is Hamlet really mad?" (the question is approached without a preconception of the answer). Examples of the second type might be formulated as: "Madness in *Hamlet*," "Hamlet and madness," or "The themes of *Hamlet*," or "What are the principal themes of Hamlet?" See Chapter 14 on hypotheses.

3. The general aim (usually there is only one) states the purpose of the analysis, whereas the specific objectives state the means to achieve that aim. For example, if the general aim is to verify whether Hamlet is really mad, the specific objectives may be: (1) to present the psychological method used; (2) to define madness using the criteria provided by this method; (3) to verify the presence/absence of these criteria in Hamlet, and their modalities; (4) to identify the causes in the fiction, in the author's life, etc., of this presence/absence and its particular modalities; (5) to identify the impact of one's findings on the meaning of the work (themes, action, message, etc.), on its esthetic effects, etc.

4. The state of the question (or "state of the art," or "literature review") presents the state of research on the subject at the present time. It therefore includes references to publications on the subject: books, journal articles, book chapters, dissertations and theses, databases, etc., possibly in several languages. The possible operations carried out by the literature review include listing the relevant documents; synthesizing their contents; showing what the literature emphasizes, the elements it covers, and what it overlooks; and identifying the strengths and weaknesses of the literature, its relevance or irrelevance to the current analysis, and its similarities and differences with the current analysis. The literature review can relate to the corpus, the approach, the aspect or configuration to be analyzed, and/or the proposition. It can be more general, more specific, or both at the same time. For example, for an analysis exploring whether Hamlet is really mad, one might address the state of the question in relation to the following points (in each case, first the general and then the specific element is given): Shakespeare's works / *Hamlet* (corpus), thematic analysis / thematic analysis on Hamlet (approach), the theme of madness in general / the theme of madness in *Hamlet* (configuration). Obviously, the literature review would address the state of the question in relation to the specific question of Hamlet's madness. The literature review notably serves to establish the originality—whether absolute or relative—of the proposed analysis, whether in terms of the corpus, the approach used, the configuration to be analyzed, and/or the proposition.

5. On the basis of the statement of the issue, the problematic, and the state of the question, one can establish and present the originality of the proposed analysis. One can show that, whether in the cultural sciences in general, or in arts and literary studies, or specifically in studies relating to the work or corpus at hand: the proposed approach and/or method has never been used (or is

entirely new); the aspect or configuration has never been analyzed (or has never even been identified in this or any other work); the proposition has never been analyzed or proven; or the work or corpus has never been analyzed (at least academically).

6. One can also comment on the potential outcomes of the research. These outcomes may be: theoretical or methodological (e.g., a new theory, concept, or method); related to the analyzed object (e.g., significant enhancement of knowledge of the corpus and of the generic, historical, etc. categories to which the corpus belongs); or related to the transferability of the theory, approach, or method to other corpora (literary, artistic, etc.) or to other fields (art history, film, etc.). The presentation of the originality and potential impact of the research establishes its importance and interest.

7–9. Finally, one can present: the author or authors of the corpus (life, works, etc.), the corpus (summary and generic classification of each work), and the editions chosen (qualities, defects, etc.).

Discussion of the issues, the problematic, the state of the question, and the originality and consequences of the analysis, as well as the presentation of the author and the corpus, can all be placed either in the introduction (keeping in mind the 10 percent rule) or in parts of the development. The implications of the analysis can also be placed in the conclusion. The hypothesis is generally placed in the introduction (but it can then be presented in greater detail in the development). As for aims and objectives, the former are presented only in the introduction, whereas the latter, which correspond to specific steps to be taken, are presented in the introduction, then generally accomplished in the course of the development (unless there is no need for a specific objective to be presented textually). For example, if we undertake to analyze the spaces that appear in a corpus of novels (general aim) and to do so we must create a database (one of the specific objectives), the creation of the database does not necessarily need to be presented textually, although the analysis of the data will be presented in the text. In a long work of analysis, it can be useful to divide the final bibliography and/or the state of the question (literature review) into different sections: the chosen corpus, existing analyses of that corpus, works on the chosen approach, etc. An alternative division would be: the corpus, works on the corpus, works on the chosen configuration for analysis, and works related to the proposition (these last two can be presented together).

8.6 A model analysis

I have presented below a complete, albeit rudimentary, analysis, with an introduction, development (method + description + interpretation), and conclusion. Although in this analysis, for the sake of providing a clear demonstration, I have separated the description and interpretation into separate sections, I recommend not doing so in most cases, and instead producing a development consisting of only two sections: "method" and "description and interpretation" (see p. 177 for details).

Analysis of some of the themes of "Birdcage" by Hector de Saint-Denys Garneau

★ ★ ★

Birdcage

Hector De Saint-Denys Garneau (1912–1943)

I'm a birdcage
A bone cage
With a bird
The bird in my bone cage
It's death making a nest
When nothing happens
I hear the ruffling of its wings
And when I've laughed heartily
If I suddenly stop
I hear it cooing
Deep down
Like a bell
It's a bird held captive
Death in my bone cage
Would it like to fly away
Are you the one holding it back
Is it me
What is it
It won't be able to leave
Until it's eaten everything
My heart
The source of blood
With life inside
It'll have my soul in its beak.

(de Saint-Denys Garneau (1993 [1937]: 74–75)

INTRODUCTION. [*topic lead-in*] Many literary texts associate, in various ways, the poet with a bird. For example, in "The Albatross" Baudelaire compares the poet to a bird, whereas in "Birdcage" the Quebec poet Hector de Saint-Denys Garneau presents the image of a bird, symbolizing death, existing within the narrator's own body. [*topic statement*] I shall undertake here a partial thematic analysis of Garneau's poem, focusing on some homological relations between signifieds. [*topic division*] The analysis consists of three parts: first, the presentation of the method (themes, homologation, etc.); second, the description of a thematic structure formed by a number of different oppositions (human/animal, life/death, etc.); and third, a brief interpretation of the data provided by the description, in which I will draw on the history of art.

METHOD. Let us first address the theoretical and methodological tools that are necessary for this analysis. The concept of the "theme" has been defined in a number of ways: "a repeated semantic element" (Smekens, 1987: 96), "that which is being talked about" (Todorov, quoted in Paquin and Reny, 1984: 201), etc. Semiotics (the discipline devoted to the study of signs) offers a particularly operational approach to the theme (see Greimas and Courtés, as presented in Hébert, 2019: chapter 9, and see Rastier, 2009 and 2016). In the broadest sense, a theme is an instance of isotopy, in the sense that it consists of the repetition of a seme (or group of semes); semes are elements that together constitute the signified of the sign. The signified is the semantic content of a sign, whereas the signifier is the form that conveys the signified. For example, in the phrase "the Earth is blue like an orange" (Paul Éluard), the seme /color/ is present in the signifieds of the words "blue" and, through homonymy, "orange" (since "orange" here denotes first a fruit and, second, a color). As for the Earth, although it has a color, it is not a color in itself.

In the following analysis, I shall address only the themes that can be structured by relations of opposition, and more specifically, in cases where an opposition stands in a relation of homologation to other oppositions. In practice, I shall discuss only a small number of the homological relations that are present in the text. We should recall that homologation is a relation of equivalence between at least two pairs of oppositions, wherein the first term of the first opposition is analogous to the first term of the second opposition, etc. For example, in our culture, we can observe a homologation between the oppositions life/death and positive/negative, such that we can say that life is to death as positive is to negative, etc. Methodologically, this approach therefore involves demonstrating the presence in the text of these oppositions and the homological relations between them.

DESCRIPTION. I shall now apply these tools to the study of the poem "Birdcage." As the title suggests, the poem places a man (the narrator)— who is compared to a cage—in opposition to a bird. The bird symbolizes death ("The bird [...] / It's death making a nest"); correlatively, the man is associated with life. More specifically, the bird is "alive" and, like the man, it seems to fight for its survival, but it is also the symbol and the cause of the man's death. Paradoxically, the bird is associated with the origin of life through the reference to a nest. The theme of "origin" is also found in the phrase "The source of blood / With life inside."

The man, as a "cage," is a container, whose content is the bird. This container/content relationship also joins blood (and/or the heart) and life ("My heart / The source of blood / With life inside"), the nest and the bird, the bird and the man's soul ("It'll [the bird] have my soul in its beak"), and the parts of the bell (the bell is thus a metaphor of the cage). We are therefore faced with a recursive, repetitive structure: the man contains a

1	human	animal
2	life (of the man)	death (of the man)
3	container	content
4	imprisoning (the bird)	freeing oneself (from the man)
5	+ (from the man's perspective)	– (from the man's perspective)

Figure 8.1 Some homologations in "Birdcage"

container which contains a content, etc. In this poem, the bird, as a content, is not free to leave its human container immediately ("It won't be able to leave / Until it's eaten everything"), so we also find the opposition captivity/freedom.

The positive/negative value—or euphoric/dysphoric value, in the terminology of "thymic" analysis—attributed to some of the themes is not univocal, but varies depending on the observer and on the themes to which they are applied. Thus, for the man, his life is positive and his death is negative (at least on the temporal level, since on the spiritual level death allows the soul to pass to the spiritual realm). We can assume that the death of the man is a matter of indifference for the bird (the man's death is a consequence of the bird's escape, but it is not clear that the former is an end or benefit in itself). The life of the bird is positive for the bird and negative for the man, etc. Similarly, the bird's captivity is positive for the man and negative for the bird. Figure 8.1 shows the structure of the homologous relations that have been identified.

INTERPRETATION. How can we interpret the structure that I have identified in the text?

First, note that, in this strongly oppositional text, some homologations are not "perfect" but relative, in the sense that it was necessary to specify the point of view (that of the man or the bird) and the object to which the theme is applied (life/death of the man/bird).

Second, in this poem, death is "personified" (or rather "animalized"), and presented as existing within man. This is an alternative to the more common presentation of death as being personified and external to man (in the figure of the "Grim Reaper," for example in Victor Hugo's poem "Mors" [Death]). This internalization of the "stranger" contrasts with the externalization and doubling found in the poem that follows "Birdcage" in the same collection, entitled "Accompaniment" (Saint-Denys Garneau (1993 [1937]: 79), where, for example, we find the verse "I walk beside myself in joy." A splitting of the subject is also found in the last verse of "Birdcage," "It'll have my soul in its mouth," which appears either as a second dispossession, after the bird has devoured the man's body, or as a liberation of the soul, which had been imprisoned in the body/cage.

Third, the association (this time it is not a homologation) between death and awareness/unawareness (of death) places this poem in a class of works known by the Latin term "Vanitas." A Vanitas is a work that "invites a meditation on death and the ephemeral nature of earthly goods" (Néraudau, 1985: 479–480) (e.g., in painting, these works include still lifes featuring a skull, or paintings that depict a young girl in the presence of a personification of death). The opposition awareness/unawareness (of death)—which is homologous to the oppositions negative/positive and profound/superficial—is mainly found in the verses "And when I've laughed heartily / If I suddenly stop / I hear it cooing." Note that, in the philosophical and moral context of a Vanitas, being aware of death is, on the contrary, viewed as positive.

CONCLUSION. [*summary*] To carry out this analysis, I first defined some of the central concepts of thematic analysis (theme, isotopy, homologation, etc.). Next, I identified the dominant homologations (human/animal, life/death, etc.) found in the poem. Finally, I suggested a partial interpretation of the data produced by my description of the poem. Among other things, it can be said that the association between death and awareness/unawareness inscribes this work in the transmedial genre (although it is mainly associated with the visual arts, and especially painting) of the Vanitas. [*opening up of the question*] By way of conclusion, I would like to propose a complementary analysis of this poem which would yield useful results, namely a complete "thymic" analysis (i.e., an analysis using the concepts of euphoria and dysphoria). For example, the negative value of death seems to be mitigated by the positive value attributed in Garneau's poem to the spiritual dimension: death frees the soul from its heavy and suffering (note that the poet was ill) bodily prison.

9 The pedagogical essay

9.1 Definition

The pedagogical essay is a genre of text produced in an educational context in which an evaluator asks an individual—typically a school pupil or university student—by means of a more or less restrictive writing instruction (also termed the "essay question"), to address a given question while conforming to certain restrictions (e.g., number of pages, word limit, time limit, etc.). The pedagogical essay does not address only literary topics, but can also deal with topics in philosophy, the humanities, or in fact on any subject, whether in a narrowly defined or more general subject area.

9.2 Types of pedagogical essays

There are three types of pedagogical essays, which are determined by the type of writing instruction.

1. In the *argumentative essay*, the writing instruction asks the writer to defend a certain position, defined by the evaluator, in relation to a given assertion (which may be expressed positively or negatively). Here are some examples: "Show that *Romeo and Juliet* is indeed a tragedy"; "Prove that there are several kinds of love in *Romeo and Juliet*." The type of analytical operation that is characteristic of this form of essay is obviously argumentation in support of the chosen position.

2. In the *critical essay*, the writing instruction asks the writer to take a position in relation to one or more assertions (expressed positively or negatively). For example: "Are Romeo and Juliet victims of circumstance or of their own mistakes?"; "Is *Death of a Salesman* a drama or a modern tragedy?" The characteristic analytical operation in this form of essay is that of adopting a position.

3. In the *analytical essay*, the writing instruction asks the writer, explicitly or implicitly, not to defend a specified position or to choose a position, but to carry out one or more analytical operations (examine, draw out, connect, classify, compare, etc.). Here are some examples: "Study the relationship between Frodo and Sauron in *The Lord of the Rings*"; "Analyze the different forms of love in *Romeo and Juliet*"; "What genre does *Death of a Salesman* belong to?"; "Compare the characters of Juliet and Ophelia"; "Compare these two excerpts

DOI: 10.4324/9781003179795-13

Argumentative essay	Critical essay	Analytical essay
Prove that this poem belongs to the romantic genre.	Does this poem belong to the romantic genre?	What genre does this poem belong to?
Show that Hamlet is actually mad.	Is Hamlet actually mad?	Analyze the links between Hamlet and the theme of madness.
Prove that Ophelia and Juliet are more different than they are similar.	Do Ophelia and Juliet have more differences than similarities?	Compare Ophelia and Juliet.

Figure 9.1 Examples of the three types of essay instruction

from *Othello*." The characteristic analytical operation in this form of essay is obviously analysis.

Regardless of the type of writing instruction, an essay can take the form of a comparison (intratextual, intertextual, between text and world, etc.), a classification (which also involves comparison), or some other analytical operation (for more on comparison, see Chapter 11). More precisely, we can say that essays address the following questions: (1) Does X have property Y, or what are the properties of X? (2) Is X an element of class Z, or to what class does X belong? A comparison is a complex version of the first type of question 1. Ultimately, question 2 is a version of question 1, since the fact of belonging to a given class is a property of the object that is being classified.

Although we can distinguish several types of essay, they all share certain elements of compositional structure: an introduction, a development, and a conclusion. The number of possible plans for the development is limited: the choice of plan depends on the wording of the topic, the literary text on which the topic is based (if applicable), and the position that is to be defended. Sometimes the wording of the topic suggests, recommends, or requires the adoption of a particular plan (for more detail, see Chapter 11).[1]

Figure 9.1 presents the different ways in which a given topic can be addressed in an argumentative essay, a critical essay, and an analytical essay respectively.

9.3 Types of instructions

Writing instructions vary in their degree of constraint, ranging from more open or general instructions (e.g., "Analyze a theme of your choice in *Hamlet*") to more narrow, specific instructions (e.g., "Analyze the theme of love that causes death in *Hamlet*, drawing connections with the genre of the play, the author's style, and other works that use this motif"). An excessive degree of openness runs

---

1 This paragraph was inspired by the ideas of Roxanne Roy, a professor at the Université du Québec à Rimouski, whom I would like to thank for her kind permission.

counter to the very nature of the pedagogical essay (e.g., "Analyze an element of your choice, from an angle of your choice, in a work of your choice"); aside from the time constraint involved in this exercise (and usually there is also a limit on the length of the text to be produced), with an instruction of this sort we are operating outside the realm of the pedagogical essay and moving toward some other sort of analytic text.

According to Vital Gadbois (cited in Lafortune and Cyr, 1996: vii), the writing instruction can be formulated in two ways: (1) interrogative ("To what extent can one claim that …?"; "Should we consider that …?"; "What do you think of this statement?"; "Do you agree with this statement?"), or (2) imperative or critical ("Criticize this statement"; "Comment on this established position"; "Discuss this claim"; "Evaluate this point of view"). In some cases, either of the two formulations, interrogative or imperative, can be used to express what is essentially the same writing instruction (e.g., "Is Hamlet actually mad or not?" or alternatively "Determine whether Hamlet is really mad or not").

All the elements of the writing instruction must be conformed to, both in terms of the specific topic to be addressed, and the way in which it is to be treated. In terms of the subject matter, no digression is permitted in the development.

9.4 Types of essay topic

A pedagogical essay in literary studies may take as its topic: (1) a work, (2) an analytical text (which analyzes a work, a method, or a theory), (3) a methodological text (or a method in general), (4) a theoretical text (or a theory, even if is presented in several texts), (4) a concept belonging to a particular method or theory, or a general concept (metaphor, the limits of interpretation), (5) a form (a given theme, topos, genre, etc.), or (6) other topics (the utility, functions, nature, aims, or future of literature, a literary event, etc.). When specific texts are analyzed, they may be whole texts or excerpts (which may be provided by the evaluator in class at the time of the exercise).

9.5 Stages in writing a pedagogical essay

We can distinguish four main stages in writing an essay.

1.   Understand the nature and meaning of the writing instruction. In terms of its nature, it is necessary to define whether it requires an argumentative, critical, or analytical essay, and whether it calls for a comparative analysis, an analysis by classification (e.g., classifying a text within the appropriate genre), a thematic study, a character study, etc. As for its meaning, it is important to determine the precise sense of the instruction's terms. The writing instruction often contains words with several meanings (polysemic terms) or technical terms (metalanguage). Specify the meaning of ambiguous or technical terms. Select the relevant meaning(s), inform the reader of your choice of

meaning, and justify it. Many students rush through this stage too quickly and produce essays that are at least partially off topic. Let us consider how to treat the following writing instruction: "How is the poet represented in Victor Hugo's 'The Function of the Poet'?" The writing instruction asks the student to undertake a thematic study, but what is the theme to be addressed? The expression "the poet" could potentially refer to the poet in general or to Hugo in particular. We must specify which of these potential topics we are going to discuss.

2. Recognize the type of plan that is demanded by the writing instruction, or choose an appropriate type of plan if it is not specified. Adapt the model plan into a specific plan tailored to the demands of the writing instruction. For example, if you are using the comparative model plan you would need to determine: (1) what aspects will be compared (e.g., in the case of a character: physical, psychological, etc.)?; (2) what arguments can be used to establish the various characteristics related to a given aspect (e.g., in terms of a character's physical aspect, they may be tall, handsome, strong, etc.)?; (3) what interpretive comments can be made?; and (4) in what order will the aspects, characteristics, arguments, and interpretive comments be presented?

3. Present the components of the analysis in a continuous essay, following the chosen plan. Clearly, if in the course of the exercise it turns out that the chosen plan does not work well, or if a superior plan presents itself, it can be changed at this stage.

4. Final rewrite(s) and revision(s).

10 Analysis of a theoretical element

10.1 Skills in dealing with theoretical elements

The skills required for dealing with a theoretical element in the broad sense (which could be a theory, an approach, a method, or a concept) correspond to the ability to carry out the operations listed below. For simplicity I refer here to "a theory," but these operations can be applied to any sort of theoretical element. For example, when we speak of the operation of creating a new theory, this also applies to the creation of a new approach, method, or concept.

1. Understanding a theory;
2. summarizing or synthesizing a theory, including one that was previously implicit;
3. illustrating or applying a theory;
4. explaining the reasons (historical, individual, social, etc.) why a theory was formulated in a particular way, and the effects of this particular formulation;
5. comparing a theory with other theories (similar, opposing, competing, complementary, etc.);
6. classifying a theory into one or more families of theories;
7. evaluating the relevance of a theory in general, or for a given object or class of objects (validating or invalidating it, gauging its value in terms of the quality of description it produces, the range of objects for which it is valid, etc.);
8. completing a theory (eliminating an erroneous element, adding a necessary or useful element, replacing an element with a better or more suitable one, developing an element that was previously only embryonic, etc.);
9. combining theories (as long as they are compatible);
10. creating a new theory.

All of these skills are in principle expected at the level of doctoral study, but not all of them will necessarily be used in the course of completing a doctorate (e.g., one does not necessarily have to produce a new theory in one's doctoral dissertation). At master's level, a student is not necessarily expected to be able to complete a theory (8), combine theories (9), or create theories (10). In literary

DOI: 10.4324/9781003179795-14

studies at an undergraduate level, students are expected to develop the skills to carry out operations 1, 2, and 3.

10.2 The relationship between a theory or method and the object to which it is applied

Several types of relations can be established between a given method or theory (together with that theory's implicit or explicit method, or the method that is habitually associated with it) and the particular object to which it is applied. A typology of these relations can be constructed, starting from a distinction between, on the one hand, those methods or theories that are conceived as being an end in themselves and, on the other hand, those methods or theories that are conceived as a means to an end.

1. When a theory or method is an end in itself, the emphasis is then placed on the theory. The object that is being analyzed simply serves to constitute the theory or method, validate it, invalidate it, modify it (by nuancing it, subtracting something, adding, substituting, merging, separating, etc.), and/or to illustrate it. In cases where the object serves to illustrate the theory, the analysis may even avoid discussion of a precise object, or it may refer superficially to several objects (e.g., citing a line from Baudelaire here, a sentence from Proust there, alluding to *Macbeth* as a whole without any further level of detail, etc.). In some cases, where the object manifestly resists the application of the theory or method at hand, the analysis will serve to show that the theory or method must be modified, or it will even invalidate the theory or method entirely.

2. When the theory or method is only a means to an end, the emphasis is placed on the object. The theory or method is used in order to learn more about the object to which it is applied, and not for itself. This does not prevent the analysis from validating, invalidating, or modifying the theory or method.

10.3 What to describe about an approach and how to describe it

An approach (whether it is a discipline in itself, falls within a discipline, or does not belong directly to any discipline) can be described from different broad points of view and treated from different angles. I have listed the main ones here, together with examples relating to semiotics (which is both a discipline and an approach). The same principles also apply, for the most part, to the description of a "pure" theory (as distinct from the implicit or explicit theory associated with a particular approach or method) or a concept. Note that a "research output," as a product generated by an approach or discipline, may be either abstract or empirical in nature (see section 10.3.2).

10.3.1 Points of view

1.   Diachronic (e.g., history of the discipline) or synchronic (state of a phenomenon, e.g., a discipline, at a given time).

2. A focus on production (the genesis of a discipline), immanence (the discipline in itself), or reception (e.g., its critical reception, subsequent work that is indebted to it).
3. Descriptive (what the discipline is), normative (what it should be), or explanatory (why it is such as it is), etc.
4. Benevolent (e.g., defending or praising the discipline), neutral, or polemical.

10.3.2 Angles from which to consider an approach

1. The meaning of the word and concept describing the approach or discipline (e.g., the word and concept "semiotics").
2. The constructed (abstract) object of analysis that is constitutive of the discipline (at the most general level: semiotic codes, semiosis, the sign, etc.) or the empirical object in which the constructed object is manifested (e.g., signifying products, which convey meaning, e.g., texts, images).
3. Disciplinary relations: higher-level disciplines (e.g., linguistics, logic) or lower-level disciplines, competing disciplines (e.g., disciplines taking an external, non-immanent approach to the same objects, such as sociology), partner disciplines (e.g., cognitive sciences), encompassed disciplines (e.g., linguistics, literary semiotics), or encompassing disciplines (e.g., sciences of culture and meaning).
4. Abstract research outputs:
    4.1. applications (e.g., analysis of Mallarmé's poem "Salut" by François Rastier, analysis of an advertisement for pasta by Roland Barthes). An application presupposes a method;
    4.2. methods (e.g., the actantial model, functions of language, the Greimas semiotic square). A method presupposes a theory;
    4.3. theories (e.g., theories of the sign, meaning, Charles Sanders Peirce's semiotics);
    4.4. theoretical, methodological, or application-related concepts (e.g., the sign, isotopy, seme, infinite semiosis [and infinite interpretation], signifier, signified, referent, icon/index/symbol, semiotic code).
5. Empirical research outputs (actual manifestations of the abstract research outputs): books, articles, journals, reports, lectures, interviews, correspondence, etc. (e.g., Ferdinand de Saussure's *Course in General Linguistics*, Algirdas Greimas's *Structural Semantics*). A single empirical output may develop one or more theories/methods/applications/concepts; a single abstract output may be manifested in one or more empirical outputs.
6. Agents producing research outputs: precursors; founders; restorers; those working *avant la lettre* (e.g., Aristotle discussed similar concepts long before the founding of semiotics); those working without knowledge of each other; casual or temporary contributors; those who, out of shame, disown the discipline they once followed (e.g., when it has fallen out of fashion); exclusive contributors (working only in semiotics); innovators; conservatives; those who are out of fashion; revolutionaries; "tinkerers";

cryptos (hiding their allegiance); the faithful; the unfaithful; the arrogant; individuals; groups; relationships (e.g., emulation, collaboration, rivalry, indifference, negation); etc. For semiotics, these agents might include Aristotle, Saussure, Peirce, Barthes, Greimas, Eco, Jakobson, Hjelmslev, the Paris School, or the Belgium-based Groupe μ (pronounced "mu").

7. Agents involved in the reception of research outputs: non-readers of works on semiotics, specialist or non-specialist readers, publishers, funding agencies, institutions (e.g., the Semiotic Society of America), etc.

8. Others (e.g., events: the founding of the International Association for Semiotic Studies in 1969).

10.4 Questions to consider when analyzing a theoretical element

Figure 10.1 shows some of the questions that one can, and indeed must, consider when presenting and analyzing a theoretical element (or any abstract element): a theory, a method, an approach, or a concept. I have drawn here on

	Questions	Sub-questions
1	Who?	Who are the precursors of the theory? Who are its founders? Who are its main representatives? Who is associated with the theory willingly or unwillingly? Who uses it today? Who should be interested in this theory?
2	When?	When was the theory developed? When was it most influential, or least influential? Did it have precursors? Has it come back into favor? If not, does it deserve to? How well has it aged?
3	Where?	Where did the theory originate? How is it marked by this origin? How far did it extend its influence? Which areas have resisted it?
4	What?	What are the main concepts of this theory and their relationships? What are its main axioms, postulates, and hypotheses? How do they differ from comparable elements of other earlier, contemporary, and possibly later theories?
5	How?	How can we analyze a literary text or element (e.g., a genre, a stylistic rhetorical figure) using this theory?
6	To what end?	What does it aim to accomplish? What are its goals? Does it achieve them?
7	Why?	Why is this theory important? Why should we be interested in it? What is its contribution compared to its earlier, contemporary, and possibly later competitors?
8	Applied to what?	To what types of phenomena (genres, authors, writing processes, concepts, etc.) can the theory be applied? On the basis of what kinds of phenomena, or what kinds of texts, was it constituted? How has this affected it, or determined it?
9	What is wrong with it?	What are the flaws, oversights, or limitations of the theory in its constitution (its concepts, hypotheses, postulates, axioms, presuppositions, etc.) or in its methods and applications?

Figure 10.1 Questions to consider when analyzing a theoretical element

the questions suggested by Barsky (1997: 16) for the analysis of literary theories, but the same questions are valid in principle for any theoretical element. For an example of the application of these questions to the analysis of a theoretical element (in this case, to sociocriticism), see Barsky (1997: 197–213) or Hébert (2014: 263–272).

11 The plan of the analytical text[1]

11.1 Typology of plans: overview

The plan of an argumentative text defines the way that text is broken into parts, in particular with regard to the development section, and the type of argumentative process that supports and unifies the parts of the development.

A distinction can be made between the model plan (the abstract template) and the applied plan (a particular manifestation of the template in an analytical text), which corresponds to the logical and linguistic distinction between the "type" and the "token." The model plan is an empty structure that will then be filled in, in different ways, in the actual instances of different applied plans. For example, in the dialectical model plan, a thesis is presented in opposition to an antithesis; the specific thesis and antithesis will vary in different applied plans. In one text, the thesis might be that "Hamlet is mad" while the antithesis is that "Hamlet is not mad"; in another text, the thesis might be that "Baudelaire is misogynistic in his texts" while the antithesis is that "Baudelaire is not misogynistic in his texts."

There are several types of plans. Here are some of the main ones:

1.   the comparative plan, in which the elements to be compared are considered alongside each other point by point;
2.   the dialectical plan, in which the elements to be confronted with one another are placed in opposition, point by point;
3.   the syllogistic plan, where a conclusion is reached (not to be confused with the final part of an analytical text, which is also called the "conclusion") through the interplay of the premises (i.e., the starting points of a logical progression);
4.   the step-by-step or analytical plan, in which each of the (selected) aspects of a question is dealt with in turn, and the aspects are linked to each other by a more or less strong structure (e.g., a chronological structure).

---

1 In this chapter I have reworked and extended an unpublished text by Roxanne Roy, professor at the Université du Québec à Rimouski, whom I would like to thank for her kind permission.

DOI: 10.4324/9781003179795-15

There are relationships between the different plans. For example, in a way, the classification of a text in a genre consists of a syllogistic analysis. The logical progression is as follows: texts in this genre have these characteristics (premise 1); this text has these characteristics (premise 2); therefore, this text belongs to this genre (conclusion). Furthermore, one can combine different types of plans, for example, by making a comparison in chronological order.

We also need to make a distinction between the pre-writing plan, which is produced as a tool to guide the writing of the text, and the post-writing plan, which faithfully reflects the plan that was actually carried out. The pre-writing plan and the post-writing plan may not correspond exactly. The post-writing plan is particularly useful for creating appropriate headings in the text.

11.2 Detailed typology of plans

11.2.1 *Dialectical plan*

The dialectical plan has three parts: the thesis, the antithesis, and the synthesis. In the thesis, the proposition formulated is presented and supported by arguments. Immediately afterwards, the antithesis takes a point of view opposite to that of the thesis; this second step consists in challenging what had been asserted in the thesis to raise objections on a certain aspect of the thesis. In the synthesis the thesis and the antithesis are opposed to each other in two ways. First, it is necessary to recognize the aspects of the thesis that resist refutation and identify those aspects that remain ambiguous (which have not really, or not entirely, been refuted). The second task is not a matter of juxtaposing thesis and antithesis, nor of summing them up, but rather of moving beyond the apparent contradiction to which the analysis has led. This is achieved by adding new elements, nuances, explanations of the contradiction, or a complete change of perspective. The synthesis is the most difficult part, as it involves bringing together the two opposing theses by identifying what is acceptable or not in the two positions, and moving beyond them with a stronger proposal. The thesis can correspond to an affirmation ("Hamlet loves Ophelia") or to a negation ("Hamlet is not mad"), and the same goes for the antithesis. If the synthesis, instead of bringing together thesis and antithesis and moving beyond them, only produces an attenuated version of the thesis or the antithesis (e.g., through a step-by-step assessment of their pros and cons), or only decides in favor of one or the other, we can speak of a dichotomous plan. From a logical point of view, in cases where a thesis and an antithesis form a dyadic logical opposition—which is not the case, for example, of the thesis "Hamlet has red hair" and the antithesis "Hamlet has blond hair," since red hair and blond hair are not opposites in a dyad, as hair can also be brown or black—four propositions are in fact possible: the thesis is true, the antithesis is true, both the thesis and the antithesis are true, neither the thesis nor the antithesis is true. The most striking and common type of synthesis is that which reflects the fourth proposition. It either simply invalidates the thesis and the antithesis or, more interestingly, it proposes another way.

Model plan	General example of an applied plan	Specific example of an applied plan
Thesis (initial position)	Yes	Hamlet loves Ophelia
Antithesis (intermediate position)	No	Hamlet does not love Ophelia
Synthesis (final position, conclusion of the development section)	"Yes, but …" (qualified position) or "No, but …" (qualified position) or "Neither" or "Neither, but a third thing"	Hamlet loves Ophelia badly or only with a certain kind of love

Figure 11.1 Structure of a dialectical plan

Figure 11.1 summarizes the main possibilities of the dialectical plan and provides examples.

11.2.2 Comparative plan

The comparative plan is used when it is necessary to conduct an extended comparison in the analysis. Comparison is an analytical operation where at least one subject-observer compares at least two objects with regard to at least one aspect[2] (the word "aspect" is used here in a broad sense) and attributes at least one character or property (usually only one) to the selected aspect of each object. Various types of comparative relations can be established between characteristics of the same aspect of the chosen objects for comparison. The main types of comparative relations are identity (one hydrogen atom and another), similarity (two twins), opposition (day and night), and alterity (day and a hippopotamus). In the interpretive phase, the causes and effects of the presence of these relationships must be established. The interpretive phase may also involve bringing to light a previously unnoticed nuance of alterity-opposition within relations of identity-similarity, or a nuance of similarity in relations of alterity-opposition.

The main kinds of literary comparison, which vary according to the kind of objects involved, are listed below.

1. Intratextual comparison. Comparison of two (or more) elements of the same text (e.g., in terms of the signified, the semantic content: characters, places, themes, situations, etc.).
2. Intertextual comparison. Comparison between a text and another text (in general, between very similar or, on the contrary, strongly contrasting texts).

2 The relation between the object being compared and an aspect of comparison is of a mereological nature, i.e., it is the relation between a whole and a part of that whole. The same goes for the relation between an aspect and a sub-aspect. The word "aspect" here has a more general meaning than when I use it to designate a component of a literary text.

3. Architextual comparison. Comparison between an architext (a class of text or a type of text, such as a genre) and a text. This form of comparison aims at classifying a text within a genre (or in a given class of texts which is not necessarily a genre). For example, one might demonstrate that a poem belongs, to a moderate or high degree, to both Romanticism and Symbolism. This type of analysis involves establishing the characteristics of the genre, verifying the presence or absence of those characteristics in the individual text, and addressing the causes, modes, and effects of this presence or absence.

4. Intergeneric comparison. Comparison between the characteristics of one genre and those of another genre (in general, between very similar genres— e.g., verse poetry and prose poetry—or, on the contrary, between strongly contrasting genres—e.g., the literary text and the scientific text).

5. Non-generic typological comparison. Comparison between a unit of a text and a type that is not a genre (or other class of texts). For example, a particular manifestation of love is compared and related to a type of love found in a given typology (e.g., conjugal love, filial love, friendship, etc.).

6. Text/world comparison. Comparison of elements of the text with elements of the real world. For example, one might compare: the structures and dynamics of real society with those of the society represented in the text (social analysis), the characters of a text with their possible real-life counterparts (biographical analysis), or the events of a text with those that occur in real life (historical literary analysis).

Note that comparisons can involve two textual elements or a textual element and an element pertaining to another semiotic code, thereby producing an intersemiotic comparison (e.g., text and image). This element from another semiotic code may belong to a non-literary art, thereby producing an inter-artistic comparison (e.g., comparison between the textual Ophelia and the Ophelia in John Everett Millais's painting). The same principle applies to intermedial comparison, that is, the relation between several media.

There are two main ways to construct a comparative plan. In the first case, the aspects of comparison are organized according to the nature of the comparative relationship (e.g., all the comparisons of identity-similarity are presented, then all the comparisons of opposition-alterity). This way of constructing a comparative plan is sometimes referred to as an "analogical plan." In the second case, the aspects of comparison are organized according to another criterion (e.g., first all the elements of content are compared, then all the elements of form).

We can also distinguish between a consecutive plan (where, for a given object, we move from one point of comparison to another, before doing the same thing for the second object) and an alternating plan (where, for a given point of comparison, we move from one object to another, before advancing to a second given point of comparison).

Figure 11.2 summarizes the main possibilities of the comparative plan and provides examples.

Model consecutive plan	Example of applied consecutive plan	Model alternating plan	Example of applied alternating plan
Object 1, aspect 1, characteristic x, y, or z, etc.	Hamlet, moral aspect, characteristic: good (x)	Object 1, aspect 1, characteristic x, y, or z, etc.	Hamlet, moral aspect, characteristic: good (x)
Object 1, aspect 2, characteristic x, y, or z, etc.	Hamlet, temperamental aspect, characteristic: melancholic (y)	Object 2, aspect 1, characteristic x, y, or z, etc.	Ophelia, moral aspect, characteristic: good (x)
Object 2, aspect 1, characteristic x, y, or z, etc.	Ophelia, moral aspect, characteristic: good (x)	Object 1, aspect 2, characteristic x, y, or z, etc.	Hamlet, temperamental aspect, characteristic: melancholic (y)
Object 2, aspect 2, characteristic x, y, or z, etc.	Ophelia, temperamental aspect, characteristic: romantic (z)	Object 2, aspect 2, characteristic x, y, or z, etc.	Ophelia, temperamental aspect, characteristic: romantic (z)

Figure 11.2 Structure of a comparative plan

11.2.3 Syllogistic plan

The construction of the syllogistic plan follows the structure of the syllogism. The *Merriam-Webster* dictionary defines a syllogism as follows: "a deductive scheme of a formal argument consisting of a major and a minor premise and a conclusion (as in 'every virtue is laudable; kindness is a virtue; therefore, kindness is laudable')."[3] A syllogism produces a deduction, a logical progression passing from the general to the particular (see Chapter 12 on argumentation).

Figure 11.3 summarizes the syllogistic plan and provides examples.

11.2.4 Analytical plan

Since, by definition, a plan differentiates and unifies different parts of the development within a progressive structure, any plan is analytic. However, the degree of analyticity, and thus the strength of the organizing structure, may vary. The "American plan" (as we call it in the Francophone world) is an example of a plan where the structure is looser: at the extreme, different parts are simply strung together with no strong organizing structure, and it no longer really constitutes an analytical plan. Conversely, the syllogistic plan is an example of an extremely structured plan.

---

3 "Syllogism." Merriam-Webster.com Dictionary, Merriam-Webster, https://www.merriam-webster.com/dictionary/syllogism (accessed February 3, 2022).

Model plan	Example of applied plan
Premise 1	One who truly loves thinks first of the loved one (proposition to be accompanied by arguments)
Premise 2	Hamlet does not think first of Ophelia (proposition to be accompanied by proofs)
Conclusion (of the logical progression and development section)	Therefore, Hamlet does not love Ophelia

Figure 11.3 Structure of a syllogistic plan

This being said, the comparative, syllogistic, and dialectical plans are generally considered separately from the analytical plan. On the other hand, the chronological plan, in which the treatment of the object is organized by successive periods of time, is sometimes integrated into the class of analytical plans and sometimes placed in a separate class of its own. In literary analysis, chronology can be based on different types of time: "real," historical time (the chronology of periods, forms, works, authors, literary phenomena, etc.); thematized time within the work, the time of the story told; or the succession of semiotic units themselves. These units are signifiers (forms that support the signifieds), signifieds (contents), or signs (the combination of a signifier and its signified). We are then faced with successions of units of different possible lengths: phonemes, words, sentences, verses, chapters, etc. As far as the analysis of texts is concerned, a plan that is organized such that it follows the succession of semiotic units themselves in a text can be called linear; a plan that does not directly follow such an arrangement and succession can be called tabular (see section 11.2.5).

What are the strong logical structures that will ensure that the different parts of the development follow one another in a logical order? The analytical plan can be chronological (time x, time $x + n$, etc.), causal (causes, effects), problem-consequences-solutions, dichotomous (for/against, positive qualities/flaws, etc.), based on systematically applied questions (who? what? when? where? how?, etc.); etc.

In a work with a looser analytical structure, the conclusion of the development (again, not to be confused with the conclusion of the whole text) is particularly important, as it provides an opportunity to synthesize and further unify the parts of the development.

Figure 11.4 summarizes the analytical plan and provides examples.

11.2.5 Linear and tabular plans

The interpretation of a series of units in the analyzed object (e.g., in a text, a comic strip, a film, a piece of music, a perceptual path through the figures in a

A. Model problem–consequence–solution plan	Example of applied problem–consequence–solution plan	B. Model chronological plan	Example of applied chronological plan
Problem	Hamlet's doubt about Claudius's guilt	Analysis at time 1	Analysis of verse 1 of a poem or chapter 1 of a novel, etc. / Analysis of the youth of the character / Analysis of the theater before 1945
Consequence	Revenge is constantly postponed	Analysis at time 2	Analysis of verse 2 of the poem or chapter 2 of the novel, etc. / Analysis of the character's old age / Analysis of the theater after 1945
Solution	Analyses and tests to prove Claudius's guilt	Etc.	Etc.

C. Model plan using analytical questions	Example of applied plan using analytical questions (on the gaze in Baudelaire's poem "Windows")
Who (acts, is acted upon, has a given characteristic)?	Who is watching? The narrator. Characteristics of the narrator? The narrator experiences an uneasiness that he combats by looking into the windows of his neighbors, etc. Links and differences with the author, the famous French poet?
What (what action or characteristic are we talking about?)?	What are we looking at? Windows, especially illuminated ones.
When?	Nighttime, as far as the illuminated windows are concerned; since no historical period is specified, we assume that the action takes place at the time of the writing of the text (nineteenth century); the action seems repetitive, the narrator has done this several times, etc.
Where?	In the city, in Paris (the collection is entitled *Le Spleen de Paris*); whereas the literary nineteenth century as a whole values nature, Baudelaire expresses contempt for nature (too regular, etc.).
How (manner, means, circumstances, etc.)?	The gaze is more imaginative than descriptive (the narrator imagines the life of the people he sees).
Why (intentions, goals, causes, etc.)?	The narrator looks into other people's windows and reconstructs, with the help of small clues, the possible lives of those people. He aims for (intention) and achieves (result) three goals: to get through life (dispel boredom, combat "spleen"), to feel that he exists, and to know who he is.
Results (intended or unintended effects, etc.)?	The intended goals seem to be achieved, but not completely ("spleen" is an invincible enemy in Baudelaire's work).

Figure 11.4 Structure of an analytical plan

painting) can be linear or tabular (I am here extending and adding more detail to these concepts, which were initially developed by Groupe μ [1990] for the study of texts). "Linear" and "tabular" are etymologically connected to "line" and "table" respectively.

These two types of interpretation underpin different plans. Linear analysis produces a type of analytical plan similar to the chronological plan, in the narrow sense. Tabular analysis may, depending on the particular case, be an instance of any of the types of plans discussed in this chapter, apart from the specific type of chronological plan mentioned above.

Linear interpretation consists in taking into account only or principally the interpretations that have been accumulated, produced, or anticipated at a given position in the analyzed product, generally proceeding as if this were the first "reading" of the semiotic product. For example, someone reading Rimbaud's "The Sleeper in the Valley" for the first time only learns at the last verse that the sleeper is (well and truly) dead. Even if one has already read the poem, one can try to recreate valid interpretations that could be made at a given point in the work (e.g., in verse 4) by a reader undertaking their first reading of the sonnet (and who is otherwise unaware of the content of the work).

Tabular interpretation does not take into account the position of a particular interpretation in the series of units, and does not generally try to recreate the experience of an initial interpretation. For example, within the framework of a tabular interpretation, one could draw up an inventory of all the signifieds (contents) that allude to death in Rimbaud's poem, including those that are found before the last line, where we learn (or confirm) the death of the young soldier. Here is another example of how the same object can be treated through a linear or tabular analysis: one can establish the characteristics of a given character in a global way (tabular analysis), or alternatively consider which characteristics appear first or at a given place in the text, or how they develop along the series of units (verses, lines, phrases, paragraphs, etc.).

Obviously, linear analysis is neither superior nor inferior to tabular analysis. Each type of analysis has its limitations. For example, a tabular analysis is often criticized for not taking into account the crucial development of units over the course of the work (when they arise, their duration, transformation, disappearance). As for linear analysis, it is vulnerable to certain problems. It may "jump" from one type of element to another when it passes from one unit of division to another, dropping, for example, theme A when it moves on from the first verse of the poem, but then picking up theme B when approaching the second verse of the poem; in doing so, it loses one of its main advantages, that of showing the development of a given element over the course of the units, and the meaning that can be extracted from this development. Linear analysis may merely undertake to move a perceptual "window" from one unit to another (e.g., for a poem, progressing from verse 1 to verse 2, and then from verse 2 to verse 3, etc.) without providing a description of the development taking place between units that are not directly juxtaposed (e.g., from verse 1 to verse 3). Linear analysis generally takes into account only one unit of measurement of linearity (e.g., the verses of a poem) and does not describe the interaction of the different units of measurement (e.g., non-strophic groups of verses, stanza, syntagma, sentence, etc.), which divide up and drive forward the text, and which do not necessarily coincide with each other (e.g., a sentence can end in the middle of a verse). At best, a linear analysis restricts itself to one unit of measurement which happens to be the most significant unit of measurement in a given text, but neglects other significant units of measurement; at worst, it chooses a unit of measurement that is not the most significant. Moreover, one may be led to pay greatest attention to "classical" units (e.g., the four stanzas of a sonnet) to the detriment of units that are more specific to the analyzed text, and which may be more significant (e.g., four groups of three verses and one group of two verses in such a sonnet). Finally, many linear analyses produced in schools are more analytical summaries than real analyses, but here, as elsewhere, the fault lies not with linear analysis itself, but with its misuse.

12 Argumentation

12.1 Introduction

Any text is either primarily *argumentative* (e.g., an opinion piece, scientific article, analytical text, editorial) or primarily *non-argumentative* (e.g., a simple description, newspaper article, poem, novel).

An argumentative text is not so much about giving one's opinion, even if it is well founded, as about persuading. To persuade is essentially to demonstrate the truth of a *proposition* (in the logical sense) or of an organized series of propositions that were previously considered—by the person to be persuaded, a given social group, or even humanity—as being (1) false, (2) undecidable (it was not possible to determine whether they were true or false), (3) undecided (their truthfulness had not yet been evaluated), or (4) "unconsidered" (e.g., the person or people to be persuaded were not even aware of these propositions). The study of argumentation not only helps you to learn how to persuade, but also acts as a defense against argumentation presented by another person that has no more than the appearance of truth.

12.2 Proposition, subject, predicate, and truth value

A proposition (in the logical sense) can be broken down into the *subject* (e.g., "love") and the *predicate* (love "is wonderful at any age"). A proposition always has a "truth value": it is true, false (more or less true, more or less false), undecidable (one cannot decide), undecided (one has not yet decided, or one has withdrawn a previous judgment), or unconsidered (the question has not arisen, just as, for example, a person who is not accused cannot be declared legally guilty or innocent). For a given proposition, the truth value (or another related status: undecidable, undecided, unconsidered) is likely to vary according to the usual factors of relativity: time, observer (the particular person, social group, culture), etc. For example, a contrarian claims as false whatever their interlocutor holds to be true, and vice versa.

A given proposition can be expressed in language (or other semiotic systems, such as images) in several different ways: "The Earth is round"; "Round, the

DOI: 10.4324/9781003179795-16

Earth? Of course it is!"; "The roundness of our planet ..." The proposition can also be presupposed: "I walked straight ahead without ever deviating and I came back to my starting point" (this is only possible because the Earth is round). Traditionally, a distinction is made between a presupposition (e.g., the question "How is your wife?" presupposes that the interlocutor is married) and a subtext (e.g., "it's cold" actually means "please close the window").

A proposition, formulated by the writer (or speaker) or reported by them, can be expressed positively or negatively, can be marked as true or false (or again, as undecidable, undecided, or unconsidered), and can be presented as certain or uncertain. Here are some examples of possible combinations: "The Earth is round" (positive, true, certain); "It is not known whether the Earth is round" (positive, undecidable, certain); "The Earth may not be flat" (negative, true, uncertain). If a proposition pertains to a dilemma (either X or Y is true, with no possibility of a third choice), validating the proposition effectively invalidates the opposite proposition, while invalidating the proposition effectively validates the opposite proposition. For example, proving that the Earth is flat invalidates the proposition that the Earth is round (since there is nobody arguing that it is, for example, cuboidal). Not all propositions have a dilemma (the basic dilemma involves a simple true/false opposition). For example, proving that John is not rich is not the same as proving that he is necessarily poor (he may be neither rich nor poor). Traditionally, the most complete logical structure used (although there are even more complex ones, such as the semiotic square, with ten possibilities, see Hébert, 2019: chapter 3) is the tetralemma, with its four possibilities: true, false, true and false at the same time, neither true nor false.

Although an argumentative text can be subjective on the level of the enunciator (writer, speaker, etc.) and of the ideas that are expressed (e.g., if I am the one who discovered the idea I am going to defend), it must generally be objective in terms of its demonstration. The logical approach to argumentation is therefore as follows (although it does not necessarily follow this sequence chronologically): (1) present a proposition with a truth value (explicit or implicit), (2) prove that the given truth value is the right (or wrong) one for that proposition.

The quality and quantity of the argumentation must be inversely proportional to the *obviousness* of the proposition, and proportional to the *scope* of the proposition and its *force*.

To illustrate the concept of the obviousness of a proposition, let us consider two extreme examples: a truism such as "The Earth is round" does not need any argumentation (at least nowadays, and with the exception of flat-earthers!); on the other hand, the proposition "The Earth is flat" would require a very strong case ... Other instances of obvious statements, barely requiring argumentation, include generalities, banalities, and other all-purpose propositions (which are true for just about any subject, in any culture, in any era, for any person): for example, "Quebec literature has changed a lot in the last few years."

NOTE: AXIOMS AND DOXA

The degree of obviousness is derived from the "axioms" that are assumed by a given social group at a given time. These axioms can vary according to factors of relativity. We often divide argumentative elements into facts and opinions. The axioms that are most strongly held by the group constitute facts (the Earth is round), but—as many examples from history have shown—the most fundamental "facts" may come to be contradicted later on. These "facts" are part of the doxa, the set of beliefs commonly accepted by a given group at a given time.

The scope of propositions is variable. Compare, for example, "all planets are round" and "the Earth is round." The force of propositions is also variable. Compare, for example, "the Earth is round" and "the Earth is perhaps round," or "The Earth is approximately round." It is essential to adjust the scope and force of the proposition to the degree of certainty that the demonstration is able to provide. This is done by using modifiers (in the broad sense). A modifier is a unit that increases or decreases the scope or force of the proposition, or of its truth value. Here are some modifiers: adverbs of doubt ("perhaps," etc.); expressions such as "it seems that ...," "we can say metaphorically that ..."; quantifiers such as "no" (e.g., no animal can conceive of God), "one," "some," "certain," "several," "many," "most," "almost all," "all but one," "all"; indicators of frequency and temporality: "never," "once," "rarely," "sometimes," "usually," "often," "almost always," "always"; indicators of subjectivity such as "I think," "personally"; etc. The scope in particular can be adjusted by varying the degree of generality or specificity of the elements of the proposition (compare the propositions "mammals can talk" and "humans can talk").

The sense of nuance—which is important in rational argumentation but often ineffective in emotional argumentation, as we see all too often, for example, in phone-in shows and on social media—is manifested both in the scope of the proposition (compare "all men are creeps" and "some men are creeps"), and in its truth value, if the latter happens to be graduated (with varying degrees between true and false). It is necessary to make the generality/specificity of the term used correspond to the generality/specificity of the phenomenon denoted by this term. For example, if the concept in question is "poetry," the word "literature" encompasses but goes beyond the phenomenon (since poetry is a part of literature) and is therefore too broad; on the other hand, the term "lyric poetry" is too specific (lyric poetry is only one part of poetry). To take a more complex example, to say that the literary manifestations of the psychoanalytical unconscious are to be found only in literary "images" would be excessively narrow in scope, since the unconscious can also be found elsewhere in literary texts (rhythms, sonorities, etc.). An excessive degree of generality leads, at best, to a lack of precision; an excessive degree of specificity can produce a partially false proposition, such as in the proposition "a mammal is a cow" (it can also be a man, a fox ...). In general, to provide a sufficient degree of nuance, one should avoid absolute terms such as "never," "always," "nowhere," "everywhere," "no" (e.g., no one can ...), "every," "the worst," "the best," "impossible," "all," "only one," "the least," "the most," etc. These words are "dangerous" in all areas of the cultural sciences (as opposed to the natural sciences), because they give rise to propositions that can generally be disproved.

NOTE: ARGUING, UNDER-ARGUING, OVER-ARGUING

Propositions are often taken for granted when they should be demonstrated through argumentation: a sense of perpetual doubt should be developed. It is better, at least at the beginning, to over-argue than to under-argue. Both tendencies are, however, flaws: over-arguing is a waste of time and energy (and the reader may feel that you are talking down to them). Moreover, an analysis can and should be concerned primarily with areas of doubt rather than areas of absolute certainty, as the latter are often of less interest precisely because they are obvious.

12.3 A method for generating and developing arguments

To argue well, one needs (1) a method for generating and developing arguments, and (2) a wide range of possible argumentative elements at one's disposal. It is impossible here to give a comprehensive account of this subject.

With regard to the first point, I will set out a rudimentary but effective method for producing and developing an argument for an argumentative text in general and for an opinion piece in particular.

1. Once you have chosen the topic, define the opinion to be put forward (true or false, for or against, absolute or nuanced). As one might expect, an opinion takes the form of a proposition with a truth value, or is based on such propositions. When the opinion is against something (e.g., against nuclear power), it is itself based on propositions with a truth value (e.g., one might be against nuclear power because the proposition "nuclear power is dangerous" is held to be true).

2. Gather elements for each of the following types of materials (one page per type): (2.1) specific, specialized vocabulary related to the issue; (2.2) aspects (broadly defined) and approaches (broadly defined) through which one can address the issue; (2.3) propositions (with their truth value) to be defended or invalidated, and arguments (and counter-arguments) proving or invalidating the propositions; (2.4) stylistic elements (metaphors, imagery, etc.).

Let us consider how to gather elements for a specific topic: "Was Baudelaire a misogynist?"

2.1. Specialized vocabulary: "misogyny" (different possible definitions of the term and a selection of one or more definitions); "empirical author," "constructed author" (see next point).

2.2.   Aspects: the real Baudelaire (empirical author) and the Baudelaire who emerges from his texts (constructed author), etc.; approaches: biographical history, social history, feminism, the worldview of the author being analyzed, etc.

2.3.   Propositions and arguments: for example, the figure of Baudelaire that appears in the texts does not exclusively devalue women (e.g., he shows compassion for women in the poem "The Little Old Women").

3. Select the most useful elements out of those that you have gathered (some elements can be discarded immediately), giving thought to their hierarchy (e.g., some arguments are powerful by themselves, while others are only worth using among a cluster of similar arguments), and how they can be combined, positioned, and developed.

Generally, elements of argumentation are combined on the basis of aspects or approaches. Another common combination is that of argument and counter-argument (i.e., an argument is confronted with another argument making the opposite point). To defend yourself in advance from the effects of an opponent's counter-argument, you should expect this opposition (whereas some people think their statements should just be taken for granted), anticipate its content, and counter it with (valid and persuasive) arguments. You should assume that the reader, without being hostile as such, will be skeptical.

In principle, one always counter-argues when one's position is attacked or could be attacked, except in the case of a *concession*, where we concede victory to the adversary on a particular point, generally in order to prevail on a more important point. For example, on the topic of the death penalty one might argue: "Certainly, I concede that incarcerating prisoners is expensive, but that is the cost we must pay for a system of justice that is not morally shameful." Or again, to return to our topic about Hamlet: "Certainly, Hamlet seems to be mad in this scene, but I shall demonstrate that in all the other scenes he is not mad."

Successfully developing counter-arguments involves getting "inside the head" of one's opponent. Ultimately, to be skilled in argumentation one must be able to argue any position, like an intellectual mercenary, or indeed like an advertiser paid to promote a product that they may find foolish, bad, or even disgusting … However, beyond this purely intellectual exercise, there are moral and ethical principles that prevent us from defending absolutely any cause "for real."

12.4 Qualities of effective argumentation

Pay attention to (1) *consistency*, with regard to the number of arguments used in support of each proposition, the variety of arguments, and their appropriate degree of development (ultimately, over-arguing is as useless as under-arguing, and can even be counterproductive).

Pay attention to (2) *coherence*. The argumentation must support the opinion (and not the opposite opinion) and not contain contradictions (saying one thing in one place and the opposite in another). In addition, the arguments must be relevant to the proposition.

For example, if the author argues that "one can be happy at home because some self-employed people work from home," their argument does not support the proposition. The causal link between being happy and working at home has been postulated, but not proven. The same defective argumentation is found in the following statement: "Ophelia is mad, and therefore so is Hamlet."

Pay attention to (3) *cohesion* and (4) *progression*. Some combinations of arguments are counterproductive. In particular, pay attention to the use of very bold arguments: if they are introduced too early or too late, poorly supported, prepared, or implemented, they will not be fully effective or may even be counterproductive.

Finally, pay attention to (5) the *adaptation* of the arguments to suit the reader's "reality" and—even more importantly—their values and knowledge: the defended propositions must not only be demonstrated to be true through valid argumentation (a matter of their truth status) but also appear to be true in the eyes of a typical reader (a matter of plausibility). This does not mean that one should withhold the truth if the truth does not conform to the reader's expectations, but that one should look for those parts of the truth that satisfy the expectations of the person to be persuaded.

12.5 Some types of argumentative elements

There are many types of argumentative elements. Figure 12.1 shows some of the most important ones.[1] For each type, two kinds of examples are given: one example suitable for a non-literary opinion piece (often addressing the question "Should aid to developing countries be increased, maintained, or decreased?"), and one example from literary studies. The examples are obviously crude and—it should go without saying—do not necessarily reflect my own thinking. A single passage of an argumentative text may combine several argumentative elements and draw on several types of argument. Some types overlap at least partially (e.g., litotes and euphemism).

A given type of argumentative element is not necessarily good or bad in itself (e.g., an example can be good or bad). It depends on how it is used and the context (a good argument in one context may be bad in another). Some types are generally seen as errors of argumentation, but a writer may—deliberately or not—use them to their advantage, or alternatively expose their presence in the opponent's argument: for example, the writer may surreptitiously slip in a statement of principle, a euphemism, or a sophism, even while criticizing the presence of these elements in the opponent's argument. Arguments that are intentionally designed to mislead are described as fallacious.

---

1 I have drawn here on Simonet and Simonet (1999), Blackburn (1994), Laberge (n.d.), and Everaert-Desmedt (2011), among others.

	Name, explanation	General example	Literary example
1	Abusive conclusion (1) from class to element, or (2) from element to class, or (3) from one element to another, or (4) from one class to another	(2) The players on this team are all good, so I deduce that this team is excellent. (3) This perfume smells like roses, so this other perfume smells like roses too.	(2 or 4) These works by Victor Hugo are collections of poems; I conclude that all of Hugo's works are collections of poems. (4) The genre of the novel entails a work with many pages; I conclude that the genre of poetry does so too.
2	Abusive conclusion (1) from the whole to the part, or (2) from the part to the whole, or (3) from one part to another, or (4) from one whole to another	(4) This flower smells good; I conclude that this other kind of flower smells good.	(1) This novel is said to be realistic; I conclude that each of its chapters is realistic.
3	Abusive particularization; see Abusive conclusion	Every inhabitant of a country that is generous with international aid is necessarily generous.	Racine's *Phèdre* contains a passage in the baroque style, the tirade of Théramène; we must therefore conclude that the play is baroque. (Note: the play is in the classical style, which is generally opposed to the baroque style)
4	*Ad hominem*, a judgment or attack directed against the opposition as individuals (whether truthful or not)	This party was, in the 2000s, a fierce defender of international aid. Now, this same party wants to cut this aid. Do the members of this party have a split personality? (also identifies the opponents' contradiction) This government that asks us to trust it in this area is the same one that has lied to us on many other subjects.	Jean Genet was a thief, so he cannot have been a good writer.
5	Anachronism (of techniques, knowledge, words, concepts, values, events, etc.)	When people in nineteenth-century Africa spoke of Africanness … (Note: the word and concept of Africanness emerged in the 1950s and 1960s)	Henry David Thoreau in *Walden* must have been aware that Darwin's principle of natural selection is at work everywhere. (Note: *On the Origin of Species* was published five years after *Walden*)

6	Anaculturalism (elements of one culture are applied to another culture where they are irrelevant)	This stranger did not burp while eating my food, so he is rude. (Note: burping while eating is not a mark of polite behavior in all cultures)	Among the Mayans the big toe is a symbol of fertility. This is therefore also true in Arthur Miller's work.
7	Appeal to common sense	Resources and money are not inexhaustible.	Literature meets a need, otherwise it would not exist.
8	Appeal to ignorance (an opinion is accepted simply because it has not been proven wrong)	There is no evidence that GMOs are harmful to health, therefore GMOs are good for one's health.	It has never been proven that Shakespeare was not the author of the plays attributed to him. He is therefore undoubtedly their author.
9	Appeal to novelty/tradition	We have been supporting development for decades, so now it is time to stop. Why end a decades-long tradition?	It is a new/traditional form of the novel, so it is good.
10	Appeal to the facts	Most people live in poor countries. Every day, people elsewhere die of hunger. The sun rises in the East. The Earth is round.	The narrator has blue eyes, as he states, "my eyes are the color of the sky."
11	Appeal to the majority (or the many)/minority (or the few)	Most countries are cutting back on humanitarian aid, why should we act differently? Galileo was called a fool, but he was right, so let us go against the international consensus and give more.	Most readers consider *Phèdre* to be one of Racine's masterpieces.
12	Appeal to the reader's experience	If your neighbor asked you for salt, would you turn them away? Therefore we should give to poorer countries. (Note: a metaphorical comparison)	The character is probably suffering from love. Who, among readers, has not already done so with these same symptoms?
13	Appeal to values	What distinguishes the human from the inhuman is solidarity and mutual aid.	This text is important because it shows what distinguishes good from evil.

Figure 12.1 Some types of argumentative elements

	Name, explanation	General example	Literary example
14	(1) Argument from authority (or appeal to authority); (2) appeal to false authority (outside the field of their expertise); (3) argument against (any) authority	(1) Did not Jesus tell us to "love one another"? (2) Albert Einstein said that we should give to developing countries. (3) Experts tell us that we must give. Experts know nothing, they are in the pay of the powers that be.	(1) Balzac scholars consider this novel by Balzac to be … (2) The President of the United States considers *Harry Potter* to be a great novel. (3) Experts say that Hamlet is not completely mad, so I will take the opposite position.
15	Argumentation by the absurd	They say that everything that is rare is expensive. But since an economical car is rare, it would be expensive …	If critics were certain that Hamlet is mad, we would not still be debating it.
16	(1) Assimilation of two things into one; (2) division (dissimilation) of one thing into several	(1) International aid and assistance to people in danger are one and the same thing. (2) There are several kinds of international aid: food aid, educational aid, etc.	(1) In a way, the theme and subject of a work are the same thing. (2) There are two main kinds of metaphor: *in praesentia* and *in absentia*.
17	Caricature or false representation (straw man)	According to the minister, we need to reduce our military spending to give to foreigners. Apparently, he thinks that nobody will ever attack the country.	*Hamlet* is nothing more than the story of a famous procrastinator, so why should it be considered a masterpiece?
18	Categorical correlations (with no degrees): (1) simple presupposition; (2) reciprocal presupposition; (3) mutual exclusion. Gradual correlations: (4) positive, or direct correlation (as one element increases, the other increases, etc.); (5) inverse correlation (as one element increases, the other element decreases, etc.). For details, see Chapter 8 on the general structure of analysis, or section 4.23 on structure, relation, operation.	(1) A wolf is a mammal, but a mammal is not necessarily a wolf. (2) If a sheet of paper has a front side, then it has a reverse side, and if it has a reverse side, then it has a front side. (3) If a door is closed it cannot currently be open, and if it is open it cannot currently be closed. (4) In general, the higher the salary, the higher the life expectancy. (5) In general, if the education level of a population increases, the crime rate diminishes.	(1) In *Hamlet*, whoever loves, dies (Hamlet, Ophelia, the King, the Queen); but whoever dies does not necessarily love (Polonius). (2) In a text, if there is a narrator there is a narratee, and if there is a narratee there is a narrator. (3) In Corneille's *Le Cid*, for the most part, will and duty are mutually exclusive: one must not do what one would like to do, and one must do what one would not like to do. (4) For Don Juan, the harder the woman is to catch, the more he desires her. (5) For Don Juan, the more he sleeps with a woman the less he desires her.

19	"Cauldron" argument (obvious inconsistency between different arguments; see paradox)	My client is not guilty and in fact he has extenuating circumstances.	Hamlet is not in love with Ophelia and he loves her very badly.
20	Change (justified or unjustified) of ontological category	Our enemies are not humans, but animals (unjustified animalization). Animals are sentient beings like us (justified partial humanization).	"You blocks, you stones, you worse than senseless things! O you hard hearts, you cruel men of Rome, Knew you not Pompey?" (from *Julius Caesar*, change from humans to "senseless things")
21	(1) Circular argument; (2) *petitio principii*; (3) tautology	(1) God exists because the Bible says so. And what the Bible says is true because it is the word of God. (2) If God did not exist, He would be imperfect, but God is perfect, therefore He exists. (3) A man is a man.	(1) Hamlet says he loves Ophelia, and he says so because he loves her. (2) If Hamlet did not love Ophelia, he would be wicked, but Hamlet is certainly not wicked, therefore he loves Ophelia. (3) Shakespeare is Shakespeare, that's all that needs to be said.
22	Concession	Certainly, some warlords take a bite out of international aid, but what matters is the grain of rice that still gets through and saves a life.	Certainly, the text has several characteristics of the genre, but they are not essential characteristics.
23	Confirmation bias; unconsciously or in order to deceive, we look for or retain only those phenomena that support our opinion and not those that could invalidate it	All swans are white, since the so-called black "swans" are not swans.	In this passage, Hamlet says he is going to feign madness. Obviously, one cannot believe the words of a madman. Hamlet is not faking, he is truly mad.
24	Contradiction (apparent, rhetorical, or real)	We need to help others internationally, but we need to stop international aid. I shall explain this apparent paradox …	Hamlet is not Hamlet. Indeed, the real Hamlet is not the same person his relatives see (apparent paradox).
25	Culturalism ("culture": man-made) (cf. Naturalism)	Nature is violent and cruel; what comes from humans is necessarily more humane.	By studying at university, Hamlet would necessarily soften his animal nature.

Figure 12.1 Continued

	Name, explanation	General example	Literary example
26	(1) Deduction (the rule is imposed on the facts); (2) induction (the rule results from the facts); (3) abduction (a rule posited as hypothetical would explain the facts).	(1) A criminal always returns to the scene of the crime, so this person who has returned could be the criminal. (2) Water boils at 100 degrees Celsius, as all measurements confirm. (3) I hypothesize that these beans came from this bag (when I have seen a bag of beans with beans spread next to it).	(1) Whenever there is a narrator, there is a narratee, so who is the narratee of this text? (2) The plots of famous literary texts usually end unhappily. (3) Hamlet, seeing Polonius coming out from behind the curtains, concludes that this foolish man was hiding there to spy on him.
27	Definition	International aid includes financial, material, and human aid. Often this "aid" is in reality a lucrative contract for the donor country.	A theme is a semantic element that repeats itself in a text.
28	Demagogy (often an abusive generalization)	We already pay enough of our hard-earned taxes to lazy people, now we're supposed to give more to a bunch of losers who can't even be bothered to sort out their own problems!	Writers are idlers who make fortunes by creating worlds that have nothing to do with reality.
29	Dunning-Kruger effect: the effect by which those with little or no expertise in a given area over-estimate their knowledge, and are therefore more confident in their views than those who have much greater expertise	According to surveys, a large majority of drivers think they are above average drivers (which is logically impossible)!	It doesn't take a specialist to see that Hamlet is really mad.
30	Echo chamber effect	The Facebook pages I frequent tell me that it is useless to give to poor countries. I do not see any opposing views. This view must be right.	As a psychoanalyst, it is clear to me that Hamlet and Horatio are in a homosexual relationship. All psychoanalysts will agree with me.
31	Equivocation (playing, consciously or not, on different meanings of the same word)	Since it is easy to make you smile, I conclude that you are an easy girl.	This text contains a high frequency of the "liquid" class of phonemes, and indeed the theme of liquids is important in this text.

32	Etymology or abusive lexical analysis	The word "religion" comes from *religare*, to *bind*, which means that religion can only unite.	To "consider" comes from con- and sidus, meaning *star*, so any text that uses this word contains the theme of astronomy.
33	Euphemism	Instead of talking about "developing countries," should we not rather talk about "countries that are being kept in poverty"? (Note: here the euphemism is criticized)	Hamlet is not a procrastinator, he is simply someone who takes his time.
34	Example, illustration	The major industrialized countries practice international aid. For example, every year Canada spends …	Novelists usually choose the title of their works very carefully. This was the case with Zola.
35	False alternative (failing to present at least one other possibility)	Between giving everything and giving nothing, the choice is simple: give nothing. Either you leave me or I will kill myself. You are either with us or against us.	Hamlet is either mad or a genius.
36	False analogy	It is ridiculous that people vote to elect their MPs. After all, we do not allow children to choose their teacher. Sure, we destroyed Native American cultures, but you can't make an omelet without breaking eggs.	It is impossible to interpret a literary text with precision; indeed a text is a coded message whose code has been lost.
37	False syllogism	To be human is to be autonomous (Note: implied reasoning; they are not autonomous, therefore they are not human; the definition of human is false, since a child, for example, is human but not autonomous). Giraffes have long necks, my sister has a long neck, so my sister is a giraffe.	All verse is poetry. Therefore if I put the text of this recipe into verse, it becomes poetry.

Figure 12.1 Continued

	Name, explanation	General example	Literary example
38	Generalization	This coin, this hammer, this leaf all fall down, so everything that goes up comes down. I dissected a mouse and found that it has a liver; I conclude that all mice have a liver. (Note: these are also inductions)	These highly regarded novels all have a sad ending, so we must conclude that good novels usually do not have a happy ending. (Note: this is also an induction)
39	Hasty or abusive generalization; see Abusive conclusion	A few years ago, a charity was embroiled in a scandal. Therefore all charities are dishonest.	This excellent novel ends badly. This is therefore true of all good novels.
40	Hyperbole (amplification)	If you say no to increasing international aid, you are causing the deaths of dozens of people and you are thus associating yourself with the worst dictators the world has ever known. (Note: this is also an abusive assimilation)	The whole universe shivered with disgust and delight when Baudelaire published his *Fleurs du mal.*
41	Illusory truth effect	God exists because I feel him in my heart.	Hamlet is mad, because that is my intuitive impression, and we should always follow our intuitions.
42	Invalid evidence (facts and figures are wrong, outdated, arbitrarily selected, insufficient as grounds for generalization), unreliable sources, unrepresentative sample	According to my brother-in-law, the governments of developing countries are always skimming from the funds intended for their citizens.	*Wikipedia* states that Hamlet is in fact mad. (Note: not a completely reliable source; also contains an argument from authority)
43	Irony (assumed or condemnatory)	Let them die, after all they are hardly human beings! And they are not really starving, they are just greedy! (Note: condemnatory, parodying the opponent's speech)	Of course, Hamlet does not love Ophelia and Horatio is not Hamlet's steadfast friend!
44	Lack of nuance	[see example for Hasty or abusive generalization]	Baudelaire is the greatest author of all time.

45	Litotes (understatement) (see also Euphemism)	Developing countries are experiencing a few "snags."	Charlie Chaplin was not bad as a comedy filmmaker.
46	Metaphorical comparison	[See the example for Appeal to experience (note that not every appeal to experience is a comparison).]	Popular literature is to literature what military music is to music.
47	Modalization (modifying an assertion using modal expressions)	In my view, according to this authority figure; all, most, some, few; certainly, certainly not, perhaps; always, never, often, sometimes; etc.	Hamlet, at least according to my analysis, is actually in love with Ophelia.
48	Naturalism (moving directly from a judgment of fact to a judgment of value [Hume's Law]) (cf. Culturalism)	A woman can have a child every year. So, my wife should have one every year. A human can live several days without eating, so it is good not to eat every day.	A human can live without literature, so literature is not important.
49	Making the "patient" of the action (person or thing undergoing the action) into the agent of that action (e.g., conflating victim with perpetrator, victim blaming; see Questionable causal link	The victim of this theft must accept some of the blame, as she flaunts her wealth so provocatively.	Polonius deserved to die, as he was spying on Hamlet.
50	Personal perspective or anecdote	Recently, I met someone who asked me for money ...	Recently, I wondered why I read, and the answer came to me in this book ...
51	*Post hoc ergo propter hoc* (after this therefore because of this)	I turned on the light and sneezed, therefore the light caused me to sneeze.	Ophelia commits suicide after singing songs of desperation. Her songs therefore drove her to suicide.
52	Presupposition (where a statement, question, etc. presupposes certain facts), presumption	Did you like this movie? (Note: presuming that you have seen it)	Polonius tells Ophelia to beware of Hamlet's advances, which presupposes that Hamlet has made such advances in the past.

Figure 12.1 Continued

	Name, explanation	General example	Literary example
53	Proverb, saying, etc. (see also Metaphorical comparison)	God helps those who help themselves.	As they say in French, "he who steals an egg, will steal an ox," so we can expect Jean Valjean, in *Les Misérables*, to commit a greater misdeed.
54	Questionable causal link: (1) seeing a causal link where there is only an accidental correlation; (2) seeing a causal link between two effects of the same cause; (3) *post hoc ergo propter hoc* (q.v.)	(1) In Switzerland, an abnormally high number of people die of lung disease; therefore the mountains are not good for the respiratory system. (Note: doctors send lung patients to the mountains) (2) In Quebec, the more strip clubs a city has, the more churches it has. (3) I received an email saying that I would have bad luck if I didn't pass it on to 13 friends; later, I slipped on a banana peel.	As soon as Hamlet looks at the clouds, he starts to rant and rave in the presence of Polonius; the clouds have therefore caused his madness. (Note: we can, however, speak of a symbolic causality, as if the clouds had "caused" the madness)
55	(1) Rational argument; (2) emotional argument (dramatization, appeal to sentiment, etc.)	(1) If we do not help poorer countries, we create disorder in the world and therefore uncertainty in our own countries. (2) Look at this child, her imploring look, her empty bowl. How can we remain indifferent?	(1) This character creates many psychological problems in his victims, so he is bad. (2) How can we fail to hate such a disgusting character?
56	Rebuttal	Our opponents say that countries are responsible for their own fate, but it is the colonizing countries that have destroyed the balance that existed before their arrival.	This poem is said to be romantic, but it does not have the essential characteristics of romantic poetry: lyricism, emotionality, autobiographical inspiration, etc.

57	Red herring (irrelevant argument)	Why would I donate when your donation ads are so poorly made?	How could this novel be good when its author does not even know how to dress properly?
58	Reinforcement: (1) positive; (2) negative	(1) Help and you will be a good person, enjoying high esteem in your community.	(1) People of good taste will like the novel I am about to analyze. (2) Only a fool would say that Hamlet is really mad.
59	Slippery slope	If I give $100 today, tomorrow they will ask me for $1,000, then all my money, then my whole country. We are being asked to help. Fine, let's help every last hungry mouse, let's help the microbe that wants to kill us …	If we allow that this text is a literary text, we will have to say that all texts are literary, which will devalue the truly literary texts.
60	Sophism identifying inconsistency between actions and words; see *Ad hominem*	John: You should give money to sponsor a child in the developing world. Paul: Why do you ask me to do so when you don't do that yourself? John: Because I am poor and you are rich.	Jean-Jacques Rousseau saw the child as a marvel of purity; this did not prevent him from giving all his children up for adoption.
61	Subtext	Is it getting cold? (meaning: please close the window)	"Does your faucet still work?" asked Maria Chapdelaine's father, meaning that he wanted a glass of water.
62	Syllogism (explicit or implied)	Humans help each other. (implied: humans help each other, we are humans, so we will help each other)	A criminal always returns to the scene of the crime. Our character, who returns several times to the scene of the crime, is therefore possibly the perpetrator.
63	*Tu quoque* (you too), or "two wrongs"	Why would we be ashamed of making 300 partisan appointments when you made 400?	Othello is not really cruel if we compare him to Macbeth.

Figure 12.1 Continued

13 Opinion and taking a position

13.1 Opinion

A proposition, in the logical sense of the term, consists of a subject (what is being talked about) and a predicate (what is said about it), and it is marked with a truth value: it is considered true, false (more or less true, more or less false), undecidable (one cannot decide), undecided (one has not yet decided or one has withdrawn a previous judgment), or unconsidered (the question has not arisen). Any argumentative text will contain a large number of propositions, some of which will be secondary, and some central (e.g., the claim to be defended or issue to be resolved in a pedagogical essay assigned to a student by a professor, or the central hypothesis in a doctoral dissertation).

An opinion, in a rhetorical context (as opposed to its everyday sense as being a subjective and unsubstantiated personal view), can be said to belong to one of two types: *veridical opinions*, which broadly carry a value of true, false, or undecidable (in technical terms, these are veridictory modalities); and *for/against opinions*, which correspond to a view that is for, against, or undecidable (e.g., with regard to the issue of abortions being legally permitted: I am for this; I am against this; I have no opinion on this). In both cases, the opinion is espoused, more or less explicitly, by a particular entity, usually an individual person (a personal opinion), but this entity can also be a group (e.g., in the case of public opinion). A veridical opinion is essentially a proposition marked with a truth value (e.g., "it is held to be true that humans are inconstant"). A for/against opinion does not directly constitute a proposition, since it consists only of a subject (abortion, euthanasia, nuclear power, the teaching of creative writing in universities) marked with a modality (for, against, or undecidable). Each of the modalities for/against/undecidable is underpinned by an attitudinal modality (in technical terms, a thymic or axiological modality), respectively positive/negative/undecidable; with rare exceptions, our opinion is "for" what we consider to be positive and "against" what we consider to be negative. The attitudinal modalities are themselves underpinned by veridical modalities: for example, one might be against nuclear power because one holds it to be true that nuclear power is negative.

DOI: 10.4324/9781003179795-17

In a critical text, the aim is not simply to express an opinion (e.g., "This movie is good"), but to justify that opinion (e.g., "This movie is good because ..."), ideally with the use of rational arguments and necessarily using only valid arguments (as opposed to a text that uses only emotional arguments and flawed rational arguments), with the goal of persuading a reader to espouse the same opinion.

13.2 Taking a position

Taking a position is the process (and outcome) of adopting a specific veridical or for/against modality in relation to a given proposition or topic (e.g., "Are humans inconstant [true/false]?"; "For or against euthanasia?") or in relation to several competing propositions (e.g., "Are humans inconstant or just unthinking?") or competing topics (e.g., "For ecology or for the economy?").

13.3 Characteristics of an opinion

An opinion *may* be: (1) validating (true or for) or invalidating (false or against), (2) absolute or nuanced (e.g., totally or partly against), (3) explicit or implicit, and (4) partial or global (e.g., one might be partially "for" for some reasons, but partially "against" for some other reasons, and globally "against" overall). An opinion *must* be: (5) clear rather than confused, (6) coherent rather than paradoxical or contradictory, and (7) comprehensive rather than incomplete in scope (it must cover the whole topic of the analysis rather than just part of it, at least as far as the global opinion is concerned).

Some of these characteristics warrant further explanation.

(3 and 5) An implicit opinion emerges in particular from the use of irony, and particularly sarcasm (in which one says the opposite of what one thinks): "The death penalty is clearly the perfect solution to all of humanity's problems: hunger, war, poverty, etc. Why did we not think of this sooner?" In this case it is clear, although implicit, that the writer actually has a negative opinion of the death penalty.

(2) In the case of a question whose answer is formulated as yes (true or for) or no (false or against), the writer can take one of four possible positions: yes, yes but ..., no but ..., no. These positions correspond to three critical perspectives: defending (yes), refuting (no), and nuancing (yes but ..., no but ...). Often a nuanced position is the best one, since many phenomena, especially in the cultural sciences (as opposed to the natural sciences), do not lend themselves to absolute judgments. Things are generally neither black nor white, but varying shades of grey.

(2, 5, and 6) A nuanced global opinion can be clear and coherent, even if the partial opinions vary in content from one section of the development to another. For example, I can say that I am for nuclear technologies in medicine and against them as a domestic and industrial energy source. Overall, I have a nuanced global opinion on nuclear power. However, it would be paradoxical to say first that I am for nuclear power in medicine and then to say the opposite, or to say initially that I am totally against it and then provide a nuanced judgment.

(7) An opinion must consider the entire essay question or chosen topic, not just a portion of it. Let us take the following essay question: "Is avant-garde literature necessary for the development of humanity?" The following responses to that question are merely partial opinions: "Literature is necessary" (the idea of the avant-garde is missing); "Avant-garde literature is necessary" (it is not indicated that it is necessary for the development of humanity); "Avant-garde literature is useful for the development of humanity" (here the idea of necessity has been replaced by usefulness, which is not the same thing).

13.4 Place of the opinion in the structure of the text

One possible approach is for the writer to reveal their opinion in the introduction. In this case, the opinion should be placed in the same sentence as the topic statement or in a sentence between the topic statement and the topic division (see Chapter 8 on the general structure of analysis). If the opinion is placed in the introduction, it can also be combined with the subject division: "Is the view of immigration that emerges from the novel positive (topic statement)? If we follow the opinion of the character Sassa, we find a positive view of immigration, but if we follow Yuan's opinion, we find a negative view" (topic division and expression of the writer's global opinion). Note that the opinion expressed here is relativistic, as it varies with the observers in question, and nuanced.

However, it is usually preferable to reserve the final opinion for the very end of the development: this will maintain (some) suspense and give the reader the impression that the opinion follows from the argumentation rather than being fixed beforehand. While the (global) opinion may be found only at the end of the development, it is usually recalled again in the text's conclusion. In this case the global opinion and the main lines of its justification are found in the "summary" part of the conclusion.

14 Hypothesis

14.1 Analysis with and without a hypothesis

There are two attitudes toward the characteristics to be identified by the analysis, attitudes that define two different kinds of analysis: (1) either the characteristics are initially hypothesized (or have been hypothesized by someone else) and the hypothesis is tested by analysis, or (2) they are not hypothesized but simply identified by the analysis. Although the first type of analysis involves a principal hypothesis and the second type does not, the first type generally adopts the second attitude with regard to phenomena of lesser importance than those directly relating to the hypothesis.

14.2 Global and local hypothesis

Some analytical texts focus on the validation, refutation, or selection of a global hypothesis (e.g., "I will show that Hamlet is really mad," or, "Is Hamlet's madness real? I will attempt to answer this question"). Other analytical texts do not have an aim centered on a principal hypothesis, but rather aim to provide a description of a given phenomenon (e.g., the themes in *Hamlet*, madness in *Hamlet*, the oppositions in Shakespeare's sonnets). It is necessary to know how to produce both types of analysis, each of which possesses certain advantages and disadvantages.

Whether or not they contain a global hypothesis, analyses always contain several related local hypotheses. For example, for an analysis whose aim is to describe oppositions in the work of Baudelaire, local hypotheses such as the following can be formulated: "The large number of oppositions to be found in *Les Fleurs du mal* is a consequence of Baudelaire's dichotomous vision"; "Among the oppositions in Baudelaire's work, the figure of the oxymoron is preferred to that of antithesis, because the closeness of the two terms within the oxymoron produces a more violent effect."

Whether they contain global hypotheses or not, analyses are always underpinned by research questions. For example, the aim of describing the themes of a text amounts to asking questions such as: what are the themes of the work, their relationships, the interpretations that one can make of them? See Chapter 8 on the general structure of analysis.

DOI: 10.4324/9781003179795-18

14.3 Definition of the hypothesis

A hypothesis, like any proposition (in the logical sense of the term), consists of a subject (the thing that is being talked about) and a predicate (what is being said about it), and it is assigned a truth value (true, false, or undecidable). For example, let us consider the hypothesis "smoking causes cancer of the toe." Smoking is the subject, causing cancer of the toe is the predicate, and the truth value is true (but since it is a hypothesis, the truth of the proposition remains to be validated).

The hypothesis is therefore a proposition that posits that one or more characteristics or predicates possibly applies to the subject (e.g., "water boils at 90 degrees"; "Pluto is not a planet"; "money causes happiness"), and the analysis is then used to validate or invalidate that proposition. It should be noted that sometimes, at the end of an analysis, we have not succeeded in either validating or invalidating a hypothesis; the proposition is then said to be *undecidable*.

The hypothesis is either our own or someone else's, whether it is generally held to be true, generally held to be false, or has not yet been truly validated or invalidated to date.

14.4 A priori and a posteriori hypothesis

In principle, a hypothesis is an *a priori* proposition, that is, it precedes verification. It is generated from an intuition, a first step toward understanding, a preliminary observation, a preliminary experimentation, or from deductive reasoning.

An *a posteriori* hypothesis is a proposition whose content has been discovered at the end of a thorough process of analysis and which, for the purposes of the text reporting the analysis, is presented as hypothetical. For example, through a careful analysis of a character's psychology, it might be concluded that they are paranoid. The text that presents this analysis then begins by presenting the hypothesis that the character is paranoid (even though we already know that this proposition is true). An a posteriori hypothesis may be obtained from a targeted research project (e.g., if we were looking for the character's psychological characteristics) or from a general research project (e.g., if we were analyzing themes and we "found" a thematic configuration that lends itself to a global hypothesis).

14.5 Invalidation and replacement of the characteristic

If, at the end of the analysis, the hypothesis is validated, it means that the characteristic posited as present is indeed present. If the hypothesis is invalidated, it either means that the analysis has shown that the characteristic is absent without being able to stipulate another characteristic that would replace it, or that the analysis has replaced the posited characteristic with another characteristic. For example, if a scientific experiment can prove only that water does not boil at 90 degrees Celsius, without being able to demonstrate exactly at what temperature it boils, it corresponds to the first case. If the scientific experiment proves both that water does not boil at 90 degrees Celsius, and that it instead boils at 100 degrees Celsius, it corresponds to the second case. As for any proposition about a characteristic, the perspective of the analysis may be categorical (the property is either present or not, without possible gradation) or gradual (the property can be more or less present, and therefore more or less absent).

14.6 Qualities of the hypothesis

To be fully satisfactory, an analysis with a global hypothesis must present a hypothesis that validates, clarifies, completes, or refutes current knowledge. A hypothesis that validates current knowledge demonstrates the veracity of knowledge that is held to be true or plausible, but that has not yet been proved (or has not yet been sufficiently validated). Obviously, one must avoid under-taking to prove obvious facts (e.g., that the sun rises in the East or that a poem by a Romantic author is romantic) or facts that are not self-evident but are common knowledge (e.g., that the Earth is round, or that $E=mc^2$). One should therefore avoid presenting hypotheses such as "I will demonstrate that *Hamlet* is a tragedy." In the case of such an obvious fact, one should instead change one's focus to a more interesting question. For example, taking the same example, we might wish to ascertain to what degree *Hamlet* is a tragedy, in which of its aspects in particular it is a tragedy, in what way it has the same "tragic" nature, or not, as other tragedies, and which of its aspects are not, or not completely, tragic. However, sometimes the supposed truth of obvious facts or common know-ledge should be questioned. For example, it was previously believed by many people that the Earth was flat. Even among scientists it used to be believed that the atom—as the etymology of its name suggests—was the smallest component of matter, until the discovery of sub-atomic particles (electrons, protons, etc.).

A hypothesis must be verifiable (e.g., that God exists is not verifiable), pre-cise, and—except for analyses intending to validate, or further validate, that which is believed to be true but has not been proved—novel (at least with regard to the object under analysis). It does not necessarily have to be plausible on first impression, and indeed it may be counter-intuitive; if it is implausible and yet it is correctly validated, the analysis will have the virtue of producing surprising new knowledge.

15 Paragraphs

15.1 Introduction

The textual macro-structure that I presented in Chapter 8 corresponds roughly, as we shall see, to the classic textual micro-structure of a paragraph.

NOTE: DEVELOPMENT, PARTS, AND PARAGRAPHS

The development usually contains at least two parts (or sections). A distinction must be made between parts and paragraphs. It is sometimes taught, for the sake of simplicity, that each part should be a single paragraph. Fortunately, the reality is more complex than this. In fact, a part can contain one or more paragraphs. When a part has several paragraphs, it is particularly important to take care at the transitions, since the reader will no longer be able to rely on the change of paragraphs to know when they are progressing to a new part; in other words, if the transition is not clear, the reader might believe that they are progressing to a new part when they are actually moving to another paragraph within the same part. Subheadings can be used to avoid this confusion. Trying to create a part with only one paragraph may lead you to make the following mistakes: (1) a paragraph that is too long, or (2) a paragraph that contains more than one idea, or at least too many ideas, or ideas related to different aspects of the topic. It is also important to avoid the opposite mistake, that of producing multiple paragraphs that are too short.

Just as, broadly speaking, the word is the unit that makes up the sentence, so the sentence is the unit that makes up the paragraph, and the paragraph is the unit that makes up the text. A text of any significant length is therefore divided into paragraphs. In general, a paragraph contains at least two sentences and fills at least three lines.

15.2 Forms of the paragraph

A paragraph combines general (broader, more abstract) ideas and specific (more precise, more concrete) ideas. We can say that the paragraph can take

DOI: 10.4324/9781003179795-19

four general forms, depending on the arrangement of the general and specific ideas: funnel, pyramid, hexagon, and hourglass:

> The funnel paragraph begins with a general idea that is then developed by means of examples, arguments, facts, and statistics, which all constitute specific details. The pyramid paragraph is the opposite: details and explanations are provided first, and then the general idea is brought on at the end. In the hexagon, the general idea is found in the center of the paragraph, having been introduced by means of specific examples or facts. This general idea is then supplemented by other specific details. Finally, the hourglass begins and ends with a general idea, either as a restatement of the first idea, or as a mini-conclusion and transition to what follows. In the administrative and scientific worlds, the preferred forms are the funnel and the hourglass, two types of paragraphs that begin with a general idea.
>
> (Lozier, 1994: 106–107)

15.3 Structure of the paragraph

Figure 15.1 shows a possible structure for the paragraph.

This structure is described as follows in *L'Indispensable*, a methodological handbook produced by the Collège François-Xavier-Garneau in Quebec City:

> (1) The *statement* of the idea can take the form of an assertion [in the affirmative or the negative], or more rarely the form of a question or a hypothesis. (2) In the second part, it is often necessary to provide *explanations* of the words, ideas, or concepts used in the statement of the idea: one thereby demonstrates that one has mastered the concepts or ideas in question, and defined them in a certain way that is appropriate to [the topic]; one can also present everything one knows about the concept or idea. (3) All of this needs to be *proven*, which is done in the third part. This proceeds by examples, citations, [etc.] (4) After having stated, explained, and proved, one then draws out the *consequences* or conclusions. Is the initial assertion or statement still true or false? How should we now answer the question at hand? Is the hypothesis invalidated or confirmed? In this fourth part, the aim is to indicate what can be drawn from the facts or ideas that have been proven. (5) The last part of the development provides a *transition* by indicating a (logical) connection between the idea addressed in this paragraph and the idea addressed in the next paragraph.
>
> (Department of Literature, n.d.)

NOTE: OTHER PARAGRAPH STRUCTURES

Other authors, such as Michel Frankland (1998), suggest the following structure: statement, explanation, illustration, mini-conclusion. The term "illustration" seems to me less clear than argumentation (illustrating is very

Part of the paragraph	Literary example (topic: proving that a poem is symbolist)	Non-literary example (topic: smoking)
1. Statement (of the idea)	The symbolist theme of the Bohemian ideal is present in this poem.	Second-hand smoke from cigarettes is harmful.
2. Explanation	By the Bohemian ideal, we mean a life without rules and without care for tomorrow.	Indeed, smoke inhaled involuntarily by those close to the smoker can cause serious health problems.
3. Argumentation	This theme is found in the following verse: "Like all nights, I slept under the stars."	A recent American study has confirmed this.
4. Commentary	Furthermore, this theme is also found in poems by the same author, with titles such as "Why Worry about Tomorrow?," "La *Dolce Vita*," "With the Gypsies," etc.	As a result, smoking can no longer be considered an individual choice without consequences for others.
5. Connection to the next idea	The Bohemian ideal is often linked to travel. But another typically symbolist theme is that of the North and the Orient.	But is this reason enough to ban smoking altogether? Let us look at some of the reasons against this.

Figure 15.1 The structure of the paragraph

similar to explaining, and is only one of the possible forms of argumentation). Producing a mini-conclusion can be interpreted as producing a summary of the paragraph. However, one then risks boring the reader by providing a summary that not only adds no new information, but comes at the end of a short paragraph, such that the information is still fresh in the reader's memory.

Several further comments are needed:

My own approach extends the scope of part 4, compared with its description in *L'Indispensable* cited above. The commentary or interpretation of the idea may touch on one or more of the following aspects of the idea: causes, ways (modalities) in which the phenomenon occurs, or consequences; its connection to other elements of content or form, whether from the same text, different texts by the same author, or texts by other authors; its connection with the movement, the historical or biographical context; etc. See section 8.4.4 on interpretation.

A paragraph may use this precise structure, but there is nothing to prevent a single paragraph from dealing with two similar ideas and therefore using this structure twice over. Furthermore, this can also be used as the structure for a part of the development, even if this part includes several paragraphs (remember that a part of the development can contain one or several paragraphs, even though in short texts there is often only one paragraph to each part).

Part of the paragraph	Literary example (subject: proving that a poem is symbolist)
1. Statement (of the idea)	The symbolist theme of the Bohemian ideal is present in this poem.
2. Explanation	By the Bohemian ideal, we mean a life without rules and without care for tomorrow.
3.1 Argumentation	This theme is found in the following verse: "Like all nights,
3.2 Explanation (of the argumentation)	I slept under the stars." Sleeping regularly under the stars is associated with a Bohemian lifestyle.
4. Commentary	Furthermore, this theme is also found in poems by the same author, with titles such as "Why Worry about Tomorrow?," "La *Dolce Vita*," "With the Gypsies," etc.
5. Connection to the next idea	The Bohemian ideal is often linked to travel. But another typically symbolist theme is that of the North and the Orient.

Figure 15.2 Example of a split paragraph structure

Moreover, for a given idea it may be necessary to reproduce this structure or part of this structure within one of the parts of the structure. For example, the commentary itself (part 4) may be made up of a statement of an idea (4.1), an explanation of that idea (4.2), etc. This is also possible for the explanation (2) and the argumentation (3). In fact, this is frequently found in the argumentation when it consists of a citation. In this case, it is not only a matter of providing the citation, but of explaining it (3.2) and then commenting on it (3.4). The table in Figure 15.2 illustrates this case of a duplication of structure.

In some cases, parts of the structure can be combined into a single sentence. Compare: (1) (statement) "The symbolist theme of the Bohemian ideal is present in this poem." (explanation) "By the Bohemian ideal, we mean a life without rules and without care for tomorrow." and (2) (statement + explanation) "The symbolist theme of the Bohemian ideal, that of a life without rules and without care for tomorrow, is present in this poem."

In some cases, certain parts of the paragraph may be optional, redundant, or even prohibited. For example, if the statement of the idea is very clear, the explanation becomes unnecessary, and similarly if the assertion is already held to be true (or false), then no argumentation is required. To take a crude example, the statement "Hamlet is the main character in *Hamlet*" does not require any explanation, nor any argumentation.

Finally, the transition can be placed at the beginning of the following paragraph instead.

15.4 Qualities of the paragraph

According to Gisèle Losier (1994: 105–119), a paragraph must meet three criteria: (1) unity of meaning, (2) coherence, and (3) being sufficiently engaging.

1. Unity: each sentence in a paragraph should relate to the same idea. This idea is what is retained when summarizing the paragraph.

Let us add a few nuances, related to the different possible levels of ideas (principal ideas, secondary ideas, tertiary ideas, etc.). An idea of a given level may be treated separately from other ideas, or alternatively—and this is especially common for ideas of lower levels (e.g., secondary ideas, tertiary ideas)—it can be combined with other ideas of the same level in a single paragraph. Finally, ideas of different levels can be combined in a single paragraph. For example, ideas could be combined in one paragraph as follows: "We will start with the disadvantages of nuclear power, beginning with the most important disadvantages (principal idea 1). The first disadvantage is that ... (secondary idea 1) The second disadvantage is that ... (secondary idea 2)." But the first sentence could just as easily be placed in a different paragraph from the other sentences. An idea can span more than one paragraph, just as it can begin or end in the middle of a paragraph.

2. Coherence: a paragraph may meet the criterion of unity, yet fail to be coherent if the sentences are not organized in a logical way (e.g., when one sentence seems to announce an example, but then this example never appears).

3. Relief (in the sense that some parts are more salient than others): a paragraph can meet the criteria of unity and coherence without possessing the relief necessary to make the text interesting, and therefore enjoyable, informative, and easier to absorb. For a paragraph to possess relief, (1) you must select what to place in the foreground and what to relegate to the background, and (2) you must use the means available to create that relief. This can be done, for example, by placing the most important idea in the principal proposition (and not in a subordinate proposition), avoiding sentences that are too long and in which the main idea becomes lost, using connective adverbs to form links between sentences ("however," "nonetheless," etc.), etc.

I would add that, from one paragraph to another, there must be both non-contradiction and progression (although this may be progression in the form of a spiral, where one returns to an earlier statement to qualify it). Obviously, a paragraph must be convincing on the level of its argumentation, but also appealing in terms of form and style in order to convey the argumentation effectively.

16 Citation

16.1 Parts of the citation

A citation (or quotation) has roughly five parts, which correspond to five operations:

1. the link between the citation and the citing text;
2. the citation itself;
3. the reference;
4. explanations to help understand the citation, if necessary;
5. commentary on the citation.

Here is a simple example of a citation with its five parts:

(1) In Baudelaire's poem "The Murderer's Wine," wine is directly associated with the crime in question, since it provides the motive, especially in the following passages: (2) "My wife is dead, so now I'm free / to drink until I drop"; "I threw her down a well" (3).[1] (4) In these passages we see a direct link established, through the word "so," between the murder of the woman and the possibility of drinking. (5) The narrator, forced to choose between an object and a human being, opts for the former, so great is his passion for wine. The depreciation of women is found in several of Baudelaire's other poems (such as "To She Who Is Too Gay"), but it is often forgotten that the poet also expresses compassion for women (especially older women) and sometimes associates them with divinity, or at least with transcendence.

(3) [1]Charles Baudelaire, "The Murderer's Wine," in *Les Fleurs du mal*, trans. Richard Howard (Boston, MA: David R. Godine, 1982), 115.

Let us consider the five parts in more detail:

(1) The link between the citation and the citing text: in most cases, the link between the citation and the citing text (which usually also identifies who is speaking within the citation) is placed before the citation, and introduces it. However, sometimes it is placed immediately after the citation, and therefore "introduces" the citation after the fact. The following two examples show how this link-text can either precede or come immediately after the citation

DOI: 10.4324/9781003179795-20

itself: (1) "I no longer have any responsibility for myself" (p. 22), claims Olivia. / (2) Olivia claims: "I no longer have any responsibility for myself" (p. 22).

You should generally avoid placing a citation as a stand-alone sentence in the main text (especially if the citation is syntactically incomplete as a sentence). It should instead be formally integrated into the main text, as in these examples:

- Incorrect example (citation as a stand-alone sentence): "The earth is blue like an orange" (Éluard). There is an incompatibility between the color blue and the color orange.
- Possible correct forms (citation formally integrated): "In the verse 'the Earth is blue like an orange,' there is an incompatibility between the color blue and the color orange." or "In the following verse, there is an incompatibility between the color blue and the color orange: 'The earth is blue like an orange.'" or "'The Earth is blue like an orange.' In this verse, there is an incompatibility between the color blue and the color orange."

The examples in this chapter are mostly concerned with "run-in citations," where the citation is incorporated into the main body of the text. In cases where a direct citation (see section 16.2) is several lines long or consists of one or more whole paragraphs (the specific criteria for this vary with different style guides or sets of conventions), it is more appropriate to use "set off" or "block" citations. In these instances, the citation is preceded by a colon, then separated from the rest of the main text by line breaks at the beginning and end of the cited text. The quotation marks are omitted, and sometimes the citation is formatted in a different way from the main text (e.g., written in a smaller font, inset on the left relative to the main text, etc.). In all other respects, block citations should be treated in the same way as the run-in citations discussed in this chapter.

(2) The citation: the aim is to provide either a direct citation (reproducing the cited text word for word) or an indirect citation (reproducing an idea from the cited text). In both cases it must respect the letter and the spirit of the cited text. Care must be taken in the use of quotation marks (inverted commas), the syntactic integration of the citation into the citing text, the correction of the syntax of the citation itself, and the use of square brackets to indicate an omission, substitution, or explanation.

It is also essential to avoid confusion between direct and indirect citations. In the case of a false direct citation, quotation marks are placed around words that are not reproduced precisely from the cited text, but are actually a paraphrase produced by the person citing. In the case of a false indirect citation, quotation marks are omitted even though the text is reproduced word for word from the cited text.

(3) The reference: this involves checking that a reference is present, that it provides the necessary information in the appropriate format (as determined by the chosen or assigned referencing style, e.g., Chicago, MLA, APA, etc.), and that it is correctly positioned in the text (e.g., the placement of a footnote anchor, parentheses, etc.).

(4) Explanations to help understand the citation (especially explanations of the context of the citation): this stage is necessary so that a reader who does not have access to the text from which the citation is taken can still fully understand the citation and see its relevance to the argumentation taking place in the citing text. Some contextual explanations may be incorporated into the citation itself, through substitutions or explanations indicated by the use of square brackets. Sometimes the citation is sufficiently clear by itself and requires no explanation. If there is a risk that the reader will feel as if they are being talked down to by a seemingly self-evident explanation, you can qualify the explanation with an expression such as: "As we know, ..."; "We should remember that ..."; "Obviously, ..."

A citation must be contextualized: first, it must be reproduced in a way that respects its original context, and second, it must, if necessary, be accompanied by the elements required for it to be fully understood by the reader. To respect the context of a citation, you must respect its original scope, and if its scope has been modified, this should be indicated. Here is an example of such an indication: "The following citation from Ricardou analyzing Poe fits perfectly with my present purpose, even though the work I am analyzing is not the same." Here, we must not lead or allow the reader to believe that the cited author was talking about precisely the same topic as we are discussing in our citing text.

There are four possible situations with regard to the connection between the citation and the use that the citing text makes of it (in its explanations and commentary): (a) the citation does not contain what the writer claims to find in it (the text being referred to may not contain the element at all, or it may be found elsewhere in the text but not in the passage that is cited)—this is one of the worst errors of citation; (b) the citation does not contain exactly what the writer claims to find in it; (c) the citation contains the element, but implicitly, whether by allusion or otherwise; (d) the citation contains the element clearly and explicitly.

In the first situation (a), the writer has committed an error of interpretation, which cannot be remedied by explanations in part 4 of the citation. For example:

> In Breton's poem "Sunflower" we find the theme of women being viewed negatively: "The young woman could be seen by them but badly and in profile." The woman is judged negatively because she is viewed "badly."

In fact, the term "badly" is used in this context to indicate that she is not seen clearly by the viewers, but rather from an inconvenient angle. It is simply a question of the viewers' visual field, and it does not entail any negative judgment of the woman herself.

In the second situation (b), there is a slippage between what the citation is said to contain and what it actually contains. For example, it might be claimed that the citation provides evidence of a theme containing multiple elements, whereas in fact it contains only one of those elements (e.g., the citation features the love of animals but not, as had been claimed, the love of humans).

Example: "In this poem we are told that 'two individuals are fighting,' so the theme of war is present." All war involves conflict, but this example of combat does not necessarily constitute a war.

Some assertions (including those found in writing instructions for a pedagogical essay) allow the writer some flexibility. For example, if the writing instruction for an essay on Breton's poem "Sunflower" invites the writer to address "associations between the woman and negativity," these "associations" might concern the woman being perceived as negative, causing something negative, undergoing something negative, viewing something negatively, etc. However, some extensions of meaning are excessive. For example, it would be excessive to imply that any conflict, including that between two individuals, constitutes a war.

In the third situation (c), you must demonstrate to the reader that the theme is actually there, although it is partially hidden or implicit. If you do not demonstrate that it is there, or do not demonstrate it sufficiently, then you may well be right, but you will have failed to prove that you are right, which is hardly better than being wrong.

In the fourth situation (d), an explanation (part 4 of the citation) is optional, or even to be avoided, since it is unnecessary.

(5) Providing a relevant and interesting commentary on the citation: a commentary is an interpretation, in the broad sense of the word (see Chapter 8 on the structure of the analysis). Broadly speaking, four types of commentary are possible: intratextual (where focus "remains" on the same text), intertextual (which relates the text to another text), architextual (which relates the text to a genre, a class of texts, or an abstract element such as a cliché or a stylistic rhetorical figure), and that which relates the text to the real world (e.g., the text's historical context). The first type of commentary is often the easiest since it does not require any particular research or knowledge other than knowledge of the work being analyzed.

Part 5 should focus on what was presented in parts 3 and 4, and not on anything else contained in the text being analyzed. Here is an example of an error in this regard:

> (1) The theme of the negativity of women appears in Baudelaire's poem "Windows." The woman observed in the poem is (2) "wrinkled" and (2) "poor." (4) In our culture, these are generally viewed as negative characteristics. (5) "Windows" is a prose poem, that is, it is not written in verse form. Baudelaire was one of the first French authors to use this poetic form.

Part 5 must also provide sufficient argumentation (this argumentation may make use of citation) and explanation (in particular through contextualization). Here is an example of a failure in this respect, which consists in not providing textual evidence that the soldier in Rimbaud's "The Sleeper in the Valley" is dead (the writer proves only that a soldier is mentioned) or that nature is beautiful (the writer is correct, but fails to prove this to a reader who has not read the poem):

> (1) In Rimbaud's "The Sleeper in the Valley," we find, among other things, the theme of war, since there is discussion of (2) "a soldier." (5) The dead soldier is contrasted with the beauty of nature.

You should avoid placing "raw," unconnected citations in your text. Citations should not simply be placed side by side, but made to interact with each other, and with the analysis itself. In other words, you generally need to provide localized commentary for each citation and an overarching commentary for each group of related citations. The cited text cannot stand on its own. It is not enough merely to cite; the citing text must integrate, appropriate, and make use of the citation. The citation should illustrate, support, and complete the point that is being made. Each citation should be necessary for the analysis (providing information, supporting argumentation, or even primarily enhancing the stylistic appeal of the analysis, etc.). Citations should generally therefore not appear to have been abandoned in the text, without explanation or commentary.

16.2 Types of citations

As we have seen, there are two general sorts of citations, both of which require a reference: direct, or word for word citation (surrounded by quotation marks); and indirect citation, reproducing an idea from the cited text (without quotation marks). We can also distinguish between two ways of syntactically integrating a direct citation into the citing text: citation that is syntactically dependent on the citing text and syntactically autonomous citation. The following examples illustrate this typology:

> Direct citation, autonomous syntax: "Mathurin is confused: 'I'm troubled' (p. 121)."
> Direct citation, syntax integrated into that of the citing text: "Mathurin is 'troubled' (p. 121)."
> Indirect citation (the question of the syntactic autonomy of the citation does not arise in this case): "Mathurin is confused (p. 121)."

16.3 Referencing

Any ideas and phrases (or even unusual expressions) that are not our own, and are not a matter of "common knowledge," must be marked as such; otherwise, whether we like it or not, we are guilty of "intellectual appropriation" and plagiarism. This includes ideas and phrases originating from one's professor, whether they are derived from lecture notes, words spoken in class, or individual exchanges (in person, by email, etc.). Let us consider some absurd examples illustrating things that do not need to be referenced. For the fact that the sun rises in the East, we do not need to provide the name of the first person who made this discovery, or first wrote it in a text. Similarly, in the case of proverbs such as "like father like son," one does not need to (try to) find out who first uttered it, or first recorded it. The same goes for popular expressions such as "you win some, you lose some." Finally, a phrase such as "To be or not to be, that is the question" is so well known that it is not necessary to provide a precise reference, nor even to mention the play or the author ...

Excluding the case of ideas and statements that are "common knowledge," there are three situations in which a reference must be provided: (1) direct citation, e.g., "Genette writes: '[...]' (Genette, 1979: 50)"; (2) indirect citation, reformulation of an idea from the cited text, e.g., "Genette considers that [...] (Genette, 1979: 25)"; (3) generalized reformulation or inspiration, e.g., "In the following paragraphs I will make use of Genette's presentation of these concepts (1979: 50–55)" or "I will draw inspiration in the following paragraphs from Genette's (1979: 50–55) ideas and presentation." In the case of generalized reformulation, it is not sufficient to provide a simple reference without making it clear that you are making a generalized use of the referenced text.

In addition to the ethical obligation, it is in the writer's best interest to indicate the source of each idea in their text that is taken from elsewhere, so that in all the other parts of their text, a reader can confidently attribute authorship of the ideas to the writer. This is particularly important in the context of academic or professional evaluation. Of course, the writer can emphasize that a particular idea or formulation is their own, with expressions such as: "My own view is that ..."; "On the contrary, I would argue that ..."; "I propose to call this phenomenon ...."

It is particularly important in a comparative analysis to identify in the main text which work is being discussed, even if a formal reference is provided in a footnote. Here is an example of an error in this regard (in a comparative analysis between Lamartine's poem "The Lake" and Apollinaire's "Mirabeau Bridge"): In the poems "Mirabeau Bridge" and "The Lake," time is associated with love: "And lovers / Must I be reminded."[1] The writer perhaps assumes that, because a reference is provided to "Mirabeau Bridge" in footnote 1, there is no need to indicate in the main text that this is the work being cited, but this makes life more difficult for the reader.

16.4 Ways of delimiting direct citations

Let us use the following schematic sentence to consider the different ways in which a citation can be delimited and presented:

Word-1 word-2 word-3 word-4 word-5.

Below are some examples of the possible forms of direct citations. Note the use of ellipses and square brackets, the position of quotation marks, final punctuation, etc.

A. "Word-1 word-2."
B. "Word-1 word-2 […]."
C. "word-2."
D. "word-2 […] word-5."
E. "[…] word-2 word-3 […]."
F. "[W]ord-2 word-3 […]"
G. "[…] word-2 word-3 […]"
H. "word-2 word-3."

Example F involves capitalizing the first letter of the cited text (with square brackets to indicate that this is a change from the original cited text) so that it can be integrated into the citing text at the beginning of a sentence. I suggest using only forms a, c, d, and h, which are the most concise forms. In the discussion below on the use of ellipses, I explain why the other, more cumbersome forms are not necessary.

16.5 Second-hand citation

It is possible to cite, directly or indirectly, a text that is itself making a direct or indirect citation; one then produces a citation of a citation. For example, you (Author-3) cite author Smith (Author-2) citing author Williams (Author-1). The citation of Williams produced by Smith is a first-hand citation, since it directly cites the author at the origin of the chain of citations. Your own citation is a second-hand citation, since it cites a citation (it cites Smith citing Williams).

In order to reference a second-hand citation, we provide the name of the author of the original cited text (Williams, in our example), but we also provide details of the text where the citation was found (Smith's text, in our example). This will result in a reference that looks something like this: Williams, cited directly in Smith, [*Title of Smith's Book*], [page number in Smith's book], etc. As can be seen in the example, I recommend specifying whether Smith is citing Williams directly or only reproducing Williams's ideas.

If you want to transform a second-hand citation into a first-hand citation (an ordinary citation), you must consult the original text at the start of the chain of citations (Williams's text, in our example). You should then check whether the text that cited the citation did so correctly (without changing the wording, the ideas, etc.), so as not to replicate any errors. It is surprising how often the citation turns out to be wrong. For this reason, it is always preferable to use first-hand citations whenever possible. It is therefore a weakness to have too many second-hand citations in one's text, especially if the texts at the origin of the chain of citations are easily accessible.

16.6 Direct citation within a direct citation

A citation of a citation may take the form of a direct citation that in turn contains a direct citation. In this case, it is necessary to distinguish the cited citation by enclosing it in the appropriate type of quotation marks. The conventions for this vary, but the following example demonstrates the format most commonly used in American English: According to Tremblay, "Frontenac declared to the invader, 'You will hear my answer from the mouths of my cannons.'"

16.7 Quotation marks and square brackets

Square brackets ([ ]) are punctuation marks which have several uses in relation to direct citation (among other uses). 1. Square brackets surrounding an ellipsis ([…]) are used to indicate that the writer has omitted elements (words, letters, etc.) that were present in the cited text, at the beginning, middle, or end of a direct citation. 2. Square brackets can be used to add elements to a direct citation (while making it clear that these elements were not found in the cited text), either to help integrate the citation grammatically or syntactically into the citing text, or to add information that helps the reader understand the citation. 3. Square brackets can also be used to replace elements from the cited text with other elements added by the writer of the citing text.

These three uses of square brackets are demonstrated in the following examples, each providing a modified citation of the verse "Cypris herself, flesh bare and hair wind-blown":

1. "Cypris herself, […] hair wind-blown"
2. "Cypris [an alternative name for the goddess Venus] herself, flesh bare and hair wind-blown"
3. "[Venus] herself, flesh bare and hair wind-blown."

Although parentheses can serve the same purpose, it is preferable to use square brackets to avoid ambiguity. There is potential for confusion when you are citing a text that itself contains square brackets. In this case, the most common practice is to add a note explaining the situation to the reader, as in the following example: Wolfe comments that "Polonius wrote, 'How beautiful life is […] thanks to the clouds and the trees!'" (square brackets in Wolfe's text). There is also a potential for confusion if the cited text contains ellipses without square brackets, and once again a note in parentheses can clarify the situation for the reader (e.g., "ellipses in original").

An unnecessarily long citation is as bad as one that is too short. You should cut the citations, using ellipses in square brackets ([…]) if necessary, in order to focus attention on the "center of the citation," the most important element.

It is only really necessary to indicate the omission of elements in the middle of the cited sentence. Their use is optional at the beginning and end of a citation, and need only be used if it is necessary to emphasize to the reader that an omission has been made, as in the following example:

> Lucky's monologue begins with the words "Given the existence as uttered forth in the public works of Puncher and Wattmann of a personal God quaquaquaqua […]" and runs on incoherently for several minutes without pause.

16.8 Syntax of direct citation

The citation must be syntactically and grammatically correct in itself (except where the cited text is deliberately incorrect) and it must be integrated into the citing text in such a way that it forms a syntactically and grammatically correct sentence. If this is not the case, the sentence introducing the citation must be changed, or the citation must be modified (indicated by the use of square brackets for omission, addition or substitution).

Here are some examples of errors in this regard, and some possible solutions:

Incorrect example: "The priest, before the final scene, is unimpressive:'always seemed so shy and weak.'" Possible correction: "The priest, before the final scene, is unimpressive: he 'always seemed so shy and weak.'"

Avoid inserting citations in the sentence without any form of integration. Incorrect example: "The bag is empty at the beginning 'when empty my bag was worthless' and at the end it is filled." Possible correction: "The bag is empty at the beginning ('when empty my bag was worthless') and at the end it is filled."

Incorrect example: "The author refers to Greco-Latin culture: 'only to the altar of the Muse and the temples of the gods.'" Possible correction: "The author refers to Greco-Latin culture: the poet addresses his prayers 'only to the altar of the Muse and the temples of the gods.'" or "The author refers to Greco-Latin culture in expressions such as 'the altar of the Muse' and 'temples of the gods.'"

Incorrect example: "The poet 'gilds his winged cadences with golden rhymes.' in order to produce an impression of luxury." Possible correction: "The poet 'gilds his winged cadences with golden rhymes' in order to produce an impression of luxury." The punctuation (a period) at the end of the cited verse should be omitted to form a correct sentence.

Incorrect example: "The character sees this as a 'premonition of my death.'" Possible correction: "The character sees this as a 'premonition of [his] death.'"

In particular, avoid using a period or semicolon to separate the sentence announcing the citation and the citation itself. A colon should be used instead. Incorrect example: "The narrator is young, lively, and full of energy; 'I set off at my usual brisk pace.'" Correction: "The narrator is young, lively, and full of energy: 'I set off at my usual brisk pace.'"

In principle, an explanatory element added in square brackets is not considered to have any effect on the syntax of the cited text. If it is necessary to alter the syntax of the cited text, a substitution or omission should be made as well, or instead. Incorrect example: "She 'will understand as soon as you [Yuan] get on the plane.'" Possible correction: "She 'will understand as soon as [Yuan] get[s] on the plane.'"

16.9 Citation from a text in verse

If a direct citation containing two or more verses is integrated into the citing text as a run-in citation (rather than as a block citation, where it would be formatted as it is in the cited text), it is necessary to separate the verses with a spaced slash (/), while maintaining the capitalization found in the cited text. The separation between stanzas can be indicated with a double slash (//), although in this case it may be preferable to use a block citation instead. For example: He lyrically declares his love for her: "O you, my dearest love, / I will always love you. // And never, never, / Could I hate you."

16.10 Citation from a theatrical text

It is obviously important to inform the reader who is saying what is being cited. This is especially important when a literary work contains the speech of several different characters. In the case of a theatrical text, two approaches can be used: (1) the name of the protagonist can be mentioned in the introduction to the citation, or (2) the name of the protagonist, as indicated in the script, can be included at the beginning of the citation (usually capitalized). Let us consider how to cite the following line from a play: "MARIE. *In a soft tone*: I can't take it anymore …" Citation type 1: "The theme of exasperation is present in the following words spoken by Marie: 'I can't take it anymore …'" Citation type 2: "The theme of exasperation appears here: 'MARIE. *In a soft tone*: I can't take it anymore …'" or "The theme of exasperation appears here: 'MARIE […]: I can't take it anymore …'"

16.11 The main problems relating to citation

Let us finish with an assortment of possible errors of citation, some of which overlap with errors that I have already mentioned, and some of which raise new problems:

1. indirect citation that deforms the ideas expressed in the cited text;
2. direct citation that does not accurately and precisely reproduce the original text (introducing variations in spelling, vocabulary, punctuation, word arrangement, etc.). If the cited text contains an error, or if you simply wish to express your surprise, discomfort, etc. with regard to what the cited author says, you can use the Latin expression "[*sic*]" in square brackets, which indicates that the citation is indeed accurate and transcribed together with its mistake or its surprising and/or questionable element;

3. failure to mark a direct citation appropriately (no quotation marks or reference);
4. a false direct citation (which is in reality an indirect citation);
5. a false indirect citation (which is in reality a direct citation);
6. excessive use of direct citation, as a proportion of the text (as a solution, one can use a mixture of both direct and indirect citations, and/or, of course, add more of one's own words);
7. failure to provide the source of a direct or indirect citation (with the exceptions noted above, sources must always be given, including when the ideas and/or words come from one's professor, or from the internet—even if they come from *Wikipedia*);
8. an insufficiently precise reference (e.g., a passage from a novel is cited, with the title, chapter, etc., but without indicating the page number);
9. an incomplete or erroneous reference, or references in the wrong format (relative to the chosen or assigned referencing style guide), or formatted inconsistently;
10. a false first-hand citation (which is in reality a second-hand citation);
11. excessive repetition of the same types of citation, or the same way of introducing, explaining, or commenting on the citations;
12. use of a run-in citation, rather than block citation, to reproduce a passage consisting of (depending on the specific conventions or style guide being used) one or more whole paragraphs, or more than a couple of lines of prose, or more than a couple of verses of poetry;
13. introduction of a direct citation with a semicolon rather than a colon;
14. citation of a passage that one does not understand, and therefore cannot explain and comment on in a relevant way. One must at least try to explain it. If the citation is incomprehensible or at least esoteric in itself, and not because of the inability of the citer to interpret it, one can obviously distance oneself from it and comment on it to the best of one's ability;
15. absence of any direct citations from the text being analyzed (this is generally unacceptable in literary studies);
16. making a comment about the citation that the citation does not support, or failing to make a comment that should be made, or failing to make a comment at all.

Works cited

Angenot, Marc (1989), *1889: un état du discours social*, Montréal/Longueuil (Québec), Le Préambule.

Angenot, Marc (2007), "Nouvelles figures de la rhétorique: la logique du ressentiment," *Questions de communication*, 2, 12, pp. 57–75.

Badmington, Neil (2010), "Posthumanism," in Manuela Rossini and Bruce Clarke (eds), *The Routledge Companion to Literature and Science*, Abingdon (UK), Routledge, pp. 374–384.

Barsky, Robert F. (1997), *Introduction à la théorie littéraire*, Sainte-Foy (Québec), Presses de l'Université du Québec.

Bénac, Henri and Brigitte Réauté (1993), *Vocabulaire des études littéraires*, Paris, Hachette.

Bertrand, Nathalie (2008), "Toponymie d'une Provence imaginaire selon Henri Bosco," in Yves Baudelle (ed.), *Onomastique romanesque*, Paris, L'Harmattan, pp. 69–82.

Blackburn, Pierre (1994), *Logique de l'argumentation*, St-Laurent (Québec), ERPI.

Bourdieu, Pierre (1981), *Questions de sociologie*, Paris, Minuit.

Bourdieu, Pierre (2016), *La distinction*, Paris, Minuit.

Buchanan, Ian (2018), "Queer Studies," in *A Dictionary of Critical Theory*, Oxford, Oxford University Press, n.p.

Buell, Laurence (1995), *The Environmental Imagination: Thoreau, Nature Writing, and the Formation of American Culture*, Cambridge (MA), Harvard University Press.

Capers, Bennett (2015), "Critical Race Theory," in Markus D. Dubber and Tatjana Hörnle (eds), *The Oxford Handbook of Criminal Law* (digital edition), Oxford, Oxford University Press, pp. 25–37.

Caracciolo, Marco (2018), "Degrees of Embodiment in Literary Reading: Notes for a Theoretical Model, with *American Psycho* as a Case Study," in Szilvia Csabi (ed.), *Expressive Minds and Artistic Creations: Studies in Cognitive Poetics*, Oxford, Oxford University Press, pp. 11–31.

Cerisuelo, Marc and Antoine Compagnon (n.d.), "Critique littéraire," in *Encyclopaedia Universalis*, consulted 11/25/2013, www.universalis.fr/encyclopedie/critique-litteraire/. First published in A. Compagnon (1997), *Dictionnaire des genres et notions littéraires*, Paris, Albin Michel, pp. 415–432.

Chartier, Roger (1996), "Peut-on parler de révolution de la lecture au dix-huitième siècle?" *Transactions of the Ninth International Congress on the Enlightenment* (Münster, July 23–29, 1995), Oxford, Voltaire Foundation, pp. 731–737.

Clark, Timothy (2014), "Nature, Post Nature," in Louise Westling (ed.), *The Cambridge Companion to Literature and the Environment*, Cambridge (UK), Cambridge University Press, pp. 75–89.

Courtés, Joseph (1991), *Analyse sémiotique du discours: De l'énoncé à l'énonciation*, Paris, Hachette.

Damrosch, David (2003), *What is World Literature?* Princeton (NJ), Princeton University Press.

Delcroix, Michel and Fernand Hallyn (eds) (1987), *Introduction aux études littéraires*, Paris, Duculot.

Delgado, Richard, Jean Stefancic, and Angela Harris (2017), *Critical Race Theory: An Introduction*, New York, New York University Press.

Demougin, Jacques (1992) (ed.), *Dictionnaire des littératures françaises et étrangères*, Paris, Larousse.

Derrida, Jacques (1967), *De la grammatologie*, Paris, Minuit.

Department of Literature (n.d.), *L'Indispensable*, Québec, Cégep François-Xavier-Garneau.

Diderot, Denis, *Rameau's Nephew / Le Neveu de Rameau: A Multi-Media Bilingual Edition*, ed. by Marian Hobson, trans. by Kate Tunstall and Caroline Warman, Cambridge (UK), Open Book Publishers.

Dirkx, Paul (2000), *Sociologie de la littérature*, Paris, Armand Collin.

Ducrot, Oswald and Tzvetan Todorov (1972), *Dictionnaire encyclopédique des sciences du langage*, Paris, Seuil.

Everaert-Desmedt, Nicole (2011), "La sémiotique de Peirce," in Louis Hébert (ed.), *Signo*, Rimouski (Québec), consulted 2/2/2014, www.signosemio.com/peirce/semiotique.asp.

Ferry, Luc (2014), *Sagesses d'hier*, Paris, J'ai lu.

Fouquier, Éric (1984), "Les effets du sémiologue," *Diogène*, 127, pp. 121–143.

Frankland, Michel (1998), *Comment faire une analyse de texte*, Montréal, ERPI.

Genette, Gérard (1982), *Palimpsestes*, Paris, Seuil.

Gerbier, Laurent (2006), "Féminisme," in Michel Blay (ed.), *Dictionnaire des concepts philosophiques*, Paris, Larousse, p. 320.

Gilbert, Helen and Joanne Tompkins (1996), *Post-Colonial Drama: Theory, Practice, Politics*, Abingdon (UK), Routledge.

Glotfelty, Cheryll (1996), "Introduction: Literary Studies in an Age of Environmental Crisis," in Cheryll Glotfelty and Harold Fromm (eds), *The Ecocriticism Reader: Landmarks in Literary Ecology*, Athens (GA), University of Georgia Press, pp. xv–xxxvii.

Goulet, Liliane (1987), *Cahier de méthodologie*, Montréal, Université du Québec à Montréal.

Greimas, Algirdas Julien and Joseph Courtés (1986), *Sémiotique: Dictionnaire raisonné de la théorie du langage*, vol. 2, Paris, Hachette.

Grossberg, Lawrence, Cary Nelson, and Paula A. Treichler (1992), "Cultural Studies: An Introduction," in George Lawrence, Cary Nelson, and Paula A. Treichler (eds), *Cultural Studies*, New York/London, Routledge, pp. 1–16.

Groupe μ (1990), *Rhétorique de la poésie: Lecture linéaire, lecture tabulaire*, Paris, Le Seuil [first published 1977, Brussels, Complexe].

Guillemette, Lucie and Cynthia Lévesque (2006), "La narratologie," in Louis Hébert (ed.), *Signo*, Rimouski (Québec), consulted 2/3/2014, www.signosemio.com/genette/narratologie.asp.

Guiraud, Pierre (1967), *La stylistique*, Paris, Presses Universitaires de France.

Gye, Lisa (2007), "Some Thoughts on the Evolution of Digital Media Studies," *The Fibreculture Journal*, 10, consulted 6/3/21, https://ten.fibreculturejournal.org/fcj-064-some-thoughts-on-the-evolution-of-digital-media-studies/.

Habert, Benoît (2005), *Instruments et ressources électroniques pour le français*, Paris, Ophrys.

Hall, David D. (1983), "The Uses of Literacy in New England 1600–1850," in William L. Joyce, David D. Hall, Richard Brown, and John B. Hench (eds), *Printing and Society in Early America*, Worcester (MA), American Antiquarian Society, pp. 1–47.

Hallyn, Fernand (1987), "Littérature et histoire des idées," in Maurice Delcroix and Fernand Hallyn (eds), *Introduction aux études littéraires: Méthodes du texte*, Paris, Duculot, pp. 241–252.

Hamon, Philippe (1998), *Le personnel du roman: Le système des personnages dans les Rougon-Macquart d'Émile Zola*, Geneva, Librairie Droz.

Hébert, Louis (2014), *L'analyse des textes littéraires: Une méthodologie complète*, Paris, Classiques Garnier.

Hébert, Louis (2019), *An Introduction to Applied Semiotics: Tools for Text and Image Analysis*, Abingdon (UK), Routledge.

Hébert, Louis (2020), *Cours de sémiotique: Pour une sémiotique applicable*, Paris, Classiques Garnier.

Hébert, Louis and Éric Trudel (forthcoming), *Onomastique textuelle: Théories et méthodes pour l'analyse des noms propres*, Paris, Classiques Garnier.

Hickman, Miranda (2012), "Introduction: Rereading the New Criticism," in Miranda Hickman and John McIntyre (eds), *Rereading the New Criticism*, Columbus, The Ohio State University Press, pp. 1–21.

Hickman, Miranda and John McIntyre (2012) (eds), *Rereading the New Criticism*, Columbus, The Ohio State University Press.

Hugo, Victor (1912), *Odes et Ballades*, Paris, Ollendorf.

Jacques, Francis (2008), "Pragmatique," *Encyclopædia universalis*, consulted 9/29/2011, www.universalis.fr/encyclopedie/pragmatique/.

Jakobson, Roman and Claude Lévi-Strauss (1962), "'Les chats' de Charles Baudelaire," *L'Homme*, 2, 1, pp. 5–21.

Jakobson, Roman (1960), "Linguistics and Poetics," in Thomas Sebeok (ed.), *Style in Language*, Cambridge (MA), M.I.T. Press, pp. 350–377.

Kerbrat-Orecchioni, Catherine (2002), "Connotation," in André Jacob (ed.), *Encyclopédie philosophique universelle*, S. Auroux (ed.), *Les notions philosophiques, dictionnaire* (2 vols), Paris, Presses universitaires de France, vol. I, pp. 425–426.

Klinkenberg, Jean-Marie (1996), *Précis de sémiotique générale*, Paris, Seuil.

Kowzan, Tadeusz (1992), *Spectacle et signification,* Candiac (Québec), Balzac.

Laberge, Jean (n.d.), "Les sophismes," *Site du vieux Phil*, Montréal, consulted 2/3/2014, www.cvm.qc.ca/jlaberge/103/Notes_de_cours/SOPHISMES.pdf.

Lafortune, Monique and Dominique Cyr (1996), *La dissertation critique par l'exemple*, Laval (Québec), Mondia.

Lafortune, Monique and Sonya Morin (1996), *L'analyse littéraire par l'exemple*, Laval (Québec), Mondia.

Lakoff, George and Mark Johnson (1980), *Metaphors We Live By*, Chicago (IL), The University of Chicago Press.

Lessing, Gotthold Ephraim (1836) [1767], *Laocoon: or, The Limits of Poetry and Painting*, trans. by William Ross, London, Ridgeway.

Losier, Gisèle (1994), *Écrire: Découverte du processus*, Montréal, Holt, Rinehart, & Winston.

Mayaffre, Damon (2002), "Les corpus réflexifs: Entre architextualité et hypertextualité," *Corpus*, 1, pp. 51–69.

McLuhan, Marshall (1964), *Understanding Media: The Extensions of Man*, New York, McGraw-Hill.

Méchoulan, Éric (2003), "Le temps des illusions perdues," *Intermédialités*, 1, spring, pp. 9–27, consulted 3/2/2021, https://id.erudit.org/iderudit/1005442ar.

Michon, Jacques and Denis Saint-Jacques (2002), "Média," in Paul Aron, Denis St-Jacques, and Alain Viala (eds), *Le dictionnaire du littéraire*, Paris, Presses universitaires de France, pp. 362–363.

Moeschler, Jacques and Anne Reboul (1994), *Dictionnaire encyclopédique de pragmatique*, Paris, Seuil.

Molino, Jean (2018), *Ce que nous appelons littérature … Pour une théorie de l'œuvre de langage*, Paris, L'Harmattan.

Moretti, Franco (2000), "Conjectures on World Literature," *New Left Review*, 1, January–February, consulted 3/1/2021, https://newleftreview.org/issues/ii1/articles/franco-moretti-conjectures-on-world-literature.

Murji, Karim and John Solomos, "Introduction: Situating the Present," in Karim Murji and John Solomos (eds) (2014), *Theories of Race and Ethnicity: Contemporary Debates and Perspectives*, Cambridge (UK), Cambridge University Press, pp. 1–22.

Nattiez, Jean-Jacques (1997), "De la sémiologie générale à la sémiologie musicale: L'exemple de *La Cathédrale engloutie* de Debussy," *Protée*, 25, 2, fall, pp. 7–20.

Nayar, Pramod (2015), *The Postcolonial Studies Dictionary*, Hoboken (NJ), Wiley.

Néraudau, Jean-Pierre (1985), *Dictionnaire d'histoire de l'art*, Paris, Presses universitaires de France.

Neveu, Franck (2004), *Dictionnaire des sciences du langage*, Paris, Armand Colin.

Paquin, Michel and Roger Reny (1984), *La lecture du roman; une initiation*, Mont-Saint-Hilaire (Québec), La lignée.

Pavis, Patrice (2002), *Dictionnaire du théâtre*, Paris, Armand Colin.

Pelckmans, Paul (1987), "Littérature et histoire des mentalités," in Maurice Delcroix and Fernand Hallyn (eds), *Introduction aux études littéraires: Méthodes du texte*, Paris, Duculot, pp. 253–265.

Pilote, Carole (1997), *Français ensemble I*, n.p., Études vivantes.

Poirier-Roy, Arthur (2020), "En complément à la géocritique et la géopolitique, la géoesthétique: L'influence des lieux sur la réception sémiotique," *Semiotica*, 234, pp. 199–215, https://doi.org/10.1515/sem-2019-0059.

Ransome, John Crowe (1937), "Criticism, Inc.," *The Virginia Quarterly Review*, 13, 4, pp. 586–602.

Rastier, François (2001), *Arts et sciences du texte*, Paris, Presses universitaires de France.

Rastier, François (2004), "Enjeux épistémologiques de la linguistique de corpus," *Texto!*, June, www.revue-texto.net/Inedits/Rastier/Rastier_Enjeux.html.

Rastier, François (2009), *Sémantique interprétative*, Paris, Presses universitaires de France.

Rastier, François (2011), *La mesure et le grain: Sémantique de corpus*, Paris, Honoré Champion.

Rastier, François (2016) [first published 1989], *Sens et textualité*, Limoges, Lambert-Lucas.

Rastier, François (forthcoming), "Glossaire" in *Décrire le sens: Introduction à la sémantique interpretative*.

Renault, Emmanuel, "Marxisme," in Michel Blay (ed.), *Dictionnaire des concepts philosophiques*, Paris, Larousse, pp. 490–496.

Ricardou, Jean (1975), "'Claude Simon' textuellement," in Jean Ricardou (ed.), *Claude Simon: Analyse, théorie*, Paris, Union générale d'éditions, pp. 7–19.

Rooney, Ellen (2006), "Introduction," in Ellen Rooney (ed.), *The Cambridge Companion to Feminist Literary Theory*, Cambridge (UK), Cambridge University Press, pp. 1–26.

Said, Edward (1978), *Orientalism*, New York, Pantheon Books.

Saint-Denys Garneau, Hector de (1993) [first published 1937], *Regards et jeux dans l'espace*, Montréal, Boréal.

Saint-Gelais, Richard (2007) [first published 1994], "La lecture erratique," in Bertrand Gervais and Rachel Bouvet (eds), *Théories et pratiques de la lecture littéraire*, Québec, Presses de l'Université du Québec, pp. 175–190.

Saint-Gelais, Richard (2011), *Fictions transfuges: La transfictionnalité et ses enjeux*, Paris, Seuil.

Simonet, Renée and Jean Simonet (1999), *Savoir argumenter*, Paris, Éditions d'organisation.

Smekens, Wilfried (1987), "Thématique," in Michel Delcroix and Fernand Hallyn (eds), *Méthodes du texte: Introduction aux études littéraires*, Paris, Duculot, pp. 96–112.

Somerville, Siobhan B. (2020), "Introduction," in *The Cambridge Companion to Queer Studies*, Cambridge (UK), Cambridge University Press, pp. 1–13.

Stockwell, Peter (2019), *Cognitive Poetics: An Introduction*, 2nd edition, Abingdon (UK), Taylor and Francis.

Thomsen, Mads Rosenthal (2011), "Franco Moretti and the Global Wave of the Novel," in Theo D'haen, David Damrosch, and Djelal Kadir (eds), *The Routledge Companion to World Literature*, Abingdon (UK), Routledge, pp. 136–144.

Todorov, Tzvetan (1970), *Introduction à la littérature fantastique*, Paris, Seuil.

University of Montréal Department of Comparative Literature (n.d.), "Qu'est-ce que la littérature comparée?" consulted 12/30/2013, http://littco.umontreal.ca/departement/la-litterature-comparee/.

Vinaver, Michel (ed.) (1993), *Écritures dramatiques: Essais d'analyse de textes de théâtre*, Arles (France), Actes Sud.

Von Uexküll, Jakob (2010), *Milieu animal et milieu humain*, Paris, Payot et Rivages.

Worringer, Wilhelm (1907), *Abstraktion und Einfühlung: Ein Beitrag zur Stilpsychologie*, Neuwied, Heuser.

Index